Praise for the "Kids Love" Guidebook travel series
On-Air Personality Comments (Television Interviews)

"The great thing about these books is that your whole family actually lives these adventures" – (**WKRC-TV**, Cincinnati)

"Very helpful to lots of families when the kids say, I'm bored...and I don't want to go to same places again!" – (**WISH-TV**, Indianapolis)

"Dividing the state into many sections, the book has something for everyone...everywhere." – (**WLVT-TV**, Pennsylvania)

"These authors know first-hand that it's important to find hands-on activities that engage your children..." (**WBNS-TV**, Columbus)

"You spent more than 1000 hours doing this research for us, that's really great – we just have to pick up the book and it's done..."
(**WTVR-TV**, Richmond)

"A family that's a great source for travel ideas..."
(**WBRA-TV**, Roanoke)

"What a great idea...this book needed to be done a long time ago!"
(**WKYT-TV**, Lexington)

"A fabulous idea...places to travel that your kids will enjoy"
(**WOOD-TV**, Grand Rapids)

"The Zavatskys call it a dream come true, running their own business while keeping the family together. Their goal, encourage other parents to create special family travel memories." - (**WLVT-TV**, Pennsylvania)

"It's a wonderful book, and as someone who has been to a lot of these places...you hit it right on the money!" – (**WKRC-TV**, Cincinnati)

Praise for the "Kids Love" Guidebook travel series
Customer Comments (actual letters on file)

"I wanted to tell you how helpful all your books have been to my family of 6. I rarely find books that cater to families with kids. I have your Indiana, Ohio, Kentucky, Michigan, and Pennsylvania books. I don't want to miss any of the new books that come out. Keep up the great ideas. The books are fantastic. I have shown them to tons of my friends. They love them, too." – H.M.

"I bought the Ohio and Indiana books yesterday and what a blessing these are for us!!! We love taking our grandsons on Grammie & Papaw trips thru the year and these books are making it soooo much easier to plan. The info is complete and full of ideas. Even the layout of the book is easy to follow...I just wanted to thank you for all your work in developing these books for us..." – G.K

"I have purchased your book. My grandchildren and I have gone to many of the places listed in your book. They mark them off as we visit them. We are looking forward to seeing many more. It is their favorite thing to look at book when they come over and find new places to explore. Thank you for publishing this book!" - B.A.

"At a retail price of under $15.00, any of the books would be well worth buying even for a one-time only vacation trip. Until now, when the opportunity arose for a day or weekend trip with the kids I was often at a loss to pick a destination that I could be sure was convenient, educational, child-friendly, and above all, fun. Now I have a new problem: How in the world will we ever be able to see and do all the great ideas listed in this book? I'd better get started planning our next trip right away. At least I won't have to worry about where we're going or what to do when we get there!" – VA Homeschool Newsletter

"My family and I used this book this summer to explore Ohio! We lived here nearly our entire life and yet over half the book we never knew existed. These people really know what kids love! Highly recommended for all parents, grandparents, etc." – Barnes and Noble website reviewer

KIDS ♥ LOVE VIRGINIA

BONUS Includes Washington, DC Activities!

A Family Travel Guide to Exploring "Kid-Tested" Places in Virginia...Year Round!

George & Michele Zavatsky

Dedicated to the Families
of Virginia

© Copyright 2006, Kids Love Publications

For the latest major updates corresponding to the pages in this book visit our website:

www.KidsLoveTravel.com

- ❑ *REMEMBER: Museum exhibits change frequently. Check the site's website before you visit to note any changes. Also, HOURS and ADMISSIONS are subject to change at the owner's discretion. If you are tight on time or money, check the attraction's website or call before you visit.*
- ❑ *INTERNET PRECAUTION: All websites mentioned in KIDS LOVE VIRGINIA have been checked for appropriate content. However, due to the fast-changing nature of the Internet, we strongly urge parents to preview any recommended sites and to always supervise their children when on-line.*

ISBN-13: 978-0-9726854-9-8
ISBN-10: 09726854-9-9

KIDS ♥ VIRGINIA ™ Kids Love Publications

TABLE OF CONTENTS

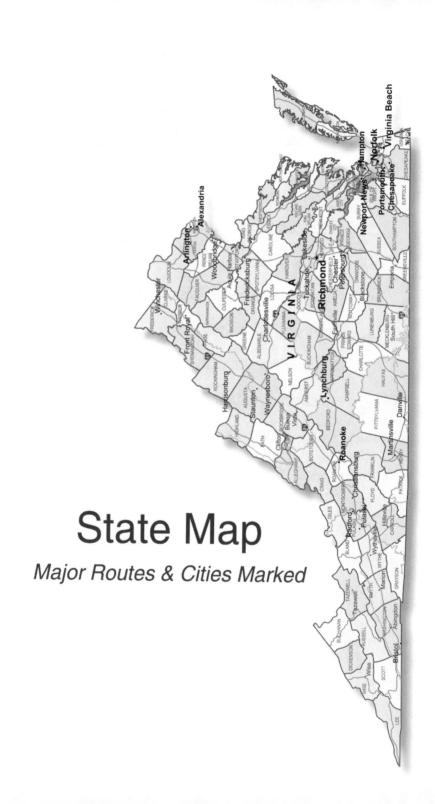

State Map

Major Routes & Cities Marked

Chapter Area
Map

CITY INDEX (Listed by City & Area)

CITY INDEX (Listed by City & Area)

Cities appearing in *italics* occur only in the Seasonal Chapter

Acknowledgements

We are most thankful to be blessed with our parents, Barbara (Darrall) Callahan & George and Catherine Zavatsky who help us every way they can – researching, proofing and babysitting. More importantly, they are great sounding boards and offer unconditional support. So many places around Virginia remind us of family vacations years ago…

We also want to express our thanks to the many Convention & Visitor Bureaus' staff for providing the attention to detail that helps to complete a project. We felt very welcome during our travels in Virginia and would be proud to call it home!

Our own kids, Jenny and Daniel, were delightful and fun children during our trips across the state. What a joy it is to be their parents…we couldn't do it without them as our "kid-testers"!

We both sincerely thank each other – our partnership has created an even greater business/personal "marriage" with lots of exciting moments, laughs, and new adventures in life woven throughout. Above all, we praise the Lord for His so many blessings through the last few years.

We think Virginia is a wonderful, friendly area of the country with more activities than you could imagine. Our sincere wish is that this book will help everyone "fall in love" with Virginia.

In a Hundred Years…
It will not matter, The size of my bank account…
The kind of house that I lived in, the kind of car that I drove…
But what will matter is…
That the world may be different
Because I was important in the life of a child.
- *author unknown*

HOW TO USE THIS BOOK

If you are excited about discovering Virginia, this is the book for you and your family! We've spent over a thousand hours doing all the scouting, collecting and compiling (*and most often visiting!*) so that you could spend less time searching and more time having fun.

Here are a few hints to make your adventures run smoothly:

- ❑ Consider the **child's age** before deciding to take a visit.
- ❑ Know **directions** and parking. Call ahead (or visit the company's website) if you have questions *and* bring this book. Also, don't forget your camera! *(please honor rules regarding use).*
- ❑ **Estimate the duration** of the trip. Bring small surprises (favorite juice boxes) travel books, and toys.
- ❑ Call ahead for **reservations** or details, if necessary.
- ❑ Most listings are **closed major holidays** unless noted.
- ❑ Make a **family "treasure chest"**. Decorate a big box or use an old popcorn tin. Store memorabilia from a fun outing, journals, pictures, brochures and souvenirs. Once a year, look through the "treasure chest" and reminisce. "Kids Love Travel Memories!" is an excellent travel journal & scrapbook that your family can create. *(See the order form in back of this book).*
- ❑ Plan **picnics** along the way. Many state history sites and state parks are scattered throughout Virginia. Allow time for a rural /scenic route to take advantage of these free picnic facilities.
- ❑ Some activities, especially tours, require **groups** of 10 or more. To participate, you may either ask to be part of another tour group or get a group together yourself (neighbors, friends, organizations). If you arrange a group outing, most places offer discounts.
- ❑ For the latest **updates** corresponding to the pages in this book, visit our website: **www.KidsLoveTravel.com.**
- ❑ Each chapter represents an area of the state. Each listing is further identified by city, zip code, and place/event name. Our popular **Activity Index** in the back of the book **lists places by Activity Heading** (i.e. State History, Tours, Outdoors, Museums, etc.).

MISSION STATEMENT

At first glance, you may think that this is a book that just lists hundreds of places to travel. While it is true that we've invested thousands of hours of exhaustive research (*and drove over 3000 miles in Virginia*) to prepare this travel resource…just listing places to travel is <u>not</u> the mission statement of these projects.

As children, Michele and I were able to travel extensively throughout the United States. We consider these family times some of the greatest memories we cherish today. We, quite frankly, felt that most children had this opportunity to travel with their family as we did. However, as we became adults and started our own family, we found that this wasn't necessarily the case. We continually heard friends express several concerns when deciding how to spend "quality" and "quantity" family time. 1) What to do? 2) Where to do it? 3) How much will it cost? 4) How do I know that my kids will enjoy it?

Interestingly enough, as we compare our experiences with our families when we were kids, many of our fondest memories were not made at an expensive attraction, but rather when it was least expected.

It is our belief and mission statement that if you as a family will study and <u>use</u> the contained information <u>to create family memories</u>, these memories will grow a stronger, tighter family. Our ultimate mission statement is, that your children will develop a love and a passion for quality family experiences that they can pass to another generation of family travelers.

We thank you for purchasing this book, and we hope to see you on the road (*and hear your travel stories!*)   God bless your journeys and happy exploring!

George, Michele, Jenny and Daniel

GENERAL INFORMATION

- Virginia Tourism Corporation. (804) VISIT-VA or **www.virginiaisforlovers.com**
- Virginia Historical Society. **www.vahistorical.org**
- Virginia State Parks – Richmond. (800) 933-PARK or **www.dcr.virginia.gov**
- Virginia Campground Directory. **www.virginiacampgrounds.org**
- Virginia Game and Inland Fisheries. (804) 367-1000 or **www.dgif.virginia.gov**
- Virginia Marine Resources Commission. (757) 247-2200 or **www.mrc.state.va.us**
- Virginia Trails Association. (804) 798-4160 or **www.waba.org**
- **NE** – Alexandria CVB. (800) 388-9119 or **www.funside.com**
- **NE** – Arlington CVB. **www.stayarlington.com**
- **NE** – Fredericksburg Tourism. **www.visitfred.com**
- **NE** – Hanover County Parks & Recreation. (804) 537-6195
- **NE** – Louisa County Park & Recreation. (540) 967-3447
- **NE** – Prince William County/Manassas CVB. (800) 432-1792 or **www.visitpwc.com**
- **NE-DC** – Washington, D.C. CVB. **www.washington.org**
- **NE-DC** – Fairfax County CVC. **www.fxva.com**
- **NW** – Albemarle County Parks /Charlottesville. (434) 296-5844
- **NW** – Charlottesville/Albemarle County CVB (877) 386-1103 or **www.SoVeryVirginia.com**
- **NW** – Fluvanna County Parks & Recreation. (434) 842-3150
- **NW** – Lexington CVB. (877) 4LEXVA2 or **www.lexingtonvirginia.com**
- **NW** – Staunton CVB. (540) 332-3865 or **www.staunton.va.us**
- **NW** – Winchester/Frederick County CVB. (877) 871-1326 or **www.winchesterva.com**

GENERAL INFORMATION (*cont.*)

- ❑ **SC** – Lynchburg Parks & Recreation (Percivals Island). (434) 847-1640 or **www.lynchburgva.gov/parksandrec**
- ❑ **SC** – Lynchburg Regional CVB. (800) 732-5821 or **www.DiscoverLynchburg.org**
- ❑ **SC** – Roanoke Valley CVB. (800) 635-5535 or **www.visitroanokeva.com**
- ❑ **SE** – Chesterfield County Parks & Recreation. (804) 748-1623
- ❑ **SE** – Hampton Conventions & Tourism. (800) 487-8778 or **www.hamptoncvb.com**
- ❑ **SE** – Henrico County Parks & Recreation. (804) 501-7275 or **www.co.henrico.va.us/rec**
- ❑ **SE** – Jamestown-Yorktown Foundation. **www.historyisfun.org**
- ❑ **SE** – Newport News Tourism. (888) 493-7386 or **www.newport-news.org**
- ❑ **SE** – Norfolk CVB. (800) 368-3097 or **www.norfolkcvb.com**
- ❑ **SE** – Portsmouth CVB. (800) PORTS-VA or **www.portsva.com**
- ❑ **SE** – Richmond CVB. (800) 370-9004 or **www.Visit.Richmond.com**
- ❑ **SE** – Richmond Parks & Recreation. (804) 646-5733
- ❑ **SE** – Surry County Parks & Recreation. (757) 294-3002
- ❑ **SE** – University of Richmond Sports. (804) 289-8388
- ❑ **SE** – Virginia Beach Tourism. (800) VA-BEACH or **www.vbfun.com**
- ❑ **SE** – Williamsburg Area CVB (800) 368-6511 or **www.visitwilliamsburg.com**
- ❑ **SW** – Heart of Appalachia. (888) 798-2386 or **www.heartofappalachia.com**
- ❑ Camping – KOA Campgrounds, **www.koa.com**

Check out these businesses / services in your area for tour ideas:

AIRPORTS

All children love to visit the airport! Why not take a tour and understand all the jobs it takes to run an airport? Tour the terminal, baggage claim, gates and security / currency exchange. Maybe you'll even get to board a plane.

ANIMAL SHELTERS

Great for the would-be pet owner. Not only will you see many cats and dogs available for adoption, but a guide will show you the clinic and explain the needs of a pet. Be prepared to have the children "fall in love" with one of the animals while they are there!

BANKS

Take a "behind the scenes" look at automated teller machines, bank vaults and drive-thru window chutes. You may want to take this tour and then open a savings account for your child.

CITY HALLS

Halls of Fame, City Council Chambers & Meeting Room, Mayor's Office and famous statues.

ELECTRIC COMPANY / POWER PLANTS

Modern science has created many ways to generate electricity today, but what really goes on with the "flip of a switch". Because coal can be dirty, wear old, comfortable clothes. Coal furnaces heat water, which produces steam, that propels turbines, that drives generators, that make electricity.

FIRE STATIONS

Many Open Houses in October, Fire Prevention Month. Take a look into the life of the firefighters servicing your area and try on their gear. See where they hang out, sleep and eat. Hop aboard a real-life fire engine truck and learn fire safety too.

HOSPITALS

Some Children's Hospitals offer pre-surgery and general tours.

NEWSPAPERS

You'll be amazed at all the new technology. See monster printers and robotics. See samples in the layout department and maybe try to put together your own page. After seeing a newspaper made, most companies give you a free copy (dated that day) as your souvenir. National Newspaper Week is in October.

RESTAURANTS

PIZZA HUT & PAPA JOHN'S

❑   Participating locations

Telephone the store manager. Best days are Monday, Tuesday and Wednesday mid-afternoon. Minimum of 10 people. Small charge per person. All children love pizza – especially when they can create their own! As the children tour the kitchen, they learn how to make a pizza, bake it, and then eat it. The admission charge generally includes lots of creatively made pizzas, beverage and coloring book.

KRISPY KREME DONUTS

❑   Participating locations

Get an "inside look" and learn the techniques that make these donuts some of our favorites! Watch the dough being made in "giant" mixers, being formed into donuts and taking a "trip" through the fryer. Seeing them being iced and topped with colorful sprinkles is always a favorite with the kids. Contact your local store manager. They prefer Monday or Tuesday. Free.

SUPERMARKETS

Kids are fascinated to go behind the scenes of the same store where Mom and Dad shop. Usually you will see them grind meat, walk into large freezer rooms, watch cakes and bread bake and receive free samples along the way. Maybe you'll even get to pet a live lobster!

TV / RADIO STATIONS

Studios, newsrooms, Fox kids clubs. Why do weathermen never wear blue clothes on TV? What makes a "DJ's" voice sound so deep and smooth?

WATER TREATMENT PLANTS

A giant science experiment! You can watch seven stages of water treatment. The favorite is usually the wall of bright buttons flashing as workers monitor the different processes.

U.S. MAIN POST OFFICES

Did you know Ben Franklin was the first Postmaster General (over 200 years ago)? Most interesting is the high-speed automated mail processing equipment. Learn how to address envelopes so they will be sent quicker (there are secrets). To make your tour more interesting, have your children write a letter to themselves and address it with colorful markers. Mail it earlier that day and they will stay interested trying to locate their letter in all the high-speed machinery.

Chapter 1
North East Area

Our Favorites...

* Alexandria Historic Area - (Gadsby's Tavern & Christ Church) - Alexandria

* Fredericksburg Trolley Tours - Fredericksburg

* Harper's Ferry Nat'l Historical Park - Harper's Ferry

* Manassas National Battlefield Park - Manassas

* Mt. Vernon & Hands-On History Tent - Mt. Vernon

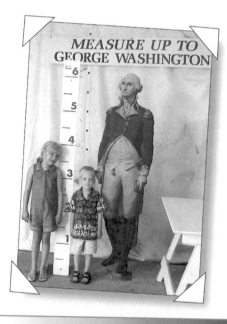

"Standing tall" with President George Washington

FORT WARD MUSEUM & HISTORIC SITE

Alexandria - *4301 West Braddock Road (I-395, Seminary Road exit), 22304. Phone: (703) 838-4848 or (703) 838-4831 (park). Web: http://ci.alexandria.va.us/oha/fortward. Hours: Museum: Tuesday-Saturday 9:00am-5:00pm, Sunday Noon-5:00pm. Park: Daily, 9:00am-Sunset. Admission: FREE.* The museum, patterned after a Union headquarters building, houses a Civil War collection and exhibits. Fort Ward was originally constructed as one of a series of forts providing for the defense of Washington, DC during the Civil War. The Fort's Northwest Bastion has been completely restored and the grounds also feature a reconstructed ceremonial gate and Officer's Hut. Climb the stockade into the fort and check out the cannon.

GREAT WAVES AT CAMERON RUN REGIONAL PARK

Alexandria - *4001 Eisenhower Avenue (I-95/495 exit 3A), 22304. Phone: (703) 960-0767. Web: www.nvrpa.org/cameron.html. Hours: Pool: (Memorial Day weekend - Labor Day). Batting cage and Mini golf: (mid-March - October). Hours vary. Peak season hours generally between 11:00am-7:00pm. Admission: Pool is $11.00-$13.00. Batting and Mini Golf are $1.00 or more added to pool price. Miscellaneous: Concessions and picnic areas.* This park offers something for everyone - waterslide, wave pool, lap pool, Play Pool (climb on snakes or alligators in shallow waters), Tad Pool, batting cages and miniature golf.

ALEXANDRIA SEAPORT FOUNDATION

Alexandria - *1000 South Lee Street, Jones Point Park (waterfront, south of Founders Park), 22313. Web: www.alexandriaseaport.org. Phone: (703) 549-7078. Hours: Daily 9:00am-4:00pm. Admission: Observation FREE. Special programs or events - call for details.* This floating museum includes a boat building shop, a marine science lab and traditional boats on the water. Volunteers build boats, teach boat building to youths, restore old boats, skipper and crew the 42' dory boat and the 15' Federalist, teach rowing and sailing, conduct marine science courses and offer boat rentals.

ALEXANDRIA ARCHAELOGY MUSEUM

105 North Union Street, #327 (on Potomac River @ the corner of King & Union Sts.- Torpedo Factory Art Center, 3rd Floor)

Alexandria 22314

❑ Phone: (703) 838-4399

    Web: www.AlexandriaArchaeology.org

❑ Hours: Tuesday-Friday 10:00am-3:00pm, Saturday 10:00am-5:00pm, Sunday 1:00-5:00pm.

❑ Admission: FREE

Interact with the City archaeologists and volunteers working in the public laboratory (and occasional public dig days). Experience Alexandria using maps, oral history, heritage through exhibits, self-guided tours, and hands-on discovery kits. View the latest finds from current excavations where archaeologists reconstruct history.

ALEXANDRIA SYMPHONY ORCHESTRA

Alexandria - *1900 North Beauregard Street Schlesinger Center & Various locations (indoors and out) around town. 22314. Phone: (703) 845-8005. Web: www.alexsym.org.* Charismatic virtuosity has guided the ASO through critically-acclaimed performances full of passion, power and emotion. They have an annual Children's Holiday Concert and Children's Art Festival each year. Students are inspired to create beautiful artwork while listening to the music.

ALEXANDRIA WALKING TOUR

221 King Street (Ramsay House Visitors Center)

Alexandria 22314

❑ Phone: (703) 838-4200 **Web: www.funside.com**

❑ Admission: $10.00 adult. Parking: Obtain a FREE pass at the Visitor's Center.

❑ Tours: Daily tour departs Monday-Saturday at 10:30am and Sunday at 2:00pm from the garden. (March-November) weather permitting.

Learn history beginning from the French / Indian War even through current events. Questions will be answered about: Why are there

For updates & travel games, visit: **www.KidsLoveTravel.com**

"snowbirds" on roofs? Why are some of the drainpipes marked, Alexandria, DC instead of Virginia? During the Civil War, how was Alexandria used by Union troops? Why is Christ Church considered, "in the woods" even though it is located right in town? Where did the first Union soldier die in the Civil War? Ever heard of an ice well? Where did Washington stay when he was in town? Where did he hold birthday parties? Be sure to look for a "busybody" and the sign of the "pineapple story". As you can tell, the facts and history about Alexandria during the tour will be extensive. It is presented in a fun way to hold your attention by some very enthusiastic and energetic tour guides! Note: The 1½ tour is delightful for about 4th graders and up (who have studied American History). Younger children (particularly without strollers) will tire quickly.

ATLANTIC CANOE & KAYAK CO.

1201 North Royal Street, **Alexandria** 22314

- ❑   Phone: (703) 838-9072 or (800) 297-0066
     Web: www.atlantickayak.com
- ❑   Hours: Monday-Saturday 10:00am-6:00pm, Thursday & Friday Noon-8:00pm, Sunday 11:00am-5:00pm. (April-October)
- ❑   Admission: $40.00+ per person.
- ❑   Miscellaneous: Groups may wish to picnic or barbecue following a tour. Bring a picnic or make arrangements for a catered meal.

Their short trips are great for first-time kayakers and those seeking a light adventure. All tours include a brief lesson and a relaxing tour. No experience is required, and all equipment is included. See osprey, great blue heron, beaver and eagles. A sampling of short tours:

DYKE MARSH WILDLIFE AREA: Glide into the quiet hidden channels of Dyke Marsh, a freshwater wetlands just downriver from Alexandria.

GEORGETOWN MONUMENTS & BRIDGES: Explore Georgetown's vibrant waterfront--paddle under the beautiful Key and Memorial bridges, in view of the George Washington and Lincoln monuments, around forested Roosevelt Island and back along Georgetown.

Atlantic Canoe & Kayak Co. (*cont.*)

<u>PISCATAWAY CREEK:</u> Go on one of two routes, depending on river conditions. One route takes you out to the mouth of Piscataway Creek, former tribal grounds of the Piscataway Indian Nation. Paddle across the wide Potomac to George Washington's Mount Vernon estate. The other route takes you upstream towards the headwaters, meandering through marsh plants into a narrow creek overhung by trees.

<u>POHICK BAY:</u> Paddle into the Mason Neck wildlife area. Saturday morning and afternoon trips, sunset trip.

<u>JULY FIREWORKS</u> - Alexandria, Georgetown, Piscataway. Experience the surreal of tranquil paddling as the fireworks light up the distant skies. Sign up early for these - they always have a waiting list.

CHRIST CHURCH

118 North Washington Street (Olde Town), **Alexandria** 22314

- ❑ Phone: (703) 549-1450, **Web: www.historicchristchurch.org**
- ❑ Hours: Daily, 9:00am-4:00pm, Sunday, 2:00-4:30pm plus visitors are welcome to attend services at 8:00am, 9:00am, 11:15am, and 5:00pm. (Visitors can actually sit in the Washington family pew - first come, first served).
- ❑ Admission: FREE, donations accepted.
- ❑ Miscellaneous: Gift shop, Tuesday-Saturday, 10:00am-4:00pm.

Built in 1773, George Washington attended church here (pew #60) when in town and Robert E. Lee was also confirmed here. In the early days, rent was charged for a family pew in lieu of tithes (and if you didn't show up for church...everyone knew!). Notice the wine goblet shaped pulpit with a sounding board overhead. No microphone was used - then or today. The Union army took over this church during the Civil War. Although the structure suffered no serious damage, the grave markers were removed and stacked to make room for the camps. No records exist of where the markers were...so it's anybody's guess if the graves are now correctly marked. Find the grave that shows a woman living to be 156 years old...what's up with that?

GADSBY'S TAVERN & MUSEUM

134 North Royal Street (Olde Town, Corner at Cameron St)

Alexandria 22314

- ❏ Phone: (703) 838-4242, Restaurant: (703) 548-1288
  Web: http://oha.ci.alexandria.va.us/gadsby/
- ❏ Hours: Museum: Tuesday-Saturday 10:00am-5:00pm, Sunday
  and Monday 1:00-5:00pm. (April-October). Tuesday-Saturday
  11:00am-4:00pm, Sunday 1-4:00pm (November-March)
  Restaurant: 7 days for lunch/dinner. Colonial entertainment in the
  evenings.
- ❏ Admission: Museum: $4.00 adult, $2.00 child (11-17).
  Restaurant prices: Lunch $8.00-$15.00 (for a unique
  carpetbaggers lunch). child's menu $5-10.00 all day. Dinner
  prices: Average $20.00.
- ❏ Miscellaneous: Part of the historic walking tours and museum has
  a separate admission and tour. Great combo for lunchtime with
  families.

"General Washington's steward had recommended me an inn kept
by Mr. Gadsby..." This is the place if you're in the mood for
authentic colonial dining (fresh fish, crabcakes, Virginia ham and
pyes - potpie puff pastry) that is served by a costumed wait staff
who speak old English. The museum is in the 1770 City Tavern
and City Hotel where many political and social events occurred
(even Washington's birthday parties). Notice the ice well where
they kept ice all year long and could serve cold beverages in the
heat of summer (something very few establishments could do).
Notable guests and stories of visits included on tour are George
Washington, Thomas Jefferson, Robert E. Lee, and their wives.
March-November (on Friday nights) they offer tours by lantern for
the family.

POTOMAC RIVERBOAT COMPANY

Union & Cameron Streets (City Marina), **Alexandria** 22314

- ❑   Phone: (703) 548-9000 or (877) 502-2628
     Web: www.potomacriverboatco.com
- ❑   Admission: $10.00-$30.00 adult, $8.00-$28.00 senior, $5.00-
     $17.00 child (2-12)
- ❑   Tours: 5 times daily (each way) - Tuesday-Sunday, 11:30am-
     9:00pm (May-September). Plus Monday Holidays and Weekends
     (April & October)

Some of the tours offered include:

- ❑   ALEXANDRIA BY WATER - 50 minute, narrated sightseeing
     cruise of Alexandria's historic waterfront aboard the Admiral
     Tilp.
- ❑   MOUNT VERNON - cruise aboard the Miss Christin from "old
     town" to the Mount Vernon Estate. 50 minutes each way. (Mt.
     Vernon admission included in ticket price)
- ❑   WASHINGTON BY WATER - round trip, 60 minute cruise
     (each way) aboard the Matthew Hayes past Washington's
     majestic landmarks. Can get off in Georgetown for a spell and
     catch a later boat.

All tours are narrated with fun facts, history and legends. Sailing
schedule is subject to weather and river conditions. Contact by
website, brochure or telephone is suggested to obtain current sailing
schedule. Some younger children may prefer this method of touring.

TORPEDO FACTORY ART CENTER

Alexandria - *105 North Union Street, 22314. Phone: (703) 838-
4565. Web: www.torpedofactory.org. Hours: Daily 10:00am-
5:00pm. closed on Easter, July 4th, Thanksgiving, Christmas, and
New Year's Day. Admission: FREE. Miscellaneous: Art Camps.*
Constructed in 1918 for the manufacturing of torpedoes, the
factory now serves as working studios for over 84 professional
artists. Visitors can purchase wares onsite or simply watch the
creative process in action.   Watch anything from sculpture, to
painting, jewelry, stained glass, weaving, printmaking, ceramics, to
photography being created.

For updates & travel games, visit: **www.KidsLoveTravel.com**

GUNSTON HALL

Alexandria (Mason Neck) - *10709 Gunston Road (I-95 or US Rte. 1 to SR 242 east), 22079. Phone: (703) 550-9220 or (800) 811-6966. Web: www.gunstonhall.org. Hours: Daily 9:30am-5:00pm. Closed New Years, Thanksgiving, and Christmas. Admission: $8.00 adult, $7.00 senior, $4.00 student (6-18).* The colonial plantation home of George Mason, author of the Virginia Declaration of Rights and a framer of the United States Constitution. The house has elaborately carved woodwork. Reconstructed outbuildings help to illustrate the work of domestic servants and slaves. There's a nature trail and a short orientation film presented in the Visitors Center. Special events make this even more interesting.

MOUNT VERNON, GEORGE WASHINGTON'S

(end of George Washington Memorial Parkway)

Alexandria (Mount Vernon) 22121

❑   Phone: (703) 780-2000, **Web: www.mountvernon.org**

❑   Hours: Daily 8:00am-5:00pm (April - August), 9:00am-5:00pm (March, September, October), 9:00am-4:00pm (rest of the year).

❑   Admission: $13.00 adult, $12.00 seniors (62+), $6.00 Child (6-11).

❑   Miscellaneous: The latest additions include a working 18th-century mill at George Washington's Gristmill and the new Food Court Pavilion and expanded Shops at Mount Vernon. George Washington's Gristmill is 3 miles away and features guides leading historic tours. Meet a miller and watch the water-wheel operate the stones grinding grain into flour. Learn about the slaves and millers who ground grain 200 years ago. (small additional fee).

Explore history and get to know the "real" George Washington. Located just inside the main entrance to Mount Vernon, the Ford Orientation Center introduces visitors to the personality and character of George Washington as his contemporaries knew him with a dramatic 15-minute film. The large-format, Hollywood-style film will provide action-oriented insight into the story of Washington's life and enable visitors to "meet" the real George

Washington. Another new attraction is the "Mount Vernon in Miniature," an authentic, one-twelfth scale version of the Mansion. Now, look upon the view and take a guided tour featuring:

❑   **HANDS ON HISTORY** - (10:00am-1:00pm - Summers only) - Learn how to bridle and sit on a mule; The Root Cellar - What archeological items could be found in a cellar? (answer: bottles, keys, bones from cooked food); Dress up, Photo-OP - Measure up to see how tall you were when you visited Mt. Vernon. Most folks don't know that George Washington was over 6' tall.

❑   **PIONEER FARMER** - Ever see a round barn? How about a barn where horses walk the 2nd floor? Crack corn, thresh wheat or take a wagon ride. Livestock are authentic to George Washington's times (some are heirloom varieties).

❑   **OUTBUILDINGS** - Dung Depository (Washington was one of the first composters), coach house and stable, laundry yard, smokehouse, clerk's office and kitchen

❑   **GEORGE WASHINGTON'S TOMB** - See the original site and see the actual vault where George Washington's body now lies.

Of course, the true highlight of this visit will be your **HOUSE TOUR**. During peak season, be prepared for a 30-90 minute wait to enter. Once inside, you'll learn the history of this very famous house. See mostly authentic furnishings, Washington's unique color choices for rooms (many are bright and cheerful like the giant green room where he and Martha loved to dance!) Look for the letter press (a carbon copy like machine) that General Washington used to make copies of all letters that were sent. (He wrote so many…and at that time they took so long to get delivered that sometimes you could forget what you wrote if you didn't keep a copy!). You'll also see a giant globe in his office that strangely is missing one entire continent (could it be that it wasn't discovered yet?). Near the end of the tour, you'll see Washington's private family chambers and the bed in which he died. You'll enjoy this site the most as a family if you participate in the Hands-On-History tent (in the summer) or during a special event (otherwise there aren't any re-enactments going on). Also, be sure your children receive the Adventure Map which has puzzles to solve…the kids love it because the map looks like a treasure map!

For updates & travel games, visit: **www.KidsLoveTravel.com**

ARLINGTON NATIONAL CEMETERY & DC TOURMOBILE

Arlington 22211 (Includes Washington DC Area)

- ❏ Phone: (703) 697-2131, (202) 554-5100 or (888) 868-7707
  Web: www.tourmobile.com
- ❏ Hours: Daily 8:30am-4:30pm (April-September), 9:30-4:30pm (rest of year).
- ❏ Admission: Walking tour is FREE. Tourmobiles fare is $5.00-$6.00 adult, $3.00 child (3-11) (Arlington Tour). If you add Washington DC to the tour the fees are: $20.00 adult, $10.00 child.
- ❏ Tours: Begin at Visitor Center on Memorial Drive starting one half hour after cemetery opens until one half hour before cemetery closes. Last tour begins 30 minutes before closing. Closed on Christmas.
- ❏ Miscellaneous: The tourmobile is suggested for kids because the walking tour is too long. The on/off all day service is perfect for families touring the many sites in the DC area.

This is the best spot to visit (especially by tourmobile), to get to the heart of Arlington. Many sites are on, or near the grounds, and some can be toured individually or part of the tourmobile tour. Why are some of the headstones smaller and empty? The tour includes the Kennedy gravesites; the Tomb of the Unknowns for the Changing of the Guard ceremony (24/7 - Look how still the guards are!); the Arlington House, The Robert E. Lee Memorial [where Lee lived for 30 years, where he chose to resign his commission in the US Army to defend Virginia in the Civil War, and where Union troops occupied it during the Civil War - Open daily, 9:30am-4:30pm, Free, (703) 557-0613]. Narrators on the tourmobile relate accounts of personal sacrifice and heroism as you ride past the important sites. Lots of little known facts and anecdotes. Check out the newer "Women in Military Service for America Memorial" were you'll see an emotional, patriotic film and learn many little known stories of women who served as water bearers, nurses, and POW's (the building is entirely covered in a "glass ceiling"). Washington stops include: All 5 Presidential Memorials, The Capitol, several Museums and the Smithsonian.

SCOTCHTOWN, HISTORIC HOME OF PATRICK HENRY

Beaverdam - *16120 Chiswell Lane (I-95 exit 92B, off US 54, W. Patrick Henry Hwy. On SR 671), 23015. Phone: (804) 227-3500 or (800) 897-1479. Web: www.apva.org/scotchtown/. Hours: Thursday-Saturday 10:00am-4:30pm, Sunday 1:30-4:30pm (April-October). Admission: $6.00 adult, $5.00 senior, $3.00 child. FREE to Hanover County school children.* Built in 1719 by Charles Chiswell, Scotchtown was the home for Patrick Henry, Virginia's first elected governor, from 1771 to 1777, and is one of the oldest plantations houses in Virginia. Scotchtown, for a short period, was also the childhood home of Dolley Madison. The Manor houses three original Henry family pieces and is unique in that all the living quarters are on one floor.

NATIONAL AIR AND SPACE MUSEUM/ UDVAR-HAZY CENTER

14390 Air and Space Museum Parkway (near Dulles International Airport at the intersection of routes 28 and 50), **Chantilly** 20151

- ❑ Phone: (202) 633-1000 **Web: www.nasm.si.edu/museum/**
- ❑ Hours: Daily 10:00am-5:30pm, except Christmas.
- ❑ Admission: FREE. Parking Lot: Yes, public parking is $12.00 in Chantilly.
- ❑ Miscellaneous: A round-trip shuttle bus offers transportation between the Museum's National Mall building in Washington D.C. and the Udvar-Hazy Center in Chantilly, Virginia. Buses arrive/depart from the Jefferson Drive (north) side of the National Mall building and the Udvar-Hazy Center's main entrance. ($9.00-$12.00 per person fee)

The museum is designed to memorialize and inspire wonder, quicken pulses and make spirits soar. Peer inside a space capsule, get a feel of weightlessness during an IMAX film or view the hundreds of aircraft on display at both locations. The flying machines on view at the Virginia center's Aviation Hangar include the only successful supersonic airplane ever built (the Concorde), the fastest plane and the first airliner with a pressurized cabin. In the Space Hanger, you'll see the Gemini VII and Mercury 15B spacecraft and the shuttle Enterprise. Can you believe this site is just an annex to the National Mall building (they had so many extra artifacts they needed to house elsewhere)?

GEORGE WASHINGTON BIRTHPLACE NATIONAL MONUMENT

Colonial Beach - *1732 Popes Creek Road (off SR 3 south side of the Potomac River), 22443. Phone: (804) 224-1732.* **Web:** *www.nps.gov/gewa. Hours: Daily, 9:00am-5:00pm. Closed Thanksgiving Day, Christmas and New Years Day. Admission: $3.00 (age 17+) - 7 day pass.* Come to see where the first President of the United States was born. The park includes: Visitor Center: the brick foundation of the house where he was born, The Washington Family Cemetery: where George's father, grandfather, and great-grandfather are buried, and The Historical Area with the Memorial House, kitchen, and typical plantation surroundings. Also, picnic grounds with a nature trail, and the Potomac River beach area.

WATERWORKS WATERPARK

5301 Dale Blvd. (I-95 exit 156, Dale Blvd. West)

Dale City 22193

❑ Phone: (703) 680-7137, **Web: www.waterworkswaterpark.com**
❑ Hours: Opens around 10:00 or 11:00am and closes before dusk
     (Memorial Day - Labor Day).
❑ Admission: $5.00-$6.00 general (2+). Discounts after 4:00pm.
❑ Miscellaneous: Full-service concessions, rental lockers,
     lifeguards.

Located within Andrew Leitch Park, Waterworks family fun center is full of these unique water features: Spacious Beach Pool Entry, Enclosed Speed Slide, Circular Open Slide, Giant Climb-on Hippo, 3 Challenging Jungle Walks, Beach Volleyball, Shade Pavillions, 2 level Children's Wading Pool with: Colorful Crayon Sprays, Great Slides, Rope Climb, Super Geysers, Fun Bubblers.

SKY MEADOWS STATE PARK

Delaplane - *11012 Edmonds Lane (one mile south on SR 17 at Rte. 710 west), 20144. Phone: (540) 592-3556. Web: www.dcr.state.va.us/parks/skymeado.htm. Hours: 8:00am-dusk. Admission: $3.00-$4.00 per vehicle.* This park offers a peaceful getaway on the eastern side of the Blue Ridge Mountains. Rich in history, the park has rolling pastures and woodlands, and scenic vistas. The park also has access to the Appalachian Trail and a primitive hike-in campground, as well as picnicking, hiking and riding trails, interpretive programs and a visitor center in the historic Mount Bleak House (video presentation, nature walks). The historic Mount Bleak House is furnished as a middle-class farmhouse (about 1860) and serves as the park's visitor center. It is open during the summer and on weekends in the spring and fall. Tours are offered on weekends and holidays.

OLD MINE RANCH

17504 Mine Road (I-95 exit 152)

Dumfries 22026

❑   Phone: (703) 441-1382 **Web: www.oldmineranch.com**

❑   Hours: Weekdays, 10:00am-3:00pm. Weekends, 10:00am-
      5:00pm (April-December)

❑   Admission: $6.00 per person (age 2+).

Experience a family Wild West themed pony ranch and petting farm on over 40 acres. Admission includes a pony ride for kids, hay ride and animal feed, scenic picnic areas, guided river hike, garden center, western themed town, covered wagon, rope swings, mine tunnel slides, and petting farm. Come in the Spring if you love to witness new births and cuddle baby animals. Visit in the Fall for the Pumpkin Patch or the Holidays for Sleigh Rides.

FREDERICKSBURG AREA MUSEUM

Fredericksburg - *907 Princess Anne Street (corner of Princess Anne and William Streets), 22401. Phone: (540) 371-3037. Web: www.famcc.org. Hours: Monday-Saturday 10:00am-5:00pm, Sunday 1:00-5:00pm (March-November). Only open until 4:00pm (rest of year). Closed winter holidays. Admission: $5.00 adult,*

$1.00 student (6-18). Housed in the old 1816 Town Hall / Market House, the Federal building survived the destruction of the Civil War. This museum displays artifacts of the town starting with the formation of North America and proceeding to the present. Children enjoy the dinosaur footprints that were found in the area, as well as an Indian hut and Colonial fort, and period weapons used in the Revolutionary and Civil Wars. Look for the actual newspaper from 1767!

FREDERICKSBURG TROLLEY TOURS
Fredericksburg 22401

❑   Phone: (540) 898-0737, **Web: www.fredericksburgtrolley.com**
❑   Admission: $15.00 adult, $5.00 child (6-18). Cash only.
❑   Tours: Tours start at the Fredericksburg Visitor Center 600 Caroline St. 75 minute tours depart 3-4 times daily (every couple hours or so). (April - November). December (Weekends only)

Pass and hear information about Chatham House and 50 of the 100 historic homes (even the oldest one). The tavern wench (not a bad name in those times), the Apothecary assistant and "Mary Washington (George's mom)" will come out and wave as you pass by. See the original stonewall of the battlefield. Funny tidbits: Old Stone Warehouse - why is only the 3rd floor showing? Why were some homes built in layers? What happened if you didn't go to church at least twice a month in the Anglican Church? Why did they build narrow homes? What did the two numbers on the unknown soldiers graves mean? A great way to hear the Revolutionary and Civil War history of Fredericksburg with fun tidbits (also a great overview of the museums and restaurants in town). Afterwards, you'll know which spots you want to personally visit.

HISTORIC KENMORE
1201 Washington Avenue
Fredericksburg 22401

❑   Phone: (540) 373-3381, **Web: www.kenmore.org**
❑   Hours: Daily 10:00am-5:00pm (March-December). Closed major winter holidays.

Historic Kenmore (*cont.*)

- ❏ Admission: $8.00 adult, $4.00 student (ages 6-17 or with student ID).
- ❏ Tours: <u>RESTORATION DETECTIVE TOURS</u> - What two-century-old clues are hidden behind plaster and paneling? Why are there decorative brick arches in the cellar? Does the house have a secret passage? What unusual object has been stored in the attic for over 100 years? Reservations required, additional fee.

Historic Kenmore, located in the downtown area, was built in 1775 by George Washington's sister Betty and her husband, Fielding Lewis. The best time to visit is during Family Tours or special events: What did colonists use to start fires, make brushes, and protect toddlers from injury? How did the "stucco man" create the beautiful ceilings at Kenmore? Parents and children (age 4 and above) learn about the lives of 18th century Virginians in family tours designed with hands-on activities. No reservations needed. Usually summer weekday mornings or year-round weekend re-enactments.

HUGH MERCER APOTHECARY SHOP

1020 Caroline Street (Old Town)

Fredericksburg 22401

- ❏ Phone: (540) 373-3362
  Web: www.apva.org/apva/hugh_mercer.php
- ❏ Hours: Monday-Saturday 9:00am-5:00pm. Sunday 11:00am-5:00pm (March-November). Closes one hour earlier in winter. Closed winter holidays.
- ❏ Admission: $5.00 adult, $2.00 student (6-18)

Anyone could enjoy walking into this 18th century doctor's office and learning about all the interesting things that were used for medicines back then. While smelling the entertaining scents from unusual (mostly herbal) medicines, visitors may (or may not!) want to view utensils formerly used for draining blood, amputating, pulling teeth and performing operations. You will even see a saw that looks like it belongs in a tool box! On the way out, stop by the garden to view herbs and plants used for medicinal purposes (during the times and even popular now). They've got real leeches in here! Does mom ever say – "You're driving me crazy..."? They've got the perfect medicinal cure here.

MARY WASHINGTON HOUSE

1200 Charles Street (downtown)

Fredericksburg 22401

❑   Phone: (540) 373-1569

   Web: www.apva.org/apva/mary_washington_house.php

❑   Hours: Monday-Saturday 9:00am-5:00pm, Sunday 11:00 am-5:00pm. (March-November). Monday-Saturday, 10:00am-4:00pm, Sunday Noon-4:00pm (December-February). Closed January 1, Thanksgiving, December 24, 25, 31.

❑   Admission: $5.00 adult, $2.00 child (6-18).

Mary Washington spent the last 17 years of her life in this home bought for her by her son, George Washington, in 1772. Some of Mary's original personal possessions, including her "best dressing glass" and the boxwood bushes she planted years ago are present. The most interesting room is the old kitchen quarters.

RISING SUN TAVERN

1304 Caroline Street, Old Town, **Fredericksburg** 22401

❑   Phone: (540) 371-1494

   Web: www.apva.org/apva/rising_sun_tavern.php

❑   Hours: Monday-Saturday 9:00am-5:00pm, Sunday 11:00am-5:00pm (March-November). Opens 1hour later and closes 1 hour earlier (December-February).

❑   Admission: $5.00 adult, $2.00 student (6-18).

Discover popular pub phrases and terms, while learning about the life of a "tavern wench". She'll show you an early cash register, an 18th century mousetrap, and the confined sleeping quarters used then. Visitors can learn about subjects as serious as the separation of educated men from common men. There are silly things, too, like the bathing rituals of those times (they bathed completely only twice a year!). The Rising Sun was a "proper" tavern (as defined in those times)...never more than 5 to a bed!

FREDERICKSBURG AND SPOTSYLVANIA CIVIL WAR BATTLEFIELDS

(I-95 south to Rte. 3 exit east. At intersection of Rte. 3 & Bus Rte. 1)

Fredericksburg 22407

❑   Phone: (540) 373-6122, **Web: www.nps.gov/frsp**
❑   Hours: Parks open daily dawn to dusk. Visitors Centers open 9:00am-5:00pm daily except Thanksgiving, Christmas and New Years.

❑   Admission: $1.00-$2.00 per person (age 11+) per Visitors Center.

The Civil War was one of America's greatest tragedies and no region suffered more than the Fredericksburg area. Four major battles were fought here. Eventually, the cost of these battles would be too much for the South to bear. Today, the National Park Service maintains 18 miles of land in the Fredericksburg and Spotsylvania National Military Park. Two visitors centers help interpret four battlefields. A self-guided tour of the battlefields begins at the Fredericksburg Battlefield and continues into Spotsylvania County. In the battlefield parks, wayside exhibits, exhibit shelters, interpretive trails and many historic buildings help tell the story of the Civil War battles. Highlights on the map or audio (rental tape ~$3.00) tour are:

❑   WILDERNESS BATTLEFIELD - May 5-6, 1864. This conflict introduced Union General Grant to Lee in battle. Even though the battle ended in stalemate, Grant pressed southward , "On to Richmond". (Orange, 540-373-4461, Rte. 20, one mile west of Rte. 3)

❑   SPOTSYLVANIA BATTLEFIELD - May 8-21, 1864. On the most direct route to Richmond, warring troops engaged for 2 weeks including 20 hours on May 12 in the most intense hand-to-hand fighting of the war at the "Bloody Angle".

❑   CHANCELLORSVILLE BATTLEFIELD - April 27-May 6, 1863. Action included a spectacular military maneuver by Lee and his most trusted subordinate, "Stonewall Jackson", but the day ended in calamity when Jackson was fatally wounded by his own troops. (I-95, Rte. 3 west)

For updates & travel games, visit: **www.KidsLoveTravel.com**

❑ FREDERICKSBURG BATTLEFIELD - December 11-15, 1862. Called "Lee's most one-sided victory", the battle focused on Sunken Road and the Stone Wall at Marye's Heights.

❑ CHATHAM - across the Rappahannock River off SR218; mansion served as a Union headquarters and field hospital during the Civil War. Clara Burton and Walt Whitman provided care here to wounded soldiers. Daily 9:00am-5:00pm. FREE. (540) 371-0802.

GEORGE WASHINGTON'S FERRY FARM

268 Kings Highway (SR 3 east, along the Rappahannock River)

Fredericksburg 22407

❑ Phone: (540) 370-0732, **Web: www.ferryfarm.org**

❑ Hours: Daily 10:00am-5:00pm. Closed major winter holidays. (January – mid-February)

❑ Admission: $5.00 adult, $4.00 senior (60+), $3.00 student (ages 6-17 and anyone with a student ID). Discovery Workshops may be slightly more but include activity.

This is the boyhood home of the father of our country...not to mention, the reported place where the famous "cherry tree" incident (and legend) occurred. This was his father's 600 acre plantation where he grew up and later learned how to survey. The current property is under archeological excavations that are ongoing. Only facades of one home are viewed, but new artifacts turn up all the time. We suggest Discovery Workshops for the kids in the summer. Each workshop teaches hands-on activities about Colonial life at Ferry Farm and the Fredericksburg area. "I Dig George" sounds like the most fun as the focus is on visiting the archaeological site and learning techniques of archaeology. Other programs highlight investigating trees, 18th century gardening and games, surveying and wartime camp life. Best of all, the staff here are creative and energetic about the site and interpretation.

COLVIN RUN MILL

10017 Colvin Run Road (Beltway exit 47A, Rte. 7 west)

Great Falls 22066

- ❏ Phone: (703) 759-2771
  Web: www.co.fairfax.va.us/parks/crm/index.htm
- ❏ Hours: Daily (except Tuesday - Closed) 11:00am-5:00pm (March-December).
- ❏ Admission: Tour: $5.00 adult, $4.00 Student (16+ with ID), $3.00 Child and senior. Admission to park is FREE except for some special events.
- ❏ Tours: offered on the hour, last tour at 4:00pm
- ❏ Miscellaneous: On the grounds is the Colvin Run Mill General Store. It originally served the local community and continues to function today as a sales shop offering penny candy, freshly ground cornmeal and wheat flour, popcorn and an array of old-fashioned goods.

Colvin Run Mill has an early 19th century wooden water wheel and operating gristmill. The old Miller's House features an exhibit about the process of milling and the families who operated the mill. Another exhibit in the renovated 20th century dairy barn features the history of the Great Falls community. It offers daily tours, educational programs, special events, and outdoor concerts. The mill operates on a regular basis (usually Sundays). You can picnic on the grounds, feed the ducks, and learn about America's technological roots.

HARPERS FERRY NATIONAL HISTORICAL PARK

P. O. Box 65 (off US 340, confluence of the Potomac and Shenandoah rivers in the states of West Virginia, Virginia, & Maryland)

Harpers Ferry, WV 25425

- ❏ Phone: (304) 535-6029, **Web: www.nps.gov/hafe/home.htm**
- ❏ Hours: The Visitor Center is open every day, 8:00am-5:00pm, except Thanksgiving, Christmas, and New Year's Day.
- ❏ Admission: Per vehicle is $6.00 or $4.00 per individual.

For updates & travel games, visit: **www.KidsLoveTravel.com**

❑   Tours: Ranger guided tours daily (summer) and weekend
     afternoons (rest of year).
❑   Miscellaneous: Hiking, fishing, canoeing and rafting are offered
     on the Shenandoah and Potomac rivers and Appalachian Trail. To
     get the "feel" for this area, catch the short videos in Building #8
     and #15. The John Brown Wax Museum is in town and open for
     a small additional fee.

Two thousand acres of restored buildings and brick sidewalks
share exhibits, interpretive programs and hiking trails. Shuttle
buses provide transport to the Lower Town Historic District where
ranger guided tours include: John Brown's Raid, Civil War,
Stonewall Jackson, Camp Hill, Harpers Ferry and the C&O Canal.
Exhibits and museums included are: the Industry Museum, the
Marshal's Office, Dry Goods Store (they could get almost
anything…even coconuts from the Hawaiian Islands), Wetlands
museum, John Brown's Fort, Black Voices Museum (slave or free,
they still had special laws), Civil War Museum and Jefferson
Rock. The story of Harpers Ferry is more than one event or
individual, but many. Harpers Ferry witnessed the first successful
application of the Industrial Revolution, the arrival of the railroad,
John Brown's attack on slavery, the largest surrender of Federal
troops during the Civil War, and the education of former slaves.
The site interpreters do an excellent job of absorbing you into
history and teaching you little known facts of the mid-to-late 1800s
- all at one site!

FRYING PAN PARK: KIDWELL FARM AND SPRING MEETING HOUSE

2709 West Ox Road (Beltway exit 9A or C, Rte. 66 west to Rte. 50
west exit), Herndon 20171

❑   Phone: (703) 437-9101
     Web: www.co.fairfax.va.us/parks/fryingpanpark.htm
❑   Hours: Farm: 9:00am-5:00pm daily.
❑   Admission: Except for special events and some educational
     programs, Frying Pan Park and the Kidwell Farm are FREE.
     Please call for use fees and availability of the equestrian
     facilities.

Frying Pan Park: Kidwell Farm & Spring Meeting House (*cont.*)

❑ Tours: Groups are welcome and guided tours are available by appointment.

❑ Miscellaneous: The Country Store, Spring House and Blacksmith Shop are open to the public during special events and programs. The Easter Bunny hops by in the spring, fall harvest activities abound in October and Santa comes to the farm in December. Indoor and outdoor horse riding arenas and bridle trails.

Kidwell Farm recreates the era from 1920 to 1940...a time of great transition in rural America. These two decades saw the advent of tractors, milking machines, mechanical bailers and other improvements in modern agriculture. In addition to draft horses, the farm is home to chickens, peacocks, rabbits, sheep, goats, pigs, cows and other livestock common to the early farms of Fairfax County. Visitors can pet the friendly farm animals, watch the farm hands at work, enjoy a picnic or take a walk through a country setting. The four-room Schoolhouse served youngsters in grades one through seven and the first two years of high school (now the hub of the park's arts and crafts, fitness, children's classes and summer camp programs). The Moffett Blacksmith Shop served local farmers from 1904 until 1955. The shop contains much of the smithy's original equipment. Today, the bellows pump, the anvil rings and the sparks fly during demonstrations. The Spring Meeting House was built in 1791. It was used for town meetings as well as for religious services. Other attractions at Frying Pan Park include hayrides, music, living history, farm life demonstrations, games and a whole lot of good old fashioned fun!

CALEDON NATURAL AREA

King George - *11617 Caledon Road (Rte. 218), 22485. Phone: (540) 663-3861. Web: www.dcr.state.va.us/parks/caledon.htm.* Summer home to one of the largest concentrations of American bald eagles on the East Coast, Caledon attracts birdwatchers galore. However, limited tours of the eagle area are offered seasonally. A visitor center and picnic area with restrooms are available too.

PAMUNKEY RESERVATION

175 Lay Landing Road

King William 23066

- ❏ Phone: (804) 843-4792, **Web: www.baylink.org/pamunkey**
- ❏ Hours: Tuesday-Saturday, 10:00am-4:00pm., Sunday, 1:00-5:00pm.
- ❏ Admission: $1.00-$3.00
- ❏ Miscellaneous: Can be an adventure just finding it. Here are the directions from Williamsburg. I-64 West to West Point exit (Rte. 33), after crossing over Pamunkey River into West Point, turn left at first traffic light (Rte. 30), Follow signs, turn left on Rte. 632 (Mt. Olive-Cohoke Road), At stop sign, turn left on Rte. 633 (Powhatan Trail), Turn right on Rte. 673 (Pocahontas Trail). Follow to reservation.

Get out to the rural, small town feel of this authentic 75 member Pamunkey Indian Reservation. You won't see teepees or huts, but instead trailers and small home (even a church - most Indians were converted to Christianity during Capt. John Smith's time). On the property you'll pass Powhatan's gravesite (Pocahontas' father), cotton or corn crops and a fish hatchery. Many men tribe members work outside the reservation while most women tend to farm or make pottery. Inside the museum you might be greeted by "Still Waters" or "Gentle Rain" as they invite you in to watch a short video about the Pamunkeys, and then you take a self-guided tour of the exhibits. Learn that Pamunkey were the most powerful of the great Powhatan tribes. Chief Powhatan and his famous daughter (Pocahontas) lived among the Pamunkey and their tribe is proud of their heritage and bravery. Kids will probably most like the cypress tree dugout canoe, the turtle shell ceremonial rattle, and the original popcorn (small corn on the cob).

BELLE ISLE STATE PARK

Lancaster - *1632 Belle Isle Road (Rte. 3 to Rte. 354 to Rte. 683), 22503. Web: www.dcr.virginia.gov/parks/bellisle.htm. Phone: (804) 462-5030. Admission: $2.00-$3.00 per car.* With 733 acres, seven miles of shoreline and access to Mulberry and Deep creeks, visitors can explore a wide variety of tidal wetlands interspersed with agricultural fields and upland forests. Belle Isle is open daily and features three picnic shelters, hiking and bridle trails, motor boat launch, overnight lodging at the Bel Air Guest House or Mansion, bicycle, canoe and motorboat rentals, guided canoe trips, a car top launch area, restrooms, a universal access playground, and conservation education programming and other interpretive programs.

LEESBURG ANIMAL PARK

Leesburg - *19270 James Monroe Highway (Rte. 7 towards Leesburg to Rte. 15 south, next to Sunshine Farms), 20175. Phone: (703) 433-0002. Web: www.leesburganimalpark.com. Hours: Friday-Sunday 10:00am-5:00pm. (May-early November). Extended weekday summer hours. Admission: $7.00-$9.00 (age 2+). Extra $1.00-$2.50 for rides.* A petting zoo that offers the opportunity to get up close and personal with some of the friendliest animals around. Pet and feed various animals including llamas, goats, sheep, miniature donkeys, deer, antelope and many others. Meet squirrel monkeys and zebra. In the spring help feed the bottle babies and meet newborn lambs, goats, and bear cubs. There is also an opportunity to visit Giant Tortoises, Lemurs, and Serval Cat. Join in on a wagon ride or a pony ride or get up close and personal with some of the resident animals in the park at Keeper's Corner.

LOUDOUN MUSEUM

16 W. Loudoun Street

Leesburg 20175

- ❑   Phone: (703) 777-7427, **Web: www.loudounmuseum.org**
- ❑   Hours: Monday-Saturday 10:00am-5:00pm, Sunday 1:00-5:00pm.
- ❑   Admission: $1.00 or less (age 5+)

The museum currently maintains displays including Native American artifacts, furniture and silver made by Loudoun County craftsmen, Civil War artifacts, letters written by freed slaves to their former masters in Loudoun, and documents signed by George

Washington and James Monroe. The original 18th century county courthouse bell is a featured exhibit and its interpretation leads the visitor through Loudoun's history as the bell tolled for celebrations, announcements, and special activities. Girls into needlework will enjoy the sampler collection which includes early schoolgirl samplers stitched by Loudoun County girls and an extensive costume collection of dresses made as early as the late 18th century. The museum's Discovery Room features a small replica of an early 19th century Quaker kitchen (complete with hearth, cookware, and utensils), activity baskets full of reproduction tools and toys, a play area, children's books, and period costumes for role playing.

PIED PIPER THEATRE

Manassas - *9419 Battle Street, 20108. Phone: (703) 330-ARTS. Web: www.potomacstages.com/PiedPiper.htm. Performances: Fall & Spring Saturdays at 7:30pm. Sundays at 3:30 pm. See schedule on website. Performances held at area high schools. Admission: Varies. Usually around $7.00.* Students of the theatre school perform many classics each year including plays such as Charlotte's Web, The Wizard of Oz and Narnia.

MANASSAS NATIONAL BATTLEFIELD PARK

6511 Sudley Road (SR 234 - between I-66 and US 29)

Manassas 20109

- ❑ Phone: (703) 361-1339, **Web: www.nps.gov/mana**
- ❑ Hours: Daily 8:30am-5:00pm. Until 6:00pm in the summer.
- ❑ Admission: $3.00 adult (18+). FREE for everyone 17 and under.
- ❑ Miscellaneous: Visitor's Center has a museum and slide program (12 minutes) plus a 3D map of strategies (told from the soldier's point of view)

A 5000 acre park is the scene of two important Civil War battles. The first and Second Battles of Manassas were fought along the waters of Bull Run Creek. Living history demonstrations bring these dramatic events to life. It was on this battleground that General Jackson was first observed standing "like a stone wall".

Tour by walking (easy access to Henry Hill which has the best scenic viewpoint of the First Manassas Battle and the Stonehouse). Tour by driving (focuses more on the Second Battle of Manassas) or, tour by horse. This area was strategically important because of the location of the railroad junction. Initially the first battle (July 21, 1861) was not taken too seriously (more like a sporting activity) as picnickers and sightseers accompanied the well equipped (but ill-trained) Union Army as it marched out of DC to fight the Confederates. After 10 hours of deadly battle, the Union army had to retreat and the war was now taken much more seriously. One year later, with tattered uniforms, the Union was once again gravely defeated by Confederate General Lee and his worn troops. Of particular interest are the cute lights on the lighted battlefield model (easy for kids to understand and follow); the first civilian casualty (Mrs. Henry - died in her bed); the civilian picnics with Senators giving out free sandwiches; and the Stone House that started as a rest stop and turned into an aid station during the battles (many soldiers write about this "Stone House" in their diaries).

SPLASHDOWN WATERPARK

Manassas - *7500 Ben Lomond Park Drive (Exit 44 off I-66), 20109. Web: www.splashdownwaterpark.com. Phone: (703) 361-4451. Hours: Open from Memorial Day through Labor Day. Park opens at 11:00am and closes at 6:00-8:00pm. Open daily when school is out. Admission: Generally around $15.00 per person. Spectators and late afternoon entry is discounted. Miscellaneous: Funbrellas & Pavillions for shade, shower and lockers, lifeguards, volleyball, tennis, lounge chairs. Coney Island Café.* Five Water Areas, 11 Acres of Fun! Includes the Zero Depth Beach Area, Boat Slide, Water Raindrops & Bubblers, 770 ft. Lazy River, Children's Area with 4 Water Slides, Two 70 ft. Tall Waterslides, Two fast Cannonball Slides, 25 Meter Lap Pool, Log Walks & Lily Pad Walk, Two Tropical Twister Waterslides.

OLD DOMINION SPEEDWAY

Manassas - *10611 Dumfries Road (south of Manassas on Rte. 234 across from the County Fairgrounds), 20110. Phone: (703) 361-RACE or (703) 361-7753. Web: www.olddominionspeedway.com. Hours: Just about every Friday and Saturday night and some Sundays. Gates open at 5:00pm, racing at 7:00pm. (April-October). Admission: $10.00-$15.00 adult, $5.00-$8.00 student (12-16), $1.00 child (5-11).* NASCAR Winston Cup, drag racing, car shows and special events including the fun "Bug Out" can be found here.

MASON NECK STATE PARK

Mason Neck (Lorton) - *7301 High Point Road (US 1, then east to SR 242), 22079. Phone: (703) 339-2385 or (703) 339-2380 (visitor center). Web: www.dcr.virginia.gov/parks/masonnec.htm. Admission: $3.00-4.00 per car. Miscellaneous: Hiking trails, picnicking and Visitors Center.* The peninsula is the site of an active heron rookery. The park also attracts several other migrating and non-migrating species of birds, including whistling swans and assorted species of duck. Bald eagles also inhabit the area. The park boasts several hundred acres of hardwood forests consisting of oaks, holly, hickory and other species of trees. In addition, several wetland areas are also found along with birdwatching and guided canoe trips on the Potomac River. More than three miles of hiking trails wind through the park providing a glimpse of nature by the bay. Elevated walkways allow visitors to explore some of the marsh areas in the park. Ten bicycles are available for rent by the hour.

CLAUDE MOORE COLONIAL FARM AT TURKEY RUN

6310 Georgetown Pike (SR 193 east off I-495, exit 13)

McLean 22101

❏   Phone: (703) 442-7557, **Web: www.1771.org**

❏   Hours: Wednesday-Sunday 10:00am-4:30pm (April to mid-December). Closed during inclement weather and Thanksgiving.

❏   Admission: $3.00 adult, $2.00 senior and child (3-12)

Claude Moore Colonial Farm At Turkey Run (*cont.*)

❑　Miscellaneous: Market Fairs and holiday events are slightly higher admission.

This living history museum demonstrates the life of a poor family living on a small tenant farm in northern Virginia during the late colonial period. The staff wear period apparel and talk like a colonist while they go about their chores in the fields, applying basic principles of hoe agriculture. Maybe come on Dairy Day, during Wheat Harvest, Pickling Produce Day, Wash Day or Threshing Day.

THEODORE ROOSEVELT MEMORIAL AND ISLAND

McLean - *George Washington Memorial Pkwy, Turkey Run Park (east of the Key Bridge on the Potomac River), 22101. Phone: (703) 289-2500. Web: www.nps.gov/this/. Miscellaneous: Two-hour parking is available off the southbound side of the George Washington Parkway. The footbridge to the island is just minutes from the Rosslyn Metro Station. Access to the island is available only from the northbound lane of the George Washington Memorial Parkway. For a different experience, rent a canoe or kayak the perimeter of the island.* Theodore Roosevelt's deep love of nature and strong commitment to conservation are reflected throughout the 88-acre island, where 2.5 miles of hiking trails pass through dense forests and marshy swamps. The memorial features a 23-foot statue of a strong, "fit-as-a-bull-moose" Roosevelt, situated in an oval terrace with two roaring fountains. The terrace is surrounded by four granite tablets inscribed with the President's philosophy on nature, manhood, youth and the state. Rich in ecological diversity, Roosevelt Island hosts a variety of flora and fauna in its swamp, marsh, rocky shore and woodland ecosystems. Along the island's southern end, the swamp trail passes a rare tidal freshwater marsh, filled with cattails and redwing nests. The island's drier patches attract foxes, great owls, ground hogs, raccoons and opossums. Open weekdays 7:30am-4:00pm. FREE.

MONTPELIER, JAMES MADISON'S

11407 Constitution Hwy. (SR 20 SW of downtown)

Montpelier Station 22957

- ☐ Phone: (540) 672-2728, **Web: www.montpelier.org**
- ☐ Hours: Daily 9:30am-5:30pm (April-October) and until 4:30pm (November-March)
- ☐ Admission: $11.00 adult, $10.00 senior, $6.00 child (6-14)
- ☐ Tours: Behind-the-Scenes Tour (offered twice daily) including the rarely seen second floor rooms. Saturday Estate tours explore 300 years of Montpelier history.

Learn about our fourth president and the "Father of the Constitution", as well as the effervescent Dolley, who inspired the title "First Lady". Enjoy a 15 minute video documentary about the Madisons or hike two miles of trails in the old-growth forest and stroll to the cemetery and nearby slave cemetery. Look at the place Madison called "a squirrels jump from heaven" and view the historic trees in the arboretum or watch archeologists dig every summer at Mount Pleasant nearby. The Mansion is in the process of being renovated. All floors are open to witness the process.

JAMES MADISON MUSEUM

Montpelier Station (Orange) - *129 Caroline Street, 22960. Phone: (540) 672-0231. Web: www.jamesmadisonmuseum.org. Hours: Monday-Friday 9:00am-5:00pm year round, Saturdays 10:00am-5:00pm, Sundays 1:00-5:00pm (March-December). Closed New Year's, Memorial Day, Independence Day, Labor Day, Thanksgiving & Christmas. Admission: $4.00 adult, $3.00 senior, $1.00 child.* Nation's only James Madison Museum commemorates the 4th President of the U.S. and Father of the Constitution. Located in Madison's home county of Orange, Virginia. Exhibits deal with the life and times of Madison and include furnishings from Montpelier, correspondence, fashions, and books from the Madison library. Stories of truths and myths about James and Dolley are told. There is an unusual Hall of Agriculture with farm devices, machinery and tools.

WESTMORELAND STATE PARK

Montross - *1650 State Park Road (just off SR 3), 22520. Phone: (804) 493-8821. Web: www.dcr.virginia.gov/parks/westmore.htm. Admission: $3.00-$4.00 per vehicle, plus small additional swimming fee. Vehicle entrance fee is waived for overnight guests.* The park extends about one and a half miles along the Potomac River, and its 1,299 acres neighbor the former homes of both George Washington and Robert E. Lee. The park's Horsehead Cliffs provide visitors with a spectacular view of the Potomac River. Opportunities for family fun - a large swimming pool and adjacent bathhouse, launching ramp for power boats, campgrounds, climate-controlled cabins, a fishing pier and kayaking tours. The Visitor Center exhibits include marine, bird and other wildlife displays. A collection of sharks' teeth is also on display. It's open on weekends from noon until 5:00pm. during May, September and October as well as Wednesdays through Sunday from Memorial Day through Labor Day.

NATIONAL MUSEUM OF THE MARINE CORPS

Quantico - *(I-95 exit next to the U.S. Marine Corps Base), 22134. Web: www.usmcmuseum.org/Store/MCHF/experience.asp. Phone: (212) 358-0800 or (800) 397-7585.* Before entering major galleries, visitors pass through an orientation theater featuring a short, introductory film about the Corps and its history. As they exit the theater, visitors will find themselves in a replica of a recruiting station, from which they will move aboard a bus, the windows of which are television screens transmitting oral histories of Marines recounting their feelings on the verge of boot camp. If you make it through Boot Camp, immerse in realistic exhibits, examine weapons and equipment and use interactive devices to better understand how this small, elite fighting force came to make a large influence on American history.

<u>SMITH ISLAND & CHESAPEAKE BAY CRUISE</u>

382 Campground Road (departs from the KOA Campground Resort on Slough Creek), **Reedville** 22539

❑ Phone: (804) 453-3430

   Web: www.eaglesnest.net/smithislandcruise

❑ Admission: Varies. Must make e-mail or phone inquiries about rates.

❑ Tours: One and one half hour cruise, by reservation only. Seasonal, weather permitting.

❑ Miscellaneous: KOA Kampground and Kabins on departure premises.

History has recorded that Capt. John Smith sailed up the Chesapeake Bay in the year 1608, came to shore here, and gave this island his name. Known as the "Soft-Shelled Crab Capital of the World," Smith Island has 3 picturesque fishing villages: Ewell, Rhodes Point, and Tylerton, each on its own island with interlacing creeks, canals, marsh and meadow. You will see historic Smith Point where the great Potomac River meets the majestic Chesapeake Bay and Smith Point Lighthouse two miles offshore. Crossing the ships channel you may see large container ships enroute to or from Baltimore, MD. or Washington, DC., or, maybe a passing cruise ship. Your relaxing cruise across the Bay, 13½ miles out passing the 5,000 acre Glen L. Martin Waterfowl /wildlife refuge, begins your journey. Egrets, Blue Herons, Ospreys, Roseatte Spoonbills are among the Refuge's numerous waterfowl you'll see. THE CAPT. EVANS - Dock at Ewell Village for delicious seafood and other homemade delicacies at one of the island's waterfront restaurants, or, you may bring your own picnic lunch. Enjoy a guided tour, visit Smith Island Center, the museum on Ewell, or visit the Island's gift shops.

LAKE ANNA STATE PARK

6800 Lawyers Road (adjacent to Route 601 off Route 208)

Spotsylvania 22553

❑   Phone: (540) 854-5503
   Web: www.dcr.virginia.gov/parks/lakeanna.htm
❑   Admission: $3.00-$4.00 per vehicle, $2.00-$4.00 beach (per
   person). Park entrance fee waived for overnight guests.

The land in Lake Anna State Park used to be known as "Gold Hill" and contained the Goodwin Gold Mine. Gold was first discovered in 1829 with mining reaching its peak in the 1880's. The last gold to be found was in a zinc mine during the 1940s. While boating and fishing on the beautiful lake are major attractions, Lake Anna State Park also has more than 13 miles of hiking trails, lakeshore picnicking, a guarded swimming beach, a children's play area, a boat ramp, a food concession stand, a bathhouse and a children's and handicapped fishing pond. Panning for gold and nature programs are popular activities. This park's cabins became available for rent July 1, 2005. Also, a new campground and camping-cabins are under construction.

STRATFORD HALL PLANTATION

(SR 3 to SR 214), **Stratford** 22558

❑   Phone: (804) 493-8038 or (804) 493-8371
   Web: www.stratfordhall.org
❑   Hours: Daily 9:30am-4:00pm. Closed Thanksgiving, Christmas,
   New Years Eve and Day.
❑   Admission: $10.00 adult, $9.00 senior (60+) and military, $5.00
   child (6-11)
❑   Miscellaneous: The Stratford Mill will operate from 11:00am to
   2:00pm on the first full weekend of each month from July
   through September. The Gristmill grinds grain just as it has for
   250 years and the flour is sold at the Plantation Store (March-
   October). Potomac River beach nearby. A log cabin dining room
   in a wooded setting serves a plantation lunch daily.

On a high bluff above the Potomac River is the colonial house with its greatest distinction being the family of patriots who lived there.

For updates & travel games, visit: **www.KidsLoveTravel.com**

Thomas Lee, a prominent Virginia planter, built Stratford in the late 1730s. Using brick made on the site and timber cut from virgin forest, workers constructed the H-shaped great house, its four outbuildings and coach house and stables. Stratford was the home of Thomas Lee's eight children. His sons Richard Henry Lee and Francis Lightfoot Lee were the only brothers to sign the Declaration of Independence. Their cousin, "Light Horse Harry" Lee, the dashing Revolutionary cavalry leader, made Stratford his home for over twenty years. Robert Edward Lee was born in the big bedroom on the upper floor of the Great House (crib still in its place). Visitors walk through meadows where the young Lees rode their horses and follow a trail to "cool, sweet spring".

LEESYLVANIA STATE PARK

Woodbridge - *2001 Daniel Ludwig Drive (US 1 to Rte. 610 east), 22191. Web: www.dcr.virginia.gov/parks/leesylva.htm. Phone: (703) 670-0372.* Located on the Potomac River, this park offers many land and water related activities including biking, picnicking, fishing and boating. Newer boat launching facilities, concessions area, a new visitor center and an environmental education center are available. Leesylvania was a home of Virginia's legendary Lee Family. Once a year (in June), there is a Civil War Weekend at Leesylvania. Explore the park's rich Civil War history, tour Freestone Point Battery and Fairfax House, and view a re-enactment of historical happenings. See Civil War era weapons fired where similar guns once blazed.

SUGGESTED LODGING AND DINING

HAMPTON INN, Alexandria, 1616 King Street, (703) 299-9900. A nice choice for D.C./Alexandria area lodging. They offer free full continental breakfast and are a quick walk to the Metro. There's an outdoor pool, too.

BUGSY'S PIZZA, Alexandria, Just down the street from the Visitors Center is (111 King Street, 703-683-0313) with original beams in the building made from tobacco boats. Across the street is another hometown favorite - Scoops Ice Cream. After all that food, walk just one block to the riverfront.

EMBASSY SUITES, **Alexandria**. Family Fun Packages all year. Your kids get a "kid-tested" pack of goodies, an indoor pool, soft play area for toddlers, and the whole family gets a wonderful made to order full breakfast. All rooms are suites with separate bedroom, microwave, and refrigerator for around $170.00/night - (800) EMBASSY.

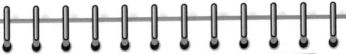

Washington, DC

Chapter 2

INTERNATIONAL SPY MUSEUM

800 F Street, NW (Metro: Gallery Place/ Chinatown),

Washington, DC 20004

❑   Phone: (202) 393-7798, **Web: www.spymuseum.org**

❑   Hours: Daily 10:00am-8:00pm (April-October); 10:00am-6:00pm
(November-March). Closed major winter holidays. Peak months
the museum opens at 9:00am.

❑   Admission: $15.00 adult (12-64), $14.00 senior (65+), Active
duty military, $12.00 child (ages 5-11). Children age 4 and under
FREE. The Permanent Exhibition is most appropriate for ages 12+.

One of Washington, DC's newest attractions is a big hit with
children and adults alike. Packed with high-tech, interactive
displays and activities, visitors can take on a spy's cover, test their
skills of observation and surveillance, while learning about the
history and the future of espionage. Examine over 200 spy gadgets,
weapons, bugs, cameras, vehicles, and technologies. Learn about the
earliest codes--who created them and who broke them. A spy must
live a life of lies. Adopt a cover identity and learn why an operative
needs one. See the credentials an agent must have to get in - or out.

NATIONAL ZOO

3001 Connecticut Avenue, NW (I-395 north to exit 8B, Washington
Blvd. To Arlington Bridge. Cross Bridge, veer left. Turn right on
Constitution, left on 17th. Metro: Zoo), **Washington, DC 20008**

❑   Phone: (202) 633-4800, **Web: http://nationalzoo.si.edu**

❑   Hours: Daily 10:00am-4:30pm. Open until 6:00pm (April-
October). Closed Christmas Day.

❑   Admission: FREE

Most of you are thinking Giant Pandas at the National Zoo. See
Tai Shan, the Zoo's newest panda, on the web cams. Information
on viewing the cub during your visit can be read here. Like babies?
Popular areas are: Dandula, the Zoo's young Asian elephant,
Cheetah cubs, Tiger cubs or animals in the Kids' Farm. It wouldn't
be the National Zoo without a Bald Eagle Refuge. While many
animals are always or usually in indoor exhibits, many others,
including giant pandas, other bears, seals, and sea lions, and great

cats, are usually outdoors. To make your walk around the Zoo more enjoyable, comfortable shoes are recommended. The Zoo is set on hilly terrain and some paths are steep. You can expect to see more animals early in the morning. Print off a scavenger hunt sheet before you visit (on the Info for Visitors web page).

ROCK CREEK PARK AND NATURE CENTER

Washington, DC - *5200 Glover Road, NW, 20008. Phone: (202) 426-6829. Web: www.nps.gov/rocr/naturecenter/. Hours: Wednesday - Sunday 9:00am-5:00pm. Closed most national holidays. FREE.* This 2,000-acre park provides a perfect setting for an urban escape or a family outing. The park has a golf course, tennis courts, picnic tables, bike trails, jogging trails, and horseback riding. The Rock Creek Nature Center is home to the only planetarium in the National Park system and a Discovery Room with a live beehive viewing area.

FRANKLIN D. ROOSEVELT MEMORIAL

900 Ohio Drive, SW (West Potomac Park at West Basin and Ohio Drive), **Washington, DC** 20024

❏   Phone: (202) 426-6841, **Web: www.nps.gov/fdrm/**
❏   Hours: Park ranger in attendance 8:00am-midnight. Wheelchair accessible. The Bookstore opens from 9:00am-6:00pm. All restroom facilities close at 11:30pm. Closed Christmas.
❏   Admission: FREE
❏   Note: The memorial did not originally feature any renderings of the president in his wheelchair. FDR did not wish to be portrayed in his wheelchair, and designers honored this request. Many people with and without disabilities were angered by this omission, and a statue of FDR in his wheelchair was installed in 2001. The statue was placed at the entrance of the monument to remind visitors that FDR was confined to a wheelchair when he became one of the country's most revered leaders.

The rambling FDR Memorial (it spans 7.5 acres) consists of four "rooms" arranged chronologically to represent the 32nd President's unprecedented four terms in office. A fountain in the first room flows peacefully, representing the healing effect water had on the president during his term in the Navy and while at Warm Springs. The second room addresses the Great Depression and the hope FDR cultivated with his extensive social programs. The third room represents the war years, 1940-1944 with choppy, unsettling stonework and water. In a stark contrast, the final room projects peace and optimism. A bas-relief resting above a pool of still water depicts FDR's funeral procession. Acknowledging FDR's own physical difficulties, his memorial was the first creation of its kind designed with easy access for people with disabilities.

JEFFERSON MEMORIAL

East Potomac Park, South end of 15th St., SW on the Tidal Basin

Washington, DC 20024

- ❑   Phone: (202) 426-6822, **Web: www.nps.gov/thje/**
- ❑   Hours: Park rangers available 8:00am-midnight.
- ❑   Admission: FREE

Easily recognizable to Jeffersonian architects, the colonnade and dome memorial reflect Jefferson's love of this architectural style. The graceful, beautiful marble design pays tribute to the third president and primary author of the Declaration of Independence. Inside, there is a large bronze statue and excerpts from his writings on the walls. Jefferson stands at the center of the temple, his gaze firmly fixed on the White House, as if to keep an eye on the institution he helped to create. Museum located in the lower lobby of the memorial.

LINCOLN MEMORIAL

900 Ohio Drive, S.W. (west end of Mall, 23rd St. and Constitution Ave., NW), **Washington, DC** 20024

- ❑   Phone: (202) 426-6841, **Web: www.nps.gov/linc/**
- ❑   Hours: Visitors Center 8:00am-midnight. Park ranger in attendance 24 hours.
- ❑   Admission: FREE

The most famous of the monuments, this site was used for several of history's greatest moments (including MLK speech). The artist opted to portray Lincoln seated, much larger than life, a symbol of mental and physical strength. As the father of a deaf child, the artist positioned Lincoln's hands in the shape of the sign language letters "A" and "L." Lincoln faces the US Capitol. Murals sculpted by Jules Guerin adorn the temple's inner walls. Emancipation is on the south wall and hangs above the inscription of the Gettysburg Address. Unification is on the north wall, above Lincoln's Second Inaugural Address.

NATIONAL MALL

Washington, DC - *(stretches from 3rd St., NW and the Capitol grounds to 14th St., between Independence and Constitution Aves.),* *20024.* Officially, the National Mall is green space that begins at 3rd Street and stretches to 14th Street. Visitors and locals, however, widely use the term to refer to the entire expanse of monuments and museums, from the grounds of the Capitol to the Lincoln Memorial. Pierre L'Enfant's original plans for the city called for this open space and parklands, which he envisioned as a grand boulevard to be used for remembrance, observance, and protest. Today, it serves this purpose, hosting concerts, rallies, festivals, as well as Frisbee matches, family outings, picnics and memorials: Vietnam Veterans Memorial (the Wall); U.S. Navy Memorial and Naval Heritage Center (701 Pennsylvania Ave., NW); Korean War Veterans Memorial (West Potomac Park, Independence Ave., beside the Lincoln Memorial; National World War II Memorial (East end of the Reflecting Pool, between the Lincoln Memorial and the Washington Monument.

UNITED STATES HOLOCAUST MEMORIAL MUSEUM

Washington, DC - *100 Raoul Wallenberg Place, SW (Metro: Smithsonian, near the National Mall, just south of Independence Ave., SW, between 14th Street and Raoul Wallenberg), 20024.* **Web: *www.ushmm.org.*** *Phone: (202) 488-0400 or (800) 400-9373. Hours: Daily 10:00am-5:30pm, except Yom Kippur and Christmas. Extended hours in the summer. Admission: FREE. Timed tickets required for permanent exhibition; available same day or in advance at **www.tickets.com**. Usually sold out by Noon.* Geared for visitors ages 11 and up, the permanent collection of the U.S. Holocaust Memorial Museum tells the moving story of the persecution of the Jewish people. A special children's exhibition, "Daniel's Story," presents the story of the Holocaust for younger visitors.

BUREAU OF ENGRAVING & PRINTING TOUR

Department of the Treasury, 14th and C Streets, SW

Washington, DC 20228

❑   Phone: (202) 874-2330 (local) or (866) 874-2330
    Web: www.bep.treas.gov/locations/index.cfm/3

❑   Hours: Public Tour: 9:00am-10:45am & 12:30pm-2:00pm (every 15 minutes). Extended Summer Hours (May-August): 5:00-7:00pm (every 15 minutes). Visitors Center: Weekdays 8:30am-3:30pm and summer early evenings. The Bureau is closed on weekends, federal holidays and the week between Christmas and New Years.

❑   Tours: Tickets are required for all tours from the first Monday in March through the last Friday in August, on a first-come, first-served basis. The ticket booth is located on Raoul Wallenberg Place (formerly 15th Street). They offer same day tickets only. The Ticket Booth opens at 8:00am - Monday through Friday, and closes when all tickets have been distributed. Lines form early and tickets go quickly; most days tickets are gone by 9:00am. Please plan accordingly. No tickets required (September-February).

❑   Miscellaneous: Please be patient with them during this time of heightened security, and be advised that all tour policies are subject to change without public notification. If the Department of Homeland Security level is elevated to CODE ORANGE, the Bureau of Engraving and Printing is CLOSED to the public unless otherwise noted.

You'll see millions of dollars being printed during a tour of the BEP. The tour features the various steps of currency production, beginning with large, blank sheets of paper, and ending with the paper money we use every day! The BEP designs, engraves and prints all U.S. paper currency. Did you know they also produce postage stamps and White House invitations? Established in 1862, the Bureau, at that time, used just six people to separate and seal notes by hand in the basement of the Treasury building. The Bureau moved to its present site in 1914. Though new printing, production and examining technologies have brought us into the 21st century, the Bureau's engravers continue to use the same traditional tools that have been used for over 125 years - the graver, the burnisher, and the hand-held glass.

WASHINGTON MONUMENT

15th & Jefferson Drive (National Mall area, Tourmobile stop, Metro Smithsonian stop), **Washington, DC** 20228

❑ Phone: (202) 426-6841 or (800) 967-2283 reservations
   Web: www.nps.gov/wamo/

❑ Hours: Washington Monument are from 9:00am-4:45pm, closed December 25th.

❑ Admission: Free tickets are distributed for that day's visit from the kiosk on the Washington Monument grounds on a first-come first-served basis. All visitors 2 years of age or older must have a ticket to enter the Monument. Hours for the ticket kiosk are 8:00am-4:30pm, but tickets run out early. Advanced tickets are available through the National Park Service Reservation System. Reservations may be made between the hours of 10:00am-10:00pm. While tickets to the Washington Monument are free of charge, callers to this number will incur a $1.50 service charge and a 50¢ shipping and handling fee.

❑ Miscellaneous: Bookstore, restrooms and concessions on site.

Take the fast elevator ride to the top of the Monument for a panoramic view of the city. Many folks like to start here as Washington was our 1st President and the view gives you a good feel for the lay of the land in D.C. The 555-foot tall obelisk is marble and is the tallest free-standing obelisk in the world. Why are there two different colors of marble used? The immense structure represents Washington's enormous contribution to the founding of our republic.

NATIONAL AQUARIUM

Washington, DC – *14th Street & Constitution Avenue, NW (Metro: Federal Triangle, only one block from the Washington Monument), 20230. Web: www.nationalaquarium.com. Phone: (202) 482-2826. Hours: Daily 9:00am-5:00pm. Admission: $5.00 adult, $4.00 senior & military, $2.00 child (2-10).* Tucked inside the United States Department of Commerce building, the National Aquarium is a hidden treat for families that displays a variety of marine life. Features more than 270 species of native and exotic fish, reptiles, amphibians, and invertebrates. The aquarium features a touch tank, videos, and children's programs. Look for a surge around 2:00pm - feeding time for the sharks or piranhas.

WHITE HOUSE

1600 Pennsylvania Avenue, NW (Metro: Metro Center, McPherson Square), **Washington, DC** 20500

- ❑ Phone: (202) 456-7041, **Web: www.whitehouse.gov**
- ❑ Hours: Visitors Center: Daily 7:30am-4:00pm.
- ❑ Tours: The White House is currently open only to groups (of 10 or more) who have made arrangements through a congressional representative. Park Rangers lead Walks Around the Park at 9:30am, 11:30am (themed) and 1:30pm each day.
- ❑ Miscellaneous: The White House presents Life in the White House, an exclusive presentation of the rich history of the White House and West Wing by video online.

White House Visitor Center: All visits are significantly enhanced if visitors stop by the White House Visitor Center located at the southeast corner of 15th and E Streets, before or after their walking or White House group tour. The Center features many aspects of the White House, including its architecture, furnishings, first families, social events, and relations with the press and world leaders, as well as a thirty-minute video. Allow between 20 minutes to one hour to explore the exhibits. The White House Historical Association also sponsors a sales area. Please note that restrooms are available, but food service is not.

CAPITOL BUILDING, UNITED STATES

(east end of the National Mall)

Washington, DC 20540

- ❑ Phone: (202) 737-2300 or (800) 723-3557
- ❑ Hours: Monday-Saturday 9:00am-4:30pm.
- ❑ Admission: FREE
- ❑ Tours: Guided tours of the building leave every 15 minutes from the Rotunda.
- ❑ Miscellaneous: A limited number of free passes to the House and Senate galleries are available by contacting your representative's office, by phone or stopping by their offices across the street from the Capitol building.

The Capitol is one of the most widely recognized buildings in the world. It is a symbol of the American people and their government, the meeting place of the nation's legislature, an art and history museum, and a tourist attraction visited by millions every year. The bright, white-domed building was designed to be the focal point for DC, dividing the city into four sectors and organizing the street numbers. Begun in 1793, the Capitol has been built, burnt, rebuilt, extended, and restored. An 180-foot dome is adorned by the fresco Brumidi painting (took him 20 years to complete). The Rotunda, a circular ceremonial space, also serves as a gallery of paintings and sculpture depicting significant people and events in the nation's history. The Old Senate Chamber northeast of the Rotunda, which was used by the Senate until 1859, has been returned to its mid-19th century appearance. The third floor allows access to the galleries from which visitors to the Capitol may watch the proceedings of the House and the Senate when Congress is in session.

LIBRARY OF CONGRESS

Washington, DC - *10 First Street, SW (Metro: Capitol South), 20540. Phone: (202) 707-8000. Web: www.loc.gov. Hours: Monday-Saturday 10:00am-5:30pm. Admission: FREE public tours. Tours: Docent-led scheduled public tours are offered Mondays through Saturdays in the Great Hall of the Thomas*

Jefferson Building of the Library of Congress. Tours are limited to 50 people. For more information on guided tours, ask at either of the information desks in the Visitors' Center of the Jefferson Building (west front entrance). You may enter this building on the ground level under the staircase at the front of the building, located directly across from the U.S. Capitol. The world's largest library is home to much more than just books. At the Library of Congress, kids can see a perfect copy of the Gutenberg Bible, a collection of Houdini's magic tricks, the Wright Brothers' flight log books and more. Equipped with new information desks, a visitors' theater features a 12 minute award winning film about the Library and interactive information kiosks. The Visitors' Center enhances the experience of approximately one million visitors each year.

ALBERT EINSTEIN PLANETARIUM

Washington, DC – *7th Street & Independence Ave., SW (within the National Air & Space Museum), 20560. Phone: (202) 633-1000.* **Web:** *www.nasm.si.edu/visit/planetarium/. Hours: Daily 10:00am -5:30pm. Admission: $7.00-$8.50 per person (students and above).* Not only does this planetarium have a spectacular star field instrument, but it has been upgraded to include a first-of-its-kind, Sky Vision™ dual digital projection system and six -channel digital surround sound. For the first time, you'll feel the sensation of zooming through the cosmos with a blanket of color and sound. Infinity Express: A 20-Minute Tour of the Universe or Stars Tonight (free) program.

NATIONAL GALLERY OF ART

Washington, DC – *6th Street & Constitution Avenue, NW (Metro: Archives/Navy Memorial, on the National Mall between Third and Seventh Streets), 20560. Phone: (202) 737-4215.* **Web:** *www.nga.gov. Hours: Monday-Saturday 10:00am-5:00pm, Sunday 11:00am-6:00pm. Closed Christmas and New Years. Admission: FREE.* Visitors with children can participate in drop-in workshops, take several postcard tours of the collection using a packet of cards with pictures of objects and questions for discussion or rent a family-oriented audio tour. This fine art museum contains a collection of European and American works in chronological order with recognizable names including da Vinci, Renoir, Monet and Whistler.

NEWSEUM

(6th Street and Pennsylvania Avenue, N.W.)

Washington, DC 20560

❑   Phone: (703) 284-3544 or (888) 639-7386
    Web: www.newseum.org
❑   Hours: Tuesday-Sunday 10:00am-5:00pm. Closed winter holidays.

The world's only interactive museum of news. The exhibits take you behind the scenes to see and experience how and why news is made. Visitors here can act as editors and put together newspaper front pages. They can also step into a reality ride to the scene of a breaking news story and test their skills as investigative reporters or photographers. In the broadcast studio, visitors can watch "in person" a live TV newscast (most folks never get this chance). Try your hand at being a TV news anchor and then take home a tape of your "broadcast". A long news bar displays news from around the world. Below the wall are the front pages of daily newspapers from every state and many countries - all diversely covering the same stories. The dome theater presents great moments in news history or another theater offers a glimpse of vintage newsreels.

SMITHSONIAN INSTITUTION

Washington, DC 20560

❑   Phone: (202) 357-2700 or (202) 633-1000 (voice)
    Web: www.smithsonian.org
❑   Hours: All museums are open from 10:00am-5:30pm, daily.
❑   Admission: FREE.

Miscellaneous: The Smithsonian has opened its final installation on the National Mall, the National Museum of the American Indian (4th Street & Independence).

A visit to Washington, DC is not complete without experiencing at least one of the 14 Smithsonian museums. The following are highlights of the myriad of exhibits and activities offered especially for children:

ON THE MALL: Outside the National Air and Space Museum, a scale model of the solar system entitled Voyage: A Journey through our Solar System helps children grasp the magnitude of the world around them. During the summer months, a ride on the world's oldest carousel, near the Arts and Industries Building, is a sure treat.

HIRSHHORN GALLERY: The Smithsonian's modern art museum's "Young at Art" program introduces young visitors to different artistic disciplines through hands-on activities. Participants can act in a play, create portraits in chocolate, make clay sculptures, and more. On Saturdays, drop in for an "Improv Art" program—including a tour of the gallery with a special activity sheet and an art project to take home. The museum also offers regularly-scheduled guided family tours.

NATIONAL AIR & SPACE MUSEUM: Provides a world-renowned collection of flying machines from the Wright Brothers' Kitty Hawk Flyer to the Apollo 11 Command Module. Kids can see a moon rock, Lindbergh's Spirit of St. Louis and a variety of special films. The museum's IMAX theatre provides large-format and 3-D glimpses of space and beyond.

NATIONAL MUSEUM OF AMERICAN HISTORY: Also known as "America's Attic," this popular museum houses such treasures as the First Ladies' inaugural gowns, Dorothy's Ruby Red Slippers, and the flag that inspired "The Star-Spangled Banner." In the museum's Hands-on History Room, young visitors can explore American history with more than 30 special activities, such as operating a cotton gin and sending a message. In the Hands-on Science Room, kids can explore the scientific and social issues addressed in the museum. A new transportation exhibition (and the largest exhibition to open in the museum), America on the Move, explores the world of transportation, including real artifacts from historic Route 66.

NATIONAL MUSEUM OF NATURAL HISTORY: After visiting the Hatcher, seeing a digitally-restored Triceratops, dining in the special dinosaur café, and "ogling" the massive Hope Diamond, check out the famous Insect Zoo. Kids can learn all about these creatures and non-squeamish types are allowed to handle them for an up-close look. The newly-renovated Mammal Hall shows some of the museum's specimens in lifelike, realistic settings.

NATIONAL POSTAL MUSEUM: Located next to Union Station, the National Postal Museum offers its young visitors insights into the interesting world of mail service. Children can create a souvenir postcard, learn about the history of the Pony Express and the legend of Owney the Postal Dog, and participate in a direct mail marketing campaign. 2 Massachusetts Ave., NE. Metro: Union Station.

SACKLER GALLERY: Through the Sackler Gallery's ImaginAsia, kids visit a featured exhibition with a special guide written for children and create an art project to take home. Other special family programs include Asian dance and music lessons, storytelling, and more.

ADDITIONAL TOUR INFORMATION: Tourmobile Sightseeing is the best way to see Washington, DC. Take a ride (on/off) along DC's National Mall area and/or Arlington Cemetery. (see page 11 in the NE Chapter for details).

Chapter 3
North West Area

Our Favorites...

* Monticello Family Tours & Michie Tavern - Charlottesville

* Lexington Carriage Tours - Lexington

* Stonewall Jackson History - Lexington

* Luray Caverns & Garden Maze - Luray

* Natural Bridge, Indian Village & Wax Museum - Natural Bridge

* Virginia Safari Park - Natural Bridge

* Walton's Mountain Museum - Schuyler

* American Celebration on Parade - Shenandoah Caverns

* Frontier Culture Museum - Staunton

* Wintergreen Resort - Wintergreen

Luray Caverns' World Famous "Fried Eggs"

BRYCE RESORT

Basye - *PO Box 3 (11 miles west of I-81, exit #273, on Rt. 263), 22810. Web: www.bryceresort.com. Phone: (540) 856-2121 or (800) 821-1444. Admission: Summer activities range $3.00-$4.00. Skiing rates based on time of day and rentals beginning at around $20.00.* Ride through rural Virginia to Bryce Resort where you can be on the links, the lake, the slopes, or the trail. Bryce has golf, skiing, hiking, dining, lodging, and great scenery. They also have 45-acre Lake Laura with a beach area, swimming, paddle boats and canoes, windsurfing, and fishing; sightseeing lift rides and grass skiing; mountain bike and in-line skate rentals. Other activities near the Resort include miniature golf and horseback riding. The slopes and beginner area provide challenges for novice, intermediate, advanced and expert skiers. Their ski program for kids is called SKIwee. In 2004, Bryce Resort added the Ridge Runner's snow tubing park, where everyone can safely slide in the snow.

SHENANDOAH RIVER STATE PARK

Bentonville - *Daughter of Stars Drive (8 miles south of Front Royal), 22610. Web: www.dcr.virginia.gov/parks/andygues.htm. Phone: (540) 622-6840. Hours: 8:00am-dusk. Admission: $2.00 per car.* Situated on the Shenandoah River with nearly 1700 acres along six miles of shoreline. A large riverside picnic area with shelters, trails, river access and a car-top launch makes this a popular destination for families, anglers and canoeists alike. 30 primitive and canoe-in campsites (individual and group) are available.

WADE'S MILL & BUFFALO SPRINGS HERB FARM

55 Kennedy-Wades Mill Loop (I-81 exit #205. Follow Rt. 606 west (Raphine Road) for 4 miles. Turn right beside Buffalo Springs Herb Farm), **Brownsburg / Raphine** 24472

❑ Phone: (540) 348-1400 (mill) or (540) 348-1083 (farm)
    Web: www.wadesmill.com or www.buffaloherbs.com
❑ Hours: Wednesday-Saturday 10:00am-5:00pm, Sunday 1:00-5:00 pm. (April-mid-December). Closed Sundays in June, July & August. Farm closed January - March.

Wade's Mill & Buffalo Springs Herb Farm (*cont.*)

❑ Admission: FREE to visit Wade's Mill or the Farm. Prices vary for specific cooking classes and special events or tours.

Wade's Mill is a working water-powered flourmill listed on the National Register of Historic Places. The shop features the mill's own flours, pottery, basketry and the "Cooks' Corner", with everything you need to cook and bake with their flours. Buy a homebaked treat and walk around the inside and outside of the mill, seeing and hearing its inner workings. Buffalo Springs Herb Farm is an 18th century farmstead offering garden tours with a variety of themes.

ASHLAWN-HIGHLAND: HOME OF JAMES MONROE

1000 James Monroe Pkwy (I-64 exit 121 SR 20 south to SR 53 east to CR 795 south, 2 miles beyond Monticello)

Charlottesville 22902

❑ Phone: (434) 293-9539, **Web: www.ashlawnhighland.org**
❑ Hours: Daily 9:00am-6:00pm (April-October). Daily 11:00am-5:00pm (November-March). Closed New Year's Day, Thanksgiving Day & Christmas Day.
❑ Admission: $9.00 adult, $8.00 senior (60+), $5.00 Child (6-11). Local resident discount and President's Pass savings.
❑ Miscellaneous: Picnicking welcome.

Tour the 535 acre estate of one home of our fifth President James Monroe. Great to visit during summer MusicFest or other living history festivals or events like Plantation Days (hands-on soap, lantern doll making, open hearth food). His neighbor, Jefferson personally picked the site for him and this place has more of a feel of an early 1800s working plantation. Guided tours of the main house full of Monroe possessions and periodic demos of cooking and spinning plus a look at the overseers house and the slave quarters and gardens are included. Be on the lookout for "President Monroe" stopping by to chat with the youngsters.

MICHIE TAVERN CA.1784

683 Thomas Jefferson Pkwy (I-64 exit SR 20 south to US 53 east, near Monticello), **Charlottesville** 22902

- ❑ Phone: (434) 977-1234, **Web: www.michietavern.com**
- ❑ Hours: The Ordinary is open year-round 11:15am-3:30pm (April-October) & 11:30am-3:00pm (November-March). Museum is open year-round. Tours are Daily 9:00am-5:00pm. Last tour: 4:20pm. Closed Christmas Day and New Year's Day.
- ❑ Admission: Admission is FREE to local residents. $8.00 adult (12-61), $7.00 senior (60+), $3.00 child (6-11). Save on the cost of adult admission to our area's historic attractions by purchasing the "Presidents' Pass" combination ticket. Lunch in the Ordinary: Buffet Only, $11.50 adult, $5.95 Child (6-11) child 5 and under eat FREE! (prices do not include beverage, dessert, sales tax or gratuity).

THE TAVERN MUSEUM - This is a must see "Family Focused Fun". When in the area, your family can cross the threshold of old Michie's Tavern and enter another time. Visitors experience the Tavern's past through an historical journey which recreates life when Mr. Michie operated his Inn. During the afternoons, April through October, visitors may be invited to dance the Virginia Reel in the Assembly Room, drink an 18th-century tavern punch (very yummy...get the recipe!), write with a quill pen, or wear a costume and play the dulcimer. After visiting the original Inn (to-o-o-o fun), the tour continues through the Tavern's dependent outbuildings, the ca. 1822 Printer's Market and the ca. 1797 Meadow Run Grist Mill. How would you make reservations at a stagecoach stop? Learn what "mind your beeswax" really means. Well done, ladies and gentlemen!

THE TAVERN'S ORDINARY - The Tavern's dining rooms, the Ordinary, feature hearty fare offered by servers in period attire in a rustic Tavern setting. Their southern buffet is based on 18th century recipes. Patterned after the southern tradition, many guests choose the bountiful midday fare as their main meal of the day. The Colonial fried chicken and stewed tomatoes are the tastiest you'll find! During the colder months guests enjoy the winter menu before a roaring fire.

MONTICELLO

Thomas Jefferson Pkwy. (I-64 exit SR 20 south to US 53east)

Charlottesville 22902

- ❏ Phone: (434) 984-9822, **Web: www.monticello.org**
- ❏ Hours: Daily 8:00am-5:00pm (March-October). Daily 9:00am- ~5:00pm (November-February). Closed Christmas Day.
- ❏ Admission: $14.00 adult & senior, $ 6.00 child (6-11). Resident discounts. Presidents Pass - A combination discount ticket for touring Monticello, Ash Lawn-Highland and Michie Tavern ca. 1784 is available at the Charlottesville/Albemarle Convention & Visitors Bureau located on Rt. 20 South in the Monticello Visitor Center building. Cost (for ages 12 and up) $26.00.
- ❏ Tours: Guided tours leave approximately every 5 minutes. A shuttle bus or hike takes you to the top of the mountain where you receive a timed entrance card for the tour. Peak season waits can exceed 45 minutes.
- ❏ Miscellaneous: Free exhibit at the Monticello Visitors Center on Rte. 20 south. Stop here first to glance over 400 objects found on the property of Monticello and to view the 40 minute film "Thomas Jefferson: The Pursuit of Liberty" shown daily on the hour in the summer and at 11:00 am and 2:00 pm the rest of the year. Travel assistance and reservations are available here too. Tours for families featuring hands-on objects are available in the summer. Plantation Community weekends throughout the year.

Monticello is the autobiographical masterpiece of Thomas Jefferson, designed and redesigned and built and rebuilt for more than forty years. Jefferson was the third president and author of the Declaration of Independence. This was his home when he wasn't serving in public affairs. Visitors to Monticello tour the mountaintop main house, seasonal plantations and gardens and his gravesite. Much of Jefferson's diversity of interests can be found in artifacts around the house's 10 rooms of the first floor (esp. the items from Lewis and Clark's journeys).

Which side is the front of the house? In fact, Jefferson never spoke of a single "front." Instead he spoke of both an "east front" and a "west front." How was the house heated? The house was heated primarily by fireplaces and wood-burning stoves in certain rooms. In the late 1790s he altered the dimensions of his fireplaces to apply the fuel-saving principles. What are the holes over Jefferson's bed? Jefferson remodeled Monticello extensively in the 1790s. In his bedroom he added a skylight and a partition wall to form a bed alcove below and a closet above. The closet was reached by a steep stair or ladder. The elliptical openings in the closet provided light and ventilation. Mulberry Row slave quarters and plantation industries are also on the tour. While you may have to wait a little while for your tour time, you can wander through the row and talk with the tradesmen and women who are making baskets or nails (from iron rods). You might also have a chance to see Virginia hams or chickens being cooked with period methods. The slave quarters are outlined on the grounds and the costumed slaves are pretty candid about life there. A discussion point might be: Advocating freedom for all people - but Jefferson held slaves?

VIRGINIA DISCOVERY MUSEUM

524 E Main St (east end of downtown Pedestrian Mall) (I-64E, exit 12B North Monticello Avenue), **Charlottesville** 22902

- ❑   Phone: (434) 977-1025, **Web: www.vadm.org**
- ❑   Hours: Tuesday-Saturday 10:00am-5:00pm, Sunday 1:00-5:00pm. Closed Mondays, day before Thanksgiving, Thanksgiving Day, Christmas Eve, Christmas Day & New Year's.
- ❑   Admission: $4.00 (age 1+).

Young people (ages 1-10 best) and their adults explore and learn together about science, history and the arts. 12 permanent hands-on exhibits include walking into a Kaleidoscope; Rainforest Hallway; a reconstructed pioneer log cabin; a take-apart table (can you get it back together?); a computer lab plus "Who am I" fun with mirror dress up; and a Jefferson exhibit and a new marine exhibit touch tank. One of the most popular permanent exhibits is See the Bees alive in their hive. A new exhibit is a hands-on The Earth in Motion that explains the solar system and how it affects weather. Especially nice for locals and during those times of year when Monticello / Michie Tavern don't have living history family exhibits.

UNIVERSITY OF VIRGINIA

University Avenue (on US 29 and US 250 Bus Routes

Charlottesville 22903

❑   Phone: (434) 924-3239 or (434) 924-7969
   Web: www.virginia.edu/academicalvillage/
❑   Admission: FREE
❑   Tours: Historical tours are offered daily at 10:00am, 11:00am,
   2:00pm, 3:00pm and 4:00pm. No tours during holidays or exam
   periods. Parking is available at the Memorial Gym parking lot at
   Emmet Street and Ivy Road.

THE KLUGE-RUHE ABORIGINAL ART COLLECTION - one of the foremost private collections of Australian Aboriginal art in the world. 400 Peter Jefferson Place, (434) 244-0234.

MCCORMICK OBSERVATORY - One of two observatories is open on the first and third Friday night of each month for about 2 hours. 1st and 3rd Fridays, 9:00pm-11:00pm, April-October; 8:00 pm-10:00pm, November-March. **www.astro.virginia.edu/pubnite**. (434) 924-7494.

UNIVERSITY OF VIRGINIA ART MUSEUM - Rugby Road, (434) 924-3592 or **www.virginia.edu/artmuseum/**. Fine arts museum of the University of Virginia, exhibits art from around the world dating from ancient times to the present day, with an emphasis on art produced during Jefferson's time.

UNIVERSITY OF VIRGINIA ROTUNDA AND CENTRAL GROUNDS - Thomas Jefferson wished to be remembered as the "Father" of the University which embodied his vision as an educator and his passion for architecture.

BEAR CREEK LAKE STATE PARK

Cumberland - *929 Oak Hill Road (from US 60, go north on Rte. 622 and then west on Rte. 629), 23040. Phone: (804) 492-4410. www.dcr.state.va.us/parks/bearcreek.htm. Admission: $2.00-$3.00 per car. Swimming $2.00-$5.00 per person (includes paddle or canoe boat rental).* Nestled in the heart of Cumberland State Forest in central Virginia is a park with activities center on a 40 acre lake with a boat launch, fishing pier, boat rentals and swimming beach, as well as lake-side camping, archery picnicking, bike rentals, a playground, hiking and a 14 mile multi-use trail.

CUMBERLAND STATE FOREST

Cumberland - *751 Oak Hill Road (north of State Route 60, west of State Route 45), 23040. Phone: (804) 492-4121. Web: www.dof.virginia.gov/stforest/index-csf.shtml.* The 16,233 acre Cumberland State Forest is located in the piedmont of Virginia. The Forest is located in Cumberland County. Bear Creek Lake State Park is located within the Forest, offering: camping, picnicking, swimming, boating, and hiking. Permanent campsites are installed inside the Park. Trails: A 16 mile Willis River Hiking Trail; and the Cumberland Multi-Use Trail (Hike, Bike, Horse). The Forest also has various gated trails and Forest Roads that can be used by hikers. Fishing: There are five lakes located within the Forest. (Bear Creek Lake located at Bear Creek Lake State Park, Oak Hill Lake located off of Route 629, Winston Lake located off of Route 629, Arrowhead Lake located off of Route 629 and Bonbrook Lake located off of Route 626.). Archery Course: Consisting of a 3-D range and a practice range.

SHENANDOAH VALLEY FOLK ART & HERITAGE CENTER

Dayton - *382 High Street (I-81, exit 245. Go west on Port Republic Road (Maryland Avenue). Turn left on VA Route 42, turn right on 732. Follow signs), 22821. Phone: (540) 879-2681. Web: www.heritagecenter.com.* Hours: *Monday-Saturday 10:00am-4:00pm, Sunday 1:00-4:00pm. Admission: $5.00 adult, $1.00 student (5-18).* "Invincible Spirit: History in the Heart of the Shenandoah" tells the history of Rockingham County and Harrisonburg from pre-Columbus times through the present. Here, you can learn which Native American groups utilized the Valley, understand the local impact of our nation's wars, explore a pioneer tool shed, discover what industries fed the pre-Civil War economy, and appreciate the many cultures and crafts of the community. And, don't miss the sixteen-foot neon pencil that formerly "pointed" the way to Service Stationers on Market Street for years. Features a permanent exhibit of traditional Valley art from the 18th century through the 1990's, as well as rotating special exhibits on folk art and Valley heritage. Also offers a large electronic map with narration about the movements and battles of Stonewall Jackson's Valley Campaign. The "Stonewall" Jackson Electric Map has been enhanced with new electronics, lights, an enhanced audio track and a corresponding multimedia slideshow.

APPOMATTOX-BUCKINGHAM STATE FOREST

Dillwyn - *Rte. 3, Box 7500 (Rte. 636), 23936. Phone: (434) 983-2175. Web: www.dof.virginia.gov/stforest/index-absf.shtml. Admission: $1.00 per vehicle weekdays, $2.00 per vehicle on weekends and holidays.* Holliday Lake State Park is located within the Forest, offering: camping, picnicking, swimming, boating, and hiking. Permanent campsites are installed inside the Park. Two shelters are available on the Forest. (Locations: Woolridge Wayside on the west end of Route 640 and Lee Wayside on Richmond Forest Road). Trails: There is one mapped trail, Carter Taylor Hike, Bike, Horse Trail. The Forest has various gated trails and Forest Roads that can be also be used. Fishing: There are two lakes located within the Forest. (Holliday Lake located at Holliday Lake State Park, and Slate River Watershed located off of Route 640 in Buckingham County.) Whether you hike on foot, ride a bike, or travel on horseback, the Carter Taylor Trail is a great place to explore. Wildlife abounds in the ever-changing oak-hickory and pine forest. Deer, turkey, and even black bear make their homes in these woods.

BELLE BOYD COTTAGE

Front Royal - *101 Chester Street (off US 340), 22630. Phone: (540) 636-1446. Hours: Monday-Friday 10:00am-3:30pm (April-October). Weekends by appointment. Admission: $1.00-2.00 (age 8+).* This cottage was the home of the famous Confederate spy, Belle Boyd, when she visited the area during the Civil War. Guided tours feature Belle's story as a spy and a glimpse of life during the 1860's. Another, more thorough, site for a peek into Belle Boyd's life history is near Harper's Ferry, WV. Ask the folks at Harper's Ferry for directions and hours.

SKYLINE CAVERNS

Front Royal - *PO Box 193 (I-81 to I-66 to Rte. 340 south), 22630. Web: www.skylinecaverns.com. Phone: (540) 635-4545 or (800) 296-4545. Hours: Open daily 9:00am. Closes at 6:00pm (mid June-Labor Day). Closes at 5:00pm (mid March - mid June & Labor Day - mid November). Wintertime closes at 4:00pm. Admission: $14.00 adult, $12.00 senior, $7.00 child (7-13). See website for discount coupons. Miscellaneous: The Skyline Arrow is a ten minute ride on a one-fifth scale miniature train that carries you around Horseshoe curve, across apache Flats, by Kissing Rock and Sinkhole Overlook, and thru Boothill tunnel. Admission is $3.00 (age 2+).* The cavern is one of the only places in the world that features a unique formations known as Anthodites, "orchids of the mineral kingdom". Other features include: the Capitol Dome, The Wishing Well, Cathedral Hall, and Rainbow Falls, which plunges over 37 feet from one of three underground streams that flow through the caverns.

JAMES RIVER STATE PARK

Gladstone - *Rte. 1, Box 787 (from Rte. 60 west turn right on Rte. 605 at the J.River Bridge, left on Rte. 606), 24553. Phone: (434) 933-4355. www.dcr.virginia.gov/parks/jamesriv.htm. Admission: $2.00-$3.00 per car. Miscellaneous: Picnicking, boat launches, primitive campgrounds, equestrian camping and fishing. New Outdoor Adventure Livery Service - canoeing, kayaking, tubing and biking rentals.* Visitors can canoe, fish or camp along the banks of the historic James River or around scenic Branch pond. The park features almost 1500 acres of rolling farm meadows, quiet forest and beautiful mountain vistas, as well as three miles along the banks of the James River.

GRAND CAVERNS

Grottoes - *PO Box 478 (I-81 exit 235 east to SR 256), 24441. Web: www.uvrpa.org/grandcaverns.htm. Phone: (540) 249-5705 or (888) 430-CAVE. Hours: Daily 9:00am-5:00pm (April-October). Weekends in March. Admission: $7.00-$11.00 (age 3+). Tours: Guided one hour tours begin every 30 minutes. Miscellaneous: Hiking and biking trails, picnic shelters, swimming* *pool, miniature golf, tennis courts and a gift shop.* The panorama of subterranean beauty has been open to the public since 1806. Cathedral Hall, 280 feet long and over 70 feet high, is one of the largest rooms of any cavern in the East. Rare "shield" formations create a variety of formations like the famous "Bridal Veil, Stonewall Jackson's Horse and Dante's Inferno". The walls point out signatures of Civil War soldiers. General Stonewall Jackson even quartered his troops at Grand Caverns. The 5000 square foot Grand Ballroom was the scene of many early 19th century dances.

MASSANUTTEN VILLAGE

Harrisonburg - *PO Box 1227 (1-81N to Rt.33E at Harrisonburg. 10 miles to Rt.644 & entrance on left), 22801. Phone: (540) 289-9441 or (800) 207-MASS. **Web: www.massresort.com**. Admission: Activity cards are available. Many activities are covered under lodging pricing. Golf and boat and ski rentals and fees are extra. Miscellaneous: Shenandoah River for a half day of fishing or just relaxing while canoeing, kayaking or river tubing. Massanutten River Adventures provides pickup service at the resort daily April 1-October 31. For more information on this please contact the Concierge. Many accommodations available from hotel rooms to condos to timeshare rentals.* Activities at the year-round resort include: Basketball, Canoe/Kayak, Fishing, Golf, Hiking, Horseback Riding, Mini-golf, Mountain Biking, Skate Boarding, Skiing, Snowboarding, Swimming, Tennis, Volleyball, Crafts, Karaoke Night and Music Shows. Kids Programs include: Child Care Services, Finger-painting, Kids Night Out Slope Sliders, Weekend Programs. As a ski area, they have 14 slopes with kids ski programs, snowboarding and tubing. There is a general store, lodging, dining including a slopeside cafeteria.

JAMES MADISON UNIVERSITY CAMPUS

Main Street (near downtown)

Harrisonburg 22802

- ❑   Phone: (434) 568-6211, **Web: www.jmu.edu**
- ❑   Hours: Open school days, some closed summers.
- ❑   Admission: FREE

For updates & travel games, visit: **www.KidsLoveTravel.com**

JMU: Permanent Attractions:

☐ EDITH J. CARRIER ARBORETUM, open daily dawn to dusk, off University Boulevard; Contains a wide variety of trees and plants native to Virginia; call (434) 568-3194 for tours.

☐ MINERALOGY MUSEUM, open daily, second floor, Miller Hall; Features mineral specimens from around the world as well as a collection of Virginia specimens; call (434) 568-6421 for tours.

☐ ANCIENT GREEK AND ROMAN COIN DISPLAY, open daily, Carrier Library lobby; Showcases 71 silver, bronze and gold coins from the JMU Foundation's Fine Art Collection.

☐ COMMUNICATION MUSEUM, open weekdays, 8:00am-5:00pm, rooms A201-202, Harrison Hall. Memorabilia dating from the 1940's provide a glimpse of the evolution of communication technology; call (434) 568-5080 for tours.

HOMESTEAD RESORT

Hot Springs - *US Route 220 Main Street, PO Box 2000 (I-64 west to exit 16 (first Covington exit), follow the signs for U.S. 220 north), 24445. Phone: (540) 839-1766 or (800) 838-1766. **Web: www.thehomestead.com**. Hours: The KidsClub is open Monday through Saturday 9:00-4:00pm, and Sunday 9:00am-1:00pm. Each Saturday, evening dinners are held from 6:30- 9:30pm. Admission: Guest rooms vary in price and most rates include breakfast and dinner daily. Packages are available to suit a variety of preferences. Almost all activities require separate fees, especially golfing and skiing.* Nine slopes here with kids ski school, snowboarding and lodging/dining at restaurants, cafes and grilles. KidsClub is the club for KIDS ONLY! Headquartered in its own Clubhouse, located on Cottage Row, KidsClub features three main areas of activity: The Children's Literary Center with a library of regional folklore. A resident storyteller and, on special occasions, a children's author may visit to read excerpts from his or her book. On International Day, kids may read and learn about life in other cultures. There's an Art & Design Center and The Science & Biology Center. There are also many other fun activities available around the resort for kids: pole fishing at the Children's Fish Pond, tennis on our mini-courts, hiking and mountain biking, hand-led horseback rides, falconry demonstrations with exotic birds, bowling, winter sports such as skiing, ice skating, snowboarding and snow tubing, swimming, nightly movies, video games, etc. A qualified babysitting service is available too.

HULL'S DRIVE IN THEATER

Lexington - *US 11 (Rte. 11 four miles north of Lexington), 24450. Phone: (540) 463-2621. Web: www.hullsdrivein.com. Hours: Weekends, Friday-Sunday (April-October). Wednesday paper lists shows playing that weekend. Gates open at 8:00pm and movies start at dark. Admission: $4.00 per person. Under 12 FREE.* A blast from the past, Hull's is an authentic 1950's drive-in movie theater. The drive-in has the distinction of being the only community operated drive-in in the U.S. and the only one with status as a non-profit organization. The prices are low and the food reasonable. Mostly G and PG movies are shown.

LEE CHAPEL AND MUSEUM

Lexington - *Washington and Lee University (US 11 Business to University), 24450. Web: http://leechapel.wlu.edu. Phone: (540) 463-8768. Hours: Monday-Saturday 9:00am-5:00pm, Sunday 1:00-5:00 pm (April-October). Closes at 4:00pm (rest of year). Closed Thanksgiving Day, day after Thanksgiving, Christmas Eve, Christmas Day and New Year's Day. Holiday hours between Christmas and New Year's Day are reduced. Admission: FREE.* Lee attended daily worship services here with the students and the lower level housed his office, the treasurer's office and the YMCA headquarters (student center). Lee's office is preserved much as he left it for the last time on September 28, 1870. The rest of the lower level is a museum exhibiting items once owned by the Lee and Washington families, an exhibition tracing the history and heritage of Washington and Lee University and a museum shop. The building houses the memorial sculpture of the recumbent Lee by Edward Valentine and includes a family crypt in the lower level where the general's remains were buried. His wife, mother, father ("Light-Horse Harry" Lee), all of his children and other relatives are now buried in the crypt as well. The remains of his beloved horse, Traveller, rest in a plot outside the museum entrance.

LEXINGTON CARRIAGE COMPANY

106 East Washington Street (downtown, across from the Visitor Center), **Lexington** 24450

- ❏ Phone: (540) 463-3777 (Visitor's Center) or (540) 463-5647
  Web: www.lexcarriage.com
- ❏ Hours: Daily including holidays (weather permitting) 11:00am-5:00pm (April-October). Summer months - slightly longer hours.
- ❏ Admission: $16.00 adult, $14.00 senior (65+), $7.00 youth (7-13).
- ❏ Tours: Normally 2-3 eight passenger carriages operate each day. Last tour at 1:00pm if temp. is 92 degrees or more. Narrated tour lasts 40-45 minutes.

This very educational and kid-friendly tour offers an intriguing way to tour the unique 19th century college town of Lexington. At an easy pace, horsedrawn carriages travel the streets and tell stories of town history while passing Stonewall Jackson House, historic downtown, past Lee Chapel, by Washington and Lee University and thru residential historic districts and finally pass by the Stonewall Jackson Memorial Cemetery where the guide points out the tomb of Stonewall Jackson. The streets of town were much higher in the 1700s - note the houses' doors and balconies. Pass the Livery Inn that was once a "hotel for horses", now for people. The Lee House has the stable open to view where Traveler (Lee's famous horse) lived. Kids like the name of the house called "Skinny". This tour is worth the price for the "inside" stories alone!

STONEWALL JACKSON HOUSE

8 East Washington Street (US 11 Bus or US 60 into downtown, just past Visitors Center), **Lexington** 24450

- ❏ Phone: (540) 463-2552, **Web: www.stonewalljackson.org**
- ❏ Hours: Monday-Saturday 9:00 am-5:00pm, Sunday 1:00-5:00 pm. (Open until 6:00 pm in June, July and August). Closed New Year's Day, Easter Sunday, Thanksgiving Day & Christmas Day.

Stonewall Jackson House (*cont.*)

- ❑ Admission: $6.00 adult, $3.00 youth (ages 6-17)
- ❑ Guided tours: Conducted on the hour and ½ hour. Last tour is ½ hour before closing.

Thomas Jonathan Jackson is known to the world as "Stonewall" Jackson. In Lexington, where Jackson lived and taught for ten years before the Civil War, he was known simply as Major Thomas Jackson, a professor at Virginia Military Institute. The Stonewall Jackson House is the only home that Thomas Jackson ever owned. Jackson and his wife, Mary Anna Morrison, moved to the house early in 1859, and shared two years there before he rode off to war on April 21, 1861, never to return alive. The kids receive a chalkboard with items to circle as they are seen on the tour. Jackson was a health food fanatic (loved fruits and veggies, kids!) and only liked bottled water from Western Virginia. Look for the rug that was cloth and painted with layers of paint (a kind of early vinyl flooring). He collected fossils, loved kids, took cold bathes every day, exercised regularly and slept sitting up. Your guide weaves comedy into the tales of this eccentric man, "Stonewall Jackson". An excellent, fun way to study a famous historical soldier, teacher, and leader.

THEATRE AT LIME KILN

Lexington - *14 South Randolph Street (office) (US 60 off I-81 or I-64 through town to Borden Road south), 24450. Phone: (540) 463-3074.* **Web: *www.theateratlimekiln.com****. Hours: All plays begin at 8:00pm. All concerts begin at 7:30 pm. Admission: Play Series: $16.00 adult (weekends), $12.00 (weeknights), $14.00 student (weekends), $10.00 (weeknights), $14.00 senior (weekends), $10.00 (weeknights), Tuesday nights, tickets for child age 16 and under are only $5.00 when accompanied by at least one paying adult. Concert Series: Admission prices range from $15.00-$24.00 depending on performance. Miscellaneous: Kiln Camp (learn about theater from the inside-Improv and Drama Camps for 1st - 12th grade). Concert series. Concessions on site. Pre-play picnics with delicious gourmet (and fun kid-friendly), $8.00-$10.00 full meal selections are also available by order at Main Street Market,*

(540) 463-5004. Several dramas to choose from, but the family favorites are usually tales about locals or the Bible. The Kiln Theater seats almost 400 people, and the natural ruins of the building with parts of the chimney still intact create a wonderful background for historical plays. Very kid friendly, hand-clapping musical numbers.

VIRGINIA HORSE CENTER

Lexington - *PO Box 1051, Rte. 39 (I-64 west to exit 55), 24450. Web: www.horsecenter.org. Phone: (540) 464-2950. Hours: Monday-Friday 9:00am-5:00pm and anytime the Coliseum is open. Admission: FREE. Some special events and tours available to the public for a small fee.* The Virginia Horse Center is set in a panoramic mountain setting and boasts 600 acres, six barns, and a coliseum that seats 4000. The Center is host to over 95 events every year (see the show schedule on their website) that provide a showcase for state, national and international horse competition. The Work Horse Museum is in the Anderson Coliseum and has a collection of over 30 farm implements used by farmers in the era before motor vehicles. Ever seen fly nets?

VIRGINIA MILITARY INSTITUTE (VMI)

(VMI Parade Grounds: Off US11 and Jefferson, I-81, exit 195)

Lexington 24450

❑ Phone: (540) 464-7334 Cadet. George Marshall Museum: (540) 463-7103, **Web: www.vmi.edu/museum**

❑ Hours: Daily, 9:00am-5:00pm. Closed Thanksgiving and Winter break

❑ Admission: Donations

❑ Miscellaneous: Cadet Museum is in Jackson Memorial Hall (next to the Barracks and Marshall Museum is on Parade Ground. Dress Parade - VMI Cadets, Fridays @ 4:00pm (September-May)

The nation's oldest state military college is home to two museums which chronicle the school's history and honor VMI educated leaders and heroes. Kids can take the "Almost 20 Questions" worksheet with them as they look for Stonewall Jackson's bullet-torn raincoat, an "air" gun, a sample cadet barracks, and George S.

Patton's cadet uniform. The brightest and biggest exhibit is Stonewall Jackson's beloved Civil War horse (actually taxidermied and preserved as it was). In the Marshall Museum, the highlights are the wall sized interactive map of WWII events, a family friendly WW II Jeep and Marshall Noble Peace Prize.

WOODSON'S MILL

Lowesville - *Rte. 778, 22951. Phone: (800) 282-8223. Web: www.angelfire.com/journal/millbuilder/video.html. Hours: Saturdays 8:00am-3:00pm. Admission: FREE.* Built in 1794, reconstructed in 1845, and still in continuous operation, Woodson's Mill uses water-driven millstones to grind wheat, corn and other grains. This four-story post-and-beam structure, which also houses an operating cider press, is a fun day trip.

LURAY CAVERNS

970 US 211 West (I-81 exit 264, Follow Signs)

Luray 22835

- ❑ Phone: (540) 743-6551, **Web: www.luraycaverns.com**
- ❑ Hours: Daily, 9:00am-6:00pm (mid-March to mid-June), 9:00am-7:00pm (mid-June to Labor Day), 9:00am-6:00pm (Labor Day to end of October), 9:00am-4:00pm (November to mid-March)
- ❑ Admission: $19.00 adult, $16.00 senior (62+), $9.00 child (age 6-12) (Under 6 FREE with an adult)
- ❑ Tours: Guided, one hour tours leave every 10-20 minutes.
- ❑ Miscellaneous: Hiking trails, Skyline Drive nearby. Caverns are a cool 54 degrees with sloped, paved walkways. Steps at the entrance are only difficult for the little ones. Paths are very easy. Luray Singing Tower: the 47 bells play concerts regularly.

In 1878, cold air rushing out of a limestone sinkhole atop a big hill, blew out a candle held by Andrew Campbell, the town tinsmith. They dug away loose rock, and candle in hand, found themselves in the largest caverns in the East. Highlights of the property include:

THE GREAT STALACPIPE ORGAN - invented in 1954 by Mr. Sprinkle, a mathematician and electronic scientist at the Pentagon.

It took three years of searching the vast chambers of the caverns, tapping potential formations with a tuning fork. Stalactites were selected to precisely match a musical scale in order to become part of what would eventually be known as the world's largest musical instrument! To listen to and sometimes, see, the rubber-tipped plunger strike a column when a key is depressed is like watching a giant child's music box. This is something to write home about! The coolest, most interesting caverns ever.

<u>FAVORITE FORMATIONS</u>: the parted drapery canopy/tent; Dream Lake reflections of stalactites in the pool (you must see this to believe the optical illusion); Wishing Well of blue/green water where your coins are given to charity (the most productive wishing well in the world); and near the end of the tour the world famous fried eggs *(not just any fried eggs, but eggs that George remembers seeing with his family as a kid...trust us, people bring kids from all over the world to see this formation... and fondly remember a childhood memory!).* Use your imagination to discover names for many other formations. We named one..."Shaggy Dog", another the "Giant Turtle".

<u>LIMAIR</u>: the first air-conditioned home in America, cooled by a five horsepower electric fan forcing cool air from the caverns into the house maintaining a temperature of 70 degrees. The limestone "filter" rock removed dust and pollen and bacteria as it passed up and out of the cave-early energy conservation and hypoallergenic air conditioning!

<u>HISTORIC CAR & CARRIAGE CARAVAN MUSEUM</u>: 140 item exhibit relating to history of transportation, including cars, carriages, coaches and costumes dating from 1725. The prize in the collection is a 1892 Benz - oldest operating car in America. (included with Caverns admission)

<u>THE GARDEN MAZE</u>: A very large maze covering one acre of ornamental gardens. The 1500 trees create a ½ mile pathway of disarray, illogical rhythm and a family project to solve the puzzle (great, fun development of math skills, mom and dad). Additional fee of $5.00-6.00 per person. It is so-o-o- fun! Clues: Look for clues near the cave, near the fountain, and elsewhere. Watch out for those cute dead end signs.

LURAY ZOO

Luray - *1087 US 211W, 22835. Phone: (540) 743-4113. **Web:** www.lurayzoo.com. Hours: Open daily 10:00am-5:00pm. Winter hours may vary. Rain or shine. Admission: $8.00 adult, $5.00 child (3-12). Miscellaneous: Gift/Nature shop.* In the half acre petting zoo you will find a unique blend of: reptiles, exotic animals, tropical birds and birds of prey. Over 87 different species are exhibited with pygmy goats, tame deer, geckos, donkeys, llamas, exotic wild animals and Virginia's largest reptile collection. Here you will find most every type of venomous snake that resides in the United States. Mammoth pythons, king cobras, and some very interesting lizards and turtle species are also on exhibit. In the outdoor section of the center, one can roam with tame animals in the petting zoo. The loose animals in the petting area love to be hand fed and loved on. African pygmy goats are the star attraction, small, cute, animated, and friendly. Also in the petting zoo are Fallow deer from Europe, Sicilian donkeys, llamas and sheep. Food for the animals may be purchased at on site feeding stations.

SHENANDOAH NATIONAL PARK

Hdqtrs. 3655 US Hwy. 211 East (Skyline Drive entrances are: Front Royal/US 340; Thornton Gap/US 211; Swift Run Gap/US 33; Rockfish Gap/US 250 & I-64), **Luray** 22835

- ❏ Phone: (540) 999-3500, **Web: www.nps.gov/shen**
- ❏ Admission: Some areas (visitors centers) require $10.00 per vehicle fee for entrance (valid for 7 days). Skyline drive is FREE.
- ❏ Miscellaneous: Nature programs, camping, fishing, hiking, lodging, picnicking and restaurants (most seasonal). National Park Info Centers are: Dickey Ridge, mile 4.6; Byrd, mile 51; and Loft Mt., mile 79.5. Speed limit is 35 mph.

Shenandoah National Park lies astride a beautiful section of the Blue Ridge Mountains, which form the eastern rampart of the Appalachian Mountains between Pennsylvania and Georgia. The Shenandoah River flows through the valley to the west, with Massanutten Mountain, 40 miles long, standing between the river's north and south forks. The rolling Piedmont country lies to the east of the park. Skyline Drive, a 105-mile road that winds along the

For updates & travel games, visit: **www.KidsLoveTravel.com**

crest of the mountains (highest point is near Front Royal, elevation 3680 feet) through the length of the park, provides many scenic stop areas to view vistas of the spectacular landscape to east and west. Skyline Drive holds more than 500 miles of trails, including 101 miles of the Appalachian Trail. Trails may follow a ridge crest, or they may lead to high places with panoramic views or to waterfalls in deep canyons (Thornton Gap area 610 foot tunnel through solid granodiorite of Mary's Rock). Many animals, including deer, black bears, and wild turkeys, flourish among the rich growth of an oak-hickory forest. In season, bushes and wildflowers bloom along the Drive and trails. Apple trees, stone foundations, and cemeteries are reminders of the families who once called this place home.

CEDAR CREEK BATTLEFIELD

Middletown - *PO Box 229, 8437 Valley Pike (Interstate 81 to Strasburg exit #298, North on Route 11), 22645. Phone: (540) 869-2064 or (888) 628-1864.* **Web: *www.cedarcreekbattlefield.org.*** *Hours: Monday-Saturday 10:00am-4:00pm, Sunday 1:00-4:00pm (April-October). Admission: $2.00 per person. Tours: Guided tours are available by appointment. Miscellaneous: Annual October re-enactment.* The Cedar Creek Visitors Center is the site of a well stocked bookstore, and an interpretive exhibit on the 1864 Valley Campaign and Battle of Cedar Creek. Admission includes viewing the historic video film shown throughout the day.

ROUTE 11 POTATO CHIPS

1758 Main Street (I-81 to Middletown exit, turn right on Reliance, left on Rte 11 - follow to center of town), **Middletown** 22645

- ❑   Phone: (540) 869-0104 or (800) 294-SPUD, **www.rt11.com**
- ❑   Hours: Monday-Saturday 9:00am-5:00pm. All varieties out for sampling along with Rte. 11 dips (best sampling on weekends).
- ❑   Admission: FREE

Come watch the spudmasters at work, watch through the window, and sample the chips. The best time to see any frying action is morning or early afternoon (sample warm chips right off the line!). Look for the bucket peeler and slicer (both automatic) that once the potatoes are peeled and sliced drops them into hot oil. Some of their specialties include fried potatoes using a blend of peanut and sunflower oil, no preservatives. The basic are lightly salted but they have a wide variety of flavors like barbeque, dill pickle (for the pregnant mommies), salt 'n vinegar, sour cream 'n chive, Chesapeake crab, Mama Zuma's (dry, hot, spicy - don't give it to the kids!), no salt, Yukon Golds and unusual sweet potato chips (salted or cinnamon and sugar- dessert chips!) or mixed vegetable chips (potpourri of sweet potatoes, taro root, beets, parsnips, carrots, and purple potatoes). When have you ever seen or tasted fried carrots being prepared? Interesting tour for all ages!

DOUTHAT STATE PARK

Millboro - *Rte. 1, Box 212 (I-64 exit 27 to SR 629 north), 24460. Web: www.dcr.virginia.gov/parks/douthat.htm. Phone: (540) 862-8100. Admission: $2.00-$3.00 per vehicle.* Amid mountain scenery, visitors can enjoy a 50 acre lake stocked with trout, a restaurant overlooking the water, a sandy swimming beach, bathhouse, cabins, picnic areas and tent/trailer campgrounds. The park also features two completely furnished lodges that accommodate 15-17 guests.

NATURAL BRIDGE

US11 (I-81 exit 175 and 180, on US 11 at jct. SR 130)

Natural Bridge 24578

- ❑ Phone: (540) 291-2121 or (800) 533-1410
  www.naturalbridgeva.com or **www.awesometoymuseum.com**
- ❑ Hours: 8:00am-dark. Toy Museum: Daily 10:00am-5:00pm. Extended hours in the summer and fall. Caverns open 10:00am-5:00pm (March-November). Wax Museum: Daily 10:00am-4:00pm (March-November) and weekends only (December-February).
- ❑ Admission: 1-2 and 3-4 way passes available Combo pricing is best value. Eaches pricing is $10.00-$12.00 adult, $6.00 child (age 6-12). Combos run $18.00-$28.00 adult and $9.00-$14.00 child.

Known by the Monacan Indians as "The Bridge of God", it started as a site of worship. In 1774, Thomas Jefferson purchased from

For updates & travel games, visit: **www.KidsLoveTravel.com**

King George III this awe inspiring "rock bridge" to preserve it as a mountain retreat. Geologists now feel that this was once a cave that collapsed to form a bridge. Today, it is considered one of the "Seven Natural Wonders of the World!"

- ❏ BRIDGE, CEDAR CREEK TRAIL & MONACAN INDIAN VILLAGE - The bridge towers some 215 feet above the Cedar Creek, making it 55 feet higher than Niagara Falls. The span between the walls is 90 feet long, and about 100 feet wide. Descend into the ravine to Cedar Creek and pass underneath it. Visit the Monacan Indians as you stroll to Lace Falls (look for blue heron along the way). Journey back 300 years as you walk and sit amongst Monacans as you learn about and assist with canoe building, shelter construction, hide tanning, mat and rope weaving, fishing, tool making, gardening, harvesting, preparing meals, making pots and bowls or making baskets. Daily activities change with the seasons.

- ❏ CAVERNS - a 45 minute guided journey into the east coast's deepest commercial cave, 34 stories into the earth. Complete with the usual stalagmites and stalactites, but also, hanging gardens, underground streams and waterfalls. Tours depart every 20 minutes.

- ❏ WAX MUSEUM - a three-dimensional trip through early American History by exploring scenes from frontier life and folklore (special focus on the Valley and American Indians) on simply narrated sets featuring over 150 life-like figures. Best of all, get a rare chance to learn how these human replicas are produced on the Factory Studio Tour (heads and legs may roll, off the shelves, that is!). See hand-made wax figures of many famous visitors to Natural Bridge including Daniel Boone, Abraham Lincoln, famous inventors, and past Presidents. Conclude you tour with a sit down presentation of the last supper.

Natural Bridge (*cont.*)

❑ THE DRAMA OF CREATION - included with a Bridge admission ticket and presented nightly (spring - fall), beneath the bridge at sunset. Symphonic music and colored lights fill the ancient Blue Ridge Mountain walls with the story of the seven days of creation. The most inspiring view of the bridge is about a ½ hour before dusk - this is when it appears the largest! Seasonal performances, mostly warm weather months.

❑ THE TOY MUSEUM - The Toy Museum has the largest collection of childhood memorabilia on display in the world! The collection features many full sets and series of collectible toys particularly since 1975. The oldest European dolls (1740) on display were played with by Revolutionary War era children. From mechanical toys and robots to modern action figures, everyone in your family will recall stories of old favorites. Memory Lane experience, especially for parents and grandparents to share.

Throughout this complex, kids will learn more about natural history and American & Indian history then they will ever remember from books!

NATURAL BRIDGE ZOO

PO Box 88 (Interstate 81 between exits 180 and 175)

Natural Bridge 24578

❑ Phone: (540) 291-2420, **Web: www.naturalbridgezoo.net**
❑ Hours: Monday-Friday 9:00am-6:00pm. Weekends 9:00am-7:00pm (mid-March through Thanksgiving weekend)
❑ Admission: $8.00 adult, $7.00 senior, $6.00 Child (3-12) Under age 3 are FREE.
❑ Miscellaneous: Largest animal petting area in Virginia. Safari Shop. Picnic grounds.

Most are attracted here to visit the baby giraffes, bottle raised bear cubs, dozens of fuzzy miniature donkey colts, wooly baby llamas, or gazing into the eyes of a huge white tiger. Also, you can watch the only breeding colony of flamingos in Virginia, building their nests and rearing their young.

For updates & travel games, visit: **www.KidsLoveTravel.com**

VIRGINIA SAFARI PARK

229 Safari Lane (Off US 11 exits 180/180B - cross over to the KOA)

Natural Bridge 24578

- ❑ Phone: (540) 291-3205, **Web: www.virginiasafaripark.com**
- ❑ Hours: Daily 9:00am-5:00pm (late March - late November). Open until 6:00pm in the summer.
- ❑ Admission: $9.00 adult, $8.00 senior (65+), $7.00 child (3-12). Buckets of food $3.00.
- ❑ Tours: Guided wagon tours at 1:00pm and 3:00pm on weekends for small additional fee.
- ❑ Miscellaneous: Camera welcome. (and highly suggested!). Also a petting zoo with monkeys, kangaroos, and tortoises. A giraffe feeding station is new in the Safari Village petting area. Climb up and feed the giraffes—on their level! Be sure to purchase your giraffe crackers.

Virginia Safari Park is a drive-thru zoo located on 180 acres of hills and valleys, pasture and woods, where hundreds of exotic animals from all over the world roam free while you remain in your car. Wagon rides (additional fee) and a petting zoo area are also available. Three miles of safari roads take you up, down, and around a gravel road. It's truly a one-of-a-kind experience as you hand feed H-U-G-E elk, ostrich (they were so greedy and mean!), reindeer, antelope, camels, deer, and our favorite...the zebras (they were so kind and well-mannered, not pushy, and took their turns!). If you really have the courage (we're told it's OK) you can hand-feed bison and long (very long) horn cattle. We chickened out, but most folks just wait till they get close and throw the feed on the ground. Save at least one bucket of food for the camels - they'll eat everything you give them! It was interesting to watch the matriarch of the herds establish their leadership roles. Other herd members will fear them and let them get most of the food.

ENDLESS CAVERNS

New Market - *PO Box 859 (I-81 exit 264, US 11 south), 22844. Phone: (540) 896-2283.* **Web:** *www.endlesscavern.com. Hours: Daily Open at 9:00am year-round. Last Tour at 5:00pm (mid-March to mid-June and early-September to mid-November), 6:00pm (mid-June to Labor Day), 4:00pm (mid-November to mid-March). Admission: $14.00 adult, $6.00 child (4-12). Online coupon discount. Miscellaneous: Campground and mountain spring water sold at gift shop.* Through the years there have been many expeditions into the Endless Caverns to try and find an end to the complex network of underground passageways. Over five miles of cave passage are mapped and no end is in sight. During the one hour fifteen minute guided tour, you will see stunning displays of calcite formations. Your guide will explain the geology, history and explorations stories of the cavern. The caverns are presented with white lighting only, allowing you to see the natural effect.

NEW MARKET BATTLEFIELD STATE HISTORICAL PARK & HALL OF VALOR

8895 Collins Drive (I-81 exit 264, US211 West, follow signs)

New Market 22844

- ❑ Phone: (540) 740-3101, **Web: www.vmi.edu/museum/nm**
- ❑ Hours: Daily 9:00am-5:00pm. Closed New Year's, Christmas and Thanksgiving.
- ❑ Admission: $8.00 adult, $6.00 senior (60+), $4.00 child (6-15). Valid for one week admission.
- ❑ Miscellaneous: Picnicking, walking (1 mile) or driving tours (small loop) of the battlefield.

This is where 257 cadets (college students) from the Virginia Military Institute aided veteran Confederate troops in victory over Union forces in 1864. Why was it called the "Field of Lost Shoes"? Farm complex - early 1800's farm where the Bushong family took refuge in the basement of the, still standing, house during the battle raging outside in his wheat fields and apple orchards. The Hall of Valor - commemorates the cadets (with a 45 minute video) and highlights every major campaign in Virginia during the four years of the Civil War (including the Valley Campaign). In the lobby, you can pick up a scavenger hunt and try on Civil War clothing (great photo op of the kids in attire at camp with tin cups and plates). Many of the displays are push button with interesting facts (like how the uniforms changed during the war - better, or worse?).

WALTON'S MOUNTAIN MUSEUM
6484 Rockfish River Road (I-64 to Rte 29 south to Route 617 southeast and Route 800), **Schuyler** 22969

❑   Phone: (434) 831-2000 or (888) 266-1981
     Web: www.waltonmuseum.org
❑   Hours: Daily 10:00am-4:00pm (first weekend in March through last weekend in November)
❑   Admission: $6.00 general (age 6+).
❑   Miscellaneous: Helpful to rent the movie "The Homecoming" before you try to teach the kids about the Waltons. Eat at the Shuyler Restaurant. In Ike's General Store purchase a postcard and mail it from there. It will be postmarked "Walton's Mountain".

The Walton's Mountain Museum - Earl Hamner, Jr. created the story behind the Waltons TV series based on his own family's experiences growing up during the Depression era in this rural village of Schuyler. The school building he and his brothers and sisters attended has been converted to a museum which contains nostalgic memorabilia, replicas of the sets created for the TV series and a 30 minute audiovisual presentation (with insightful interviews from the stars) precedes a guided tour of the museum. The show "grounded people away from the confusion of the 60's and 70's". Look For: John-Boy's Bedroom - Furnished to look like the bedroom where John-Boy retreated to write. This room has 1930's-period furniture and an old Underwood typewriter that Earl Hamner, Jr. actually used when he began writing. The Walton's Kitchen - Features a long table and benches at which the family had dinner, an old wood cook stove, period cabinet work, an antique hutch and a wooden icebox and butter churn. The Walton's Living Room - A 1930's-style family room with fireplace, sofa, piano, old Atwater Kent radio (remember they used to gather around it in the evening for programs), overstuffed chairs and other period furnishings. Ike Godsey's Store - This is a favorite for many visitors. Re-live the warmth of an old country store complete with drink box, scales, penny candy and other merchandise not found in stores today. This room doubles as a gift shop with locally produced craft items for sale. Good Night John Boy!

HATTON FERRY

Scottsville - *10082 Hatton Ferry Road (Rte. 625), 24590. Phone: (434) 296-1492* **Web: www.hattonferry.org.** *Hours: Friday, Saturday, and Sunday from 9:00am-5:00pm (mid-April through mid-October).* Hatton Ferry is one of only two poled ferries still operating in the United States. A ride on the ferry is a unique opportunity to experience times past. Ferries served Albemarle County from the mid-eighteenth century to the mid-nineteenth century, and provided a means by which European settlers could communicate with other settlers and establish commercial ventures. A small exhibit explores the history of the ferry, and visitors may ride across the river at no charge if water levels permit.

AMERICAN CELEBRATION ON PARADE

397 Caverns Road (Shenandoah Caverns, I-81exit 269, 4 miles north to New Market), **Shenandoah Caverns** 22847

❑   Phone: (540) 477-4300
       Web: www.americancelebrationonparade.com
❑   Hours: Open daily at 9:00am. Last tour 5:15pm (mid-April to
       mid-June & September and October). Last tour 6:15pm (mid-
       June to Labor Day). Last tour 4:15pm (November to mid-April).
❑   Admission: $18.00 adult, $16.00 senior, $8.00 child (6-14).
       Combo rates allow you to combine Celebration with Shenandoah
       Caverns and Main Street of Yesteryear. Currently general public
       single site pricing is not available.

Mr. Hargrove and his father founded a business building parade floats, "After building so many parade floats, I felt it was sad that these huge pieces of celebration art were often discarded after one appearance," he said. His passion has become a reality for all to view. Walk thru exhibits of animated, moving figures and displays showing the pageantry and the art of parade floats and Americana - up close! 50 years of parades all under one roof (and a large roof it is - some of the floats top 25 feet tall and measure 60 feet long!). Most floats have appeared in events such as The Tournament of Roses Parade and Presidential inaugurals. You'll learn fascinating facts: Most floats still have their natural coverings; Learn the tricks like hidden entrances for drivers, special handles to keep people from toppling off and how they keep a float balanced. Throughout the museum, you get to climb on many floats (great photo ops) and at the end you get to sit in the drivers seat and operate the float's animation. Kids love the character floats, such as Rug Rats and Cinderella in her carriage. Most of these massive floats are animated, too. The floats on display change often, so if you haven't visited in a while, you'll be sure to see something new. Bigger than life - this museum is unique, colorful, and pure family fun!

SHENANDOAH CAVERNS

261 Caverns Road (I-81 exit 269, follow signs)

Shenandoah Caverns 28847

- ❑ Phone: (540) 477-3115, **Web: www.shenandoahcaverns.com**
- ❑ Hours: Daily opening at 9:00am. Last Tour 5:15pm (mid April to mid June & the Day after Labor Day to October). Last tour 6:15pm (mid June to Labor Day). Last tour 4:15pm (November to mid-April).
- ❑ Admission: $18.00 adult, $16.00 senior, $8.00 Child. Combo rates allow you to see the Caverns, Streets of Yesteryear and American Celebration on Parade for one price. General public single site pricing is not available.
- ❑ Miscellaneous: Only caverns with an elevator so accessible to handicapped and strollers for 80% of tour. Wide, level pathways provide easy walking - but wear comfortable shoes for your 60-minute tour. The temperature in the caverns is a constant 56 degrees. Many visitors like to wear a jacket or sweater. Nice, clean picnic areas in many spots. Gift shop.

Your tour of Shenandoah Caverns begins with a ride on the only elevator in a Virginia cavern as it descends into Entrance Hall. The caverns look very much as they did when they were discovered in 1884. You'll view the famous Bacon formations featured in National Geographic (look just like fried bacon) as well as beautiful flowstone and drapery formations. Long View Hall has a series of soaring rooms. In Cascade Hall you'll be dazzled by the Diamond Cascade, one of the very beautiful calcite crystal formations in the world. One of the largest stalagmites in the caverns, known as Cardross Castle, resembles that castle in Scotland. Rainbow Lake and the Oriental Garden are colorful and different. Learn some tips on taking pictures in caverns from your guide (photos welcome). Your admission to the caverns includes a stroll down Main Street of Yesteryear to enjoy a collection of antique department store window displays (From Cinderella at the Ball to the lively Circus Parade). The focus on this vast amusement property is "family fun" for sure.

FRONTIER CULTURE MUSEUM

1290 Richmond Road (I-81, Exit 222, Route 250 West, first left after light), **Staunton** 24401

❏   Phone: (540) 332-7850, **Web: www.frontiermuseum.org**
❏   Hours: Daily, 9:00am-5:00pm. Winter Hours: 10:00am-4:00 pm
      (December 1 to mid-March) Closed on Thanksgiving Day,
      Christmas Day, certain days in January, and during severe
      weather.
❏   Admission: $10.00 adult, $6.00 child (6-12).
❏   Tours: Most families opt for the self-guided tour (approximately
      2-3 hours). Group (15+) guided tours are available.
❏   Miscellaneous: Visitor Center offers displays and a short film
      about the development of the museum. Learn also the whys and
      how these European people immigrated here and what they
      brought with them. Summertime "First Fridays" picnics (6:00-
      8:30pm Free) and many cooking schools and dances.

The Frontier Culture Museum offers an international living history experience. The museum's costumed staff demonstrate 17th, 18th, and 19th century trades and traditions in four authentic, historic farms and a blacksmith forge. Rare breed livestock, heirloom gardens, agricultural crops, and period furnishings help costumed interpreters showcase old-time ways of daily life and living with the land. Walk through Europe and the Americas in one day:

- ❑ <u>GERMAN HERITAGE</u>: The museum's German farm originally stood in the small farming village of Hordt. The farm is interpreted during the first half of the 18th century (1700-1750), the period of heaviest German emigration from this region. Kids love the "punk rock" chickens -treated like domestic pets and their unique furnace.

- ❑ <u>SCOTCH-IRISH HERITAGE</u>: The Scotch-Irish (Ulster) farm buildings show a traditional architectural form... the thatched one-story stone farmhouse. The farm's time period is the early-1700s. School was emphasized only for boys. The farmhouse walls are 2 feet thick, ceilings 20 inches thick - never gets too cold or damp.

- ❑ <u>ENGLISH HERITAGE</u>: The English exhibits time period is 1675-1700 England. An 18th century cattle shed and a house Worcestershire. Watch them make cheese just once a week or other basics as the women frantically cook for the midday feast daily.

- ❑ <u>AMERICAN HERITAGE</u>: On the American site, there are 11 buildings all original to a farm from a local county (circa mid-1800s). The museum interprets the farm by showing the lifestyle of the Shenandoah Valley farmer. The Bowman house is a recreation early pioneer home. A little of every culture's influences (esp. techniques) are brought together in this farm area. A great way to show kids how the U.S. has incorporated customs of so many into one big melting pot (literally!).

You will find this to be such a welcomed difference from typical living history museums - tying in a diversity of cultures is a wonderful way to see how our lives today are a mixture of habits from many cultures.

WOODROW WILSON BIRTHPLACE MUSEUM

18-24 North Coalter and Frederick Streets (Route 11 north; stay in the middle lane and follow North Coalter Street. The Woodrow Wilson Presidential Library will be on your left), **Staunton** 24402

❑   Phone: (540) 885-0897 or (888) 496-6376
   Web: www.woodrowwilson.org

❑   Hours: Monday-Saturday 9:00am-5:00pm, Sunday Noon-5:00pm (March thru October). Open until only 4:00pm (rest of year). Closed New Years, Christmas and Thanksgiving.

❑   Admission: $8.00 adult, $5.00 student (13-18, college), $3.00 child (6-12).

❑   Miscellaneous: While in the downtown area, head over to the Historic Staunton Station and the Pullman Restaurant (540) 885-6612 or the Depot Grill (540) 885-7332.

Woodrow Wilson's first home offers an authentic picture of family life in the pre-Civil War Shenandoah Valley. Such children's activities as scavenger hunts and trying on pre-Civil War clothing are offered. As part of your own scavenger hunt, be sure to look for the limousine (how could you miss it), his White House telephone, and the desk he used at Princeton. The Museum offers a look into Wilson's public life, from his Princeton study to his historic World War I peace efforts. Also, a computer archives presents 1850s newspapers, historic photographs, Civil War rosters, and more. Serving from 1913 to 1921 as the 28th President of the United States, Woodrow Wilson is considered one of the greatest Presidents for his pursuit of world peace and security.

MCCORMICK'S FARM, CYRUS

128 McCormick's Farm Circle (I-81or US 11 exit 205/ SR 606 - Raphine Road, heading east), **Steeles Tavern** 24476

❑   Phone: (540) 377-2255
   Web: www.vaes.vt.edu/steeles/mccormick/mccormick.html

❑   Hours: Open daily 8:30am-5:00pm. Call for guided tours.

❑   Admission: FREE

❑   Miscellaneous: Farm part of the Shenandoah Valley Agricultural Research and Extension Center.

For updates & travel games, visit: **www.KidsLoveTravel.com**

Twenty minutes north of downtown Lexington is the farm and workshop of Cyrus McCormick and his father, where he invented and marketed the first mechanized grain reaper that sparked the industrial revolution. Visitors are welcome to tour the blacksmith shop, gristmill, museum and scenic site at the McCormick farm. On a hot July day in 1831, to a crowd of neighbors and on-lookers, 22 year old Cyrus demonstrated the world's first successful mechanical reaper in fields near his farm, Walnut Grove. The reaper and other farm machines came from the McCormick Company and the later company, International Harvester. For centuries, grain had been harvested with strong arms and backs and some form of long knife like a sickle. The Reaper harvested five times faster than any previous method, with minimal physical effort. McCormick also was a pioneer in business techniques: easy credit to enable farmers to pay for machines from increased harvests; written performance guarantees; and advertising. Parents: the farm and stream water sounds are so tranquil...you might be tempted to relax for a while *(the perfect place for a nap!)*.

CRYSTAL CAVERNS AT HUPP'S HILL

Strasburg - *33231 Old Valley Pike (I-81 exit 298 on US 11 south), 22657. Web: www.waysideofva.com/crystalcaverns/. Phone: (540) 465-5884. Hours: Daily tours at 11:00am, 12:30pm, 2:00pm and 3:30pm. Closed New Years, Easter, Thanksgiving and Christmas. Admission: $10.00 adult, $8.00 senior and student (age 6+).* Touring Crystal Caverns, located in the same complex as the Stonewall Jackson Museum, lets you get up close to the formations in the Caverns as your guide educates you with the real facts about caverns in the Shenandoah Valley and the uniqueness of Crystal Caverns (mine passage and frozen falls). For a step back in the past, experience a Living History Lantern Tour (advance reservations required). Your guide, dressed in period clothing, will escort you into the past by lantern light as you meet civil war soldiers, children and other citizens of the day as well as learn about the cavern and its unique formations.

HALF MOON BEACH PARK
363 Radio Station Road (I-81 exit 298, south on US 11)
Strasburg 22657

- ❑ Phone: (540) 465-5757 or (540) 465-9537 (games)
  Web: www.halfmoonbeach.com
- ❑ Hours: Daily (weather permitting) 10:00am-6:00pm (Memorial Day-Labor Day). Paintball open year round.
- ❑ Admission: $8.00 general (age 10+), $5.00 child (4-9). Under 3 FREE with paying adult. Weekday prices $5.00 general. City resident discount. Wednesdays are Senior Day with $3.00 admission per senior.
- ❑ Miscellaneous: No alcohol and no pets.

Come out for some "Fun in the Sun" at a full-service resort area. Visit the white sand beach and sparkling green water. Come and lounge in the sand by the water or take a canoe trip and explore the lake. Activities include swimming, paddle boats, fishing, camping, volleyball, paintball, batting cages, and mini golf.

MUSEUM OF AMERICAN PRESIDENTS
130 North Massanutten Street (I-81 exit 298, south on US 11)
Strasburg 22657

- ❑ Phone: (540) 465-5999, **Web: www.waysideofva.com/presidents**
- ❑ Hours: Weekends 10:00am-5:00pm.
- ❑ Admission: $5.00 adult, $4.00 senior (55+) and child (6-16).

Info about all the presidents of the United States with highlights of Madison's desk on which he drafted the Federalist Papers, White House doors, presidential hand-written letters and lots of photos and portraits. A one-room schoolhouse offers hands-on displays for kids.

STONEWALL JACKSON MUSEUM AT HUPP'S HILL
Strasburg - *33229 Old Valley Pike (I-81 exit 298, south on US 11), 22657.* **Web: www.waysideofva.com/stonewalljackson.** *Phone: (540) 465-5884. Hours: Monday-Saturday 10:00am-5:00pm, Sunday Noon-5:00pm. Admission: $5.00 adult, $4.00*

senior (55+) and child (6-16). Part of the 10-acre site where the Battle of Cedar Creek took place in 1864. Visitors see original trenches built by troops. Inside the museum is the story of Jackson's brilliant defense of the Shenandoah Valley (one of the most famous military campaigns in history, studied the world over) brought to life with a collection of artifacts from the Valley along with interpretive text. You will not only understand the campaign, but will get a vivid impression of what life was like for the soldiers who fought. Children have their own place in the museum where they can try on period costumes, ride wooden horses complete with authentic cavalry saddles and bridles, climb into a soldier's tent. "Discovery Boxes" offer kids a chance to explore an historic topic through games, puzzles and touching artifacts.

P. BUCKLEY MOSS MUSEUM

150 P. Buckley Moss Drive (I-64 exit 94, south on US 340)

Waynesboro 22980

❑   Phone: (540) 949-6473
      Web: www.pbuckleymoss.com/museum.html
❑   Hours: Daily 10:00am-6:00pm, Sundays 12:30-5:30pm.
❑   Admission: FREE

Art from "The People's Artist" is showcased here. The works of local artist P. Buckley Moss focus mostly on subjects from the Shenandoah Valley scenery and the Amish and Mennonite people of the area - really, basic human and Christian values. Her style is now referred to as "Moss Valley" and you'll see the Shenandoah Valley all through it. Did you know Ms. Moss had a learning disability and one teacher in class noticed her artist ability and encouraged it? A Children's Art area upstairs promotes artistic techniques. A dollhouse downstairs is like a painting that came to life. Look for the 30 little mice throughout the house. All paintings on the dollhouse walls are P. Buckley Moss originals. Follow the bird - the bird was the symbol of human soul - he opens his mouth and sings his own song...What's your song?

VIRGINIA METALCRAFTERS

1010 East Main Street (I-64 exit 99, US 250 west)

Waynesboro 22980

❑   Phone: (540) 949-9432, **Web: www.vametal.com**
❑   Hours: (Showroom) Monday-Friday 9:00am-5:00pm, Saturday
    until 4:00pm, Sunday 1:00-5:00pm. Observation hours, Monday-
    Thursday. (April-Christmas).

A unique sand cast brass foundry selling Williamsburg and
Monticello reproductions made from brass and iron. No tours are
given but an observation deck overlooks pouring and molding
processes. Listen to the narration as it explains the stages of
production of the art. Although these items are brand new, they
look and feel (heavy) like they are hundreds of years old. These
pieces look great for "old-fashioned" Christmas décor.

DINOSAUR LAND

3848 Stonewall Jackson Highway (US 522 south) (US 522, 340 &
277), **White Post** 22663

❑   Phone: (540) 869-2222, **Web: www.dinosaurland.com**
❑   Hours: Opens daily at 9:30am. Closing around 5:00 or 5:30pm
    (except Memorial Day-Labor Day) when they close at 6:30pm.
    Closed January and February.
❑   Admission: $5.00 adult, $4.00 child (2-10).
❑   Miscellaneous: Giant gift shop with every dinosaur toy and book
    imaginable.

Step into a world of the prehistoric past where dinosaurs were the
only creatures that roamed the earth. See the awesome meat eaters
Giganotosaurus, Megalosaurus to the sauropiods, armored and
duckbill dinosaurs. Come face to face with the awesome
Tyrannosaurus or look into the gentle face of Apatosaurus. 50 life-
size reproductions of dinos and one 20 foot King Kong - have your
picture taken in his hand! A 60' shark with an open mouth is also a
great photo op too! So, what is a dinosaur anyway? The word
dinosaur means "Terrible Lizard" in Greek. Of 15 large reptilian
groups including dinosaurs, only lizards, snakes, turtles and
crocodiles survive at all today. Don't forget your cameras. You'll

be surprised at how many dinosaurs look like modern reptiles (just on a larger scale). Parents like the brief descriptions of every type of dinosaur, too.

GEORGE WASHINGTON'S OFFICE MUSEUM

32 West Cork Street, US 11 (Corner of Braddock & Cork Streets)

Winchester 22601

- ❏ Phone: (540) 662-4412, **Web: www.winchesterhistory.org**
- ❏ Hours: Monday-Saturday 10:00am-4:00pm, Sunday Noon-4:00pm. (April-October)
- ❏ Admission: $5.00 adult, $4.50 senior and $2.50 student. Family rate $12.00
- ❏ Miscellaneous: Visitors may purchase a block ticket for admission to Abram's Delight Museum, Stonewall Jackson's Headquarters Museum, and George Washington's Office Museum.

The center room of George Washington's Office Museum was used by Colonel George Washington, commander of the Virginia Regiment, as an office between September, 1755 and December, 1756 while he was building Fort Loudoun. The fort was being built to protect the colony of Virginia from Indian raids during the French and Indian War. George Washington first arrived in Winchester in 1748 as a surveyor's assistant at the age of sixteen. This visit began a 10-year odyssey in the Virginia Backcountry which transformed Washington from an inexperienced teenager into a seasoned businessman, soldier, and politician. Kids will best like the vast array of unusual looking instruments used for surveying back then and the real blood-stained floor when the building was used as a hospital during the Civil War.

MUSEUM OF THE SHENANDOAH VALLEY

530 Amherst Street, **Winchester** 22601

- ❏   Phone: (540) 662-1473 **Web: www.shenandoahmuseum.org**
- ❏   Hours: Tuesday-Sunday 10:00am-4:00pm. Closed Mondays and major holidays.
- ❏   Admission: $8.00 adult, $6.00 senior and child (7-18).

The new $20 million, 50,000-square-foot regional history museum is dedicated to interpreting the art, history and culture of the Shenandoah Valley. Includes five exhibit galleries, a tea room, reception hall, learning center and museum store. The story begins with an explanation of the Valley's geography and natural resources and the earliest Indians who lived here, and concludes with an overview of Valley highlights today. In one section, visitors may record their own stories and impressions of the Valley. Multi-media presentations in each section of the Main Gallery Room bring the sights and sounds of the Valley alive. Behind this main gallery, three additional Valley Decorative Arts Rooms present a wide range objects made in the Valley from the middle of the eighteenth century onward. The Miniature House gallery presents five houses, four rooms, and the work of more than seventy miniatures artisans.

SHENANDOAH SUMMER MUSIC THEATRE

Winchester - *Ohrstrom-Bryant Theatre, Shenandoah University, 22601. **Web: www.su.edu/conservatory/ssmt/index.htm**. Phone: (540) 665-4569 or (877) 580-8025. Season: Summers (June-August). Performances: Evening performances Wednesday-Saturday at 8:00pm and Sunday at 7:00pm. Matinee performances on Saturdays and select Wednesdays at 2:30pm. Admission: $18.00-$21.00.* "The Secret Garden" or "The Wizard of Oz" are samples of plays performed. The Shenandoah Summer Music Theatre is a live professional theatre featuring actors from all along the eastern seaboard.

SHENANDOAH VALLEY DISCOVERY MUSEUM

54 South Loudoun Street (Old Town), **Winchester** 22601

- ❏ Phone: (540) 722-2020, **Web: www.discoverymuseum.net**
- ❏ Hours: Monday-Saturday 9:00am-5:00pm, Sunday 1-5:00pm.
- ❏ Admission: $5.00 general
- ❏ Miscellaneous: Museum store.

A delightful place for energetic kids wanting to explore science in a fun way! Some of the things we found unique to this museum included: Picking apples, crating apples and using a large conveyor belt (lots and lots of realistic pulleys and levers here) to move them along the processing line. Kids can have fun working in teams here and it's amazing to see how fast some become the "job foreman". Send balls down ramps and around loops or over jumps in the Raceways; touch the soft fur of forest animals in the American Indian Longhouse; see how high you can climb on the rock wall; or pretend you're in a Medical Center and ambulance (with a real gurney) - Mommy was the patient - Dr. Jenny was in charge! And finally, their newest feature - the Paleo Lab is open to stop by and watch the fossil preparation of a triceratops skull. Be prepared to ask questions, the curator is a paleontologist who is assembling a real dinosaur, one piece at a time (with your help!). Too cool that so much could be packed into this kids experience. A must stop!

STONEWALL JACKSON'S HEADQUARTERS MUSEUM

Winchester - *415 North Braddock Street, 22601. Phone: (540) 667-3242,* **Web:** *http://winchesterhistory.org. Hours: Monday-Saturday 10:00am-4:00pm, Sunday Noon-4:00pm (April-October). Weekends only (Friday-Sunday) (rest of year). Admission: $5.00 adult, $4.50 senior and student, $2.50 student, $12.00 Family rate. Block tickets for admission to three area history museums are available for a discount.* The Gothic style house built in 1854 served as General Jackson's headquarters while planning the Valley Campaign.

SUGGESTED LODGING AND DINING

WINTERGREEN RESORT – **Wintergreen**. (Route 664, between Blue Ridge Parkway mileposts 13 and 14, or access from Route 151). (800) 266-2444 or **www.wintergreenresort.com**. Thinking about heading to the mountains? Wintergreen Resort is located high atop the Blue Ridge Mountains. At Wintergreen Resort, you will find golf, 18 ski slopes (kiddie tube slopes too!) and trails (kids learn to ski lessons), 24 tennis courts, 30 miles of marked hiking trails, five swimming pools and a 20-acre lake (paddleboats, canoes, kayaks, inner tubes, fishing equipment rentals), horseback riding. Whatever you do, don't miss their sunsets (to-o-o nice) and deer families prancing around (particularly early evening). This resort offers a lot for families - We especially liked their well-organized, daily children's programs (in the Treehouse with planned crafts, games, stories, explorations of area, kids campouts and babysitting services); festivals and special events, a year-round nature program "WILD!" Activities for children (fee required) - weekday and weekend programs of outdoor fun for ages 6-12 on subjects like Inspector Wild, slippery slimies, Wild Adventurers, river ecology, insects and cave exploring. Resort shops, restaurants, gameroom and recreational facilities are open to the public. Lodging packages for each season (Endless Fun Package or value season/midweek rates are best value - around $150 per night with all the regular property amenities available to use without additional charge). Almost every guest room, condo or house has an efficiency or full-size kitchen - if you're watching your budget, cook your favorite meals or order a pizza from the Black Rock Market. A great mountain retreat that's close to lots of historical attractions.

DOUBLE TREE HOTEL – **Charlottesville**. 990 Hilton Heights Road (off Rte. 29, near airport). 22901. (434) 973-2121 or **www.doubletree.com**. Nice spacious rooms w/ coffee maker and hair dryers and really comfy beds (plus tables to play or eat on). Restaurant with buffets and kid pricing. Many fast food, casual restaurants down street (for frozen custard, go to Kohr's Brothers just a few blocks away). Nice family packages that include nearby site ticket packages. Indoor and outdoor pool with cute-shaped steps for entry. Volleyball, tennis and horseshoe courts, too.

NATURAL BRIDGE HOTEL - **Natural Bridge**. US 11. (800) 533-1410 or **www.naturalbridgeva.com**. Inn and cottages with seasonal indoor pool, indoor mini golf, outdoor tennis, dining room and cafes, gift shop. We recommend staying on the property at this hotel so you can easily walk to the many sites in the complex. Lodging runs about $60.00-$120.00 per night. Discounts to museum complex is available for overnight guests. The dining room is nice for breakfast but a little "stuffy" for active kids for dinner. Seasonal snack shops and delis are nearby.

Chapter 4
South Central Area

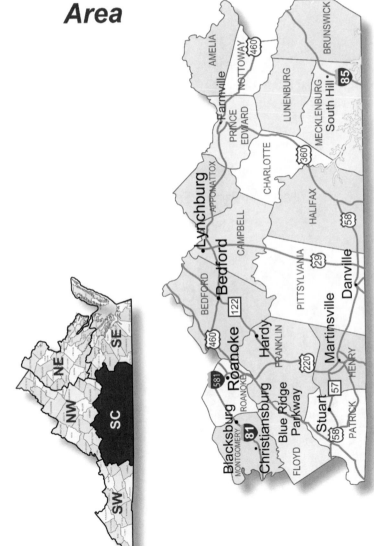

Our Favorites...

* Appomattox Court House - Appomattox

* Holyland USA - Bedford

* Popular Forest - Forest

* Booker T. Washington National Monument - Hardy

* Amazement Square Children's Museum - Lynchburg

* Virginia Museum of Natural History - Martinsville

* Art Venture (Art Museum of Western VA) - Roanoke

* Virginia Museum of Transportation - Roanoke

* Fairy Stone State Park - Stuart

"Self-Portrait" - Art Venture Fun!

APPOMATTOX COURT HOUSE NATIONAL HISTORICAL PARK

(VA 24, 2 miles northeast of the town of Appomattox)

Appomattox 24522

- ❑ Phone: (434) 352-8987, **Web: www.nps.gov/apco/index.htm**
- ❑ Hours: Daily 9:00am-5:30pm (summers). 8:30am-5:00pm (winter). Closed on Federal Holidays.
- ❑ Admission: $4.00 adult (age 17+) with $10.00 max. per vehicle (summers). $3.00/$5.00 rest of year, child and senior are FREE.
- ❑ Miscellaneous: Gift store in the tavern kitchen. It is best to walk along with ranger guided tours.

This village sits as it was in 1865, when Robert E. Lee surrendered to Ulysses S. Grant. Lee's surrender signaled the end of the Southern States attempt to create a separate nation. Learn more about each of these characters, as well as, the McLean family who ironically wanted to be removed from the war, so they moved here. There are 27 historic structures in the village, most importantly the Tavern (where parole papers were printed quickly) and the McLean House where the surrender terms were written. There are two 15 minute slide shows you can watch or listen to audio stations along the way. The map you receive will steer you with advice on touring the village, one of them being that with a lot of walking. It is suggested families with younger children explore the buildings surrounding the Courthouse/Visitors Center. The village buildings all represent various trades during that time period so it is also a history lesson on that time period. The Stacking of Arms story that occurred a few days later is interesting too. Learn why there were no papers signed here between General Grant and General Lee, what Lee's final request was the next day, and why they met at home instead of the Courthouse.

CLOVER HILL VILLAGE

Appomattox - *RR 1, Box 397 (Rte. 460 east to Rte. 24, right on Rte. 627), 24522. Phone: (434) 352-0321. Hours: Grounds open daily 9:00am-dusk, park open 10:30am-4:30pm (April-November). Admission: $2.00-$3.00 (over age 6).* Tour a 6 acre rural village where the history and heritage of Appomattox County come to life. Enjoy an educational glimpse into daily life in the past (1840 - 1920) as you browse through the general store, an extensive collection of farm equipment, and a blacksmith shop. Go back to school in a one-room schoolhouse, relax for a moment in the quiet little chapel, then stroll over to a cozy log cabin and the farm area.

FRED'S CAR MUSEUM

Appomattox - *Hwy. 24, 24522. Phone: (434) 352-0606. Web: www.appomattox.com/html/car_museum.html. Hours: Monday-Saturday 10:00am-5:00pm, Sunday 1:00-5:00pm. Admission: $5.00 general. Miscellaneous: Cruise-ins every second Saturday (May-September) 6:00-10:00pm. Classic auto souvenirs in gift shop.* More than sixty-five classic and antique automobiles made from 1906 to 1980 can be seen here. ..everything from the classic 1957 Chevrolet to very rare and seldom seen cars. One of the most rare cars in the museum is a 1939, V-12 Lincoln Limousine, one of only four ever made. See a 1906 Schacht Mfg. Company horseless carriage, a 1914 Saxton, a 1920 Piano Box Buggy, and a 1936 Packard. There is even a 1962 Rolls Royce, a classic 1946 fire engine and a Chevrolet truck that nobody can figure out the date of its manufacture.

LAUREL HILL - J.E.B. STUART BIRTHPLACE

Ararat - *PO Box 240 (SR 773, just over the border from NC), 24053. Phone: (276) 251-1833. Web: www.jebstuart.org. Hours: Daylight hours. Admission: FREE except for special events. Miscellaneous: Annual Encampments and Battle Reenactments in May and October.* Home of the Stuart family and birthplace of the famous Confederate Cavalry General J.E.B. Stuart, the "eyes" of Robert E. Lee's Army of Northern Virginia. Visitors can walk the trails where young "Jeb" learned to ride, see the swimming hole where the Stuart children played, and take in the splendor of the 80-acre core of what once was one of the largest family farms around. As the Stuart family would say, "You are most welcome to visit and picnic on our lawn".

HOLY LAND, USA

1060 Jericho Road (US 460 to US 122 south to SR 746, turn right 3 miles), **Bedford** 24523

- ❑ Phone: (540) 586-2823, **Web: www.holyland.pleasevisit.com**
- ❑ Hours: Daily 8:00am-5:00pm (mid-March thru mid-December).
- ❑ Admission: FREE for walking through on your own.
- ❑ Tours: Guided tours by appointment only. Wagon rides, vans or buses - a fee is required (but worth the extra storytelling - and less tired feet - this is a 2½ mile walking tour!)
- ❑ Miscellaneous: Picnic areas, concession machines on site. Gift shop. Art & Philosophy students will appreciate Herod's idol sculpture (made of old farm implements and "The Foolish Man - The Wise Man" Houses that really get the point across..

A 250 acre sanctuary depicts the Holy Land in Israel. In this nature sanctuary, the life, journeys and deeds of Jesus Christ are presented in a trail that begins in Bethlehem and continues north through the Judean hill country into the Shepherds' Field (you really feel like you are on the road to Jericho with Jesus). Then on to Nazareth (Jesus' hometown) where you can explore Joseph's carpenter shop and a grotto home. Now, cross the Jordan River, travel through Cana and around the Sea of Galilee, pass Capernaum, through Samaria toward Jerusalem (death, burial and resurrection of Jesus). In Jerusalem, there is a baptismal pool, the upper room, Mount Calvary and the empty garden tomb! From Jerusalem, you travel to Bethany (home of Mary, Martha and Lazarus) where you peek at Lazarus' tomb and then view the beautiful Mount of Olives (where Jesus ascended into heaven). The pleasant "journey with Jesus" is a well thought out peaceful, yet thought provoking, "gotta do that while in the area" experience. Relax and enjoy the peace!

NATIONAL D-DAY MEMORIAL

(I-460 east to Rte 122 north exit. Left off the exit and left on Tiger
Trail to Overlord Circle), **Bedford** 24523

- ❑ Phone: (540) 587-3619, **Web: www.dday.org**
- ❑ Hours: The Memorial is currently just an outdoor facility, subject
  to closing for inclement weather. Daily 10:00am-5:00pm. Closed
  on Christmas Day, New Year's Day, and Thanksgiving Day.
- ❑ Admission: $5.00 adult, $3.00 child (6-16).
- ❑ Miscellaneous: Future plans: In addition to an auditorium and
  theater, the education center will house computer and video
  stations, exhibition space for permanent and traveling exhibits,
  and three galleries for displays. The Education Center's thematic
  galleries will draw particular attention to the clergy, medicine,
  and cartooning in the context of D-Day and the broader context
  of World War II. However scattered those subjects may seem at
  first glance, the human needs they respond to - spiritual, physical,
  emotional needs - are common to all people, especially military.

Self-guided tours of the memorial are available to all visitors.
Visitors can stroll the grounds with site-brochures that offer
information on the architecture and various representations of the
memorial. Visitors can also direct questions to docents (tour
guides) stationed at specific points throughout the monument.
Guided tours are also available weather permitting (additional
$2.00 fee per person). Departing regularly throughout the day,
these 45-minute programs provide more information about the
events of June 6, 1944 and the symbolism of the Memorial itself.
Friends tell us this is the best way to visit the site with children.
The storytelling and anecdotes are so vivid, kids understand more
of the passion and history of this important day.

POPLAR FOREST, THOMAS JEFFERSON'S

SR 661 (off US 460, north on SR 811, then east on SR661)

Bedford (Forest) 24551

- ❑ Phone: (434) 525-1806 or (434) 534-8118, **www.poplarforest.org**
- ❑ Hours: Daily 10:00am-4:00pm (April-November). Closed
  Tuesdays. Summer Excavation Tent for kids open 11:00am-2:00pm.

❏   Admission: $8.00 adult, $6.00 senior (60+), $1.00 child (6-16)

Want to pretend you're an archeologist for the day? Well, this place has digging and touching galore - enough for every family member to enjoy. Poplar Forest (the first octagonal home in America) was the plantation and retreat Thomas Jefferson owned 90 miles from Monticello. What's unique about your visit here is that the house is open as a museum while (not after) restoration and archaeology continue on the grounds! Guided tours get you involved in the "detective work". For instance, can you tell where the "alcove bed" would have been, or which room has "Grandpa's chair"? You'll hear excerpts from Jefferson's grand daughter's letters when you explore the guest bedroom. The Hands-on History Tent (summers only) is worth the visit alone! The tent gives children a chance to literally put their "hands-on-history" as they make bricks (from area clay…it's kinda like "mixing and baking a cake" - says mom! Mix, "flour" the mold, pour and bake); spin wool; lie down on a slave bed (a wedding gift from the masters, along with a pot for cooking); trying on period clothes; making a bucket or a basket; or playing marbles with reproduction red clay marbles like those found on the property. Note: The Toddler Corner has coloring and puzzles. Many may not know Jefferson frequently used a polygraph (a period machine with 2 pens - one for a copy). Kids can make copies of a note using a reproduction polygraph.

HISTORIC SMITHFIELD

1000 Smithfield Plantation Road (at the edge of VA Tech Campus, take rte. 314 off US 460 bypass), **Blacksburg** 24060

❏   Phone: (540) 231-3947, **Web: http://civic.bev.net/smithfield**

❏   Hours: Thursday-Saturday 10:00am-5:00pm, Sunday 1:00-
        5:00pm (April to First weekend in December).

❏   Admission: $5.00 adult, $3.00 student (13-college), $2.00 child
        (5-12).

Take a one hour interpreted tour of a colonial frontier home built in 1775 by Colonel William Preston. Smithfield was the birthplace of two Virginia governors and the brief home of a third. The Colonel was a leader of westward expansion and a Revolutionary

War Patriot. In a land of log cabins and hardship, this homestead provided a haven of aristocratic elegances. Costumed interpreters show period furnished rooms, a colonial winter kitchen, museum, smokehouse and gardens and adjacent cabin. You'll learn how they faced threats of illness (and the odd treatments used), the Shawnee and their Tory neighbors. Notice the 14 foot high stockade fence.

VIRGINIA TECH MUSEUMS
428 North Main Street, Blacksburg 24061

- ❑ Phone: (540) 231-3001
  Web: www.unirel.vt.edu/campusguide/interest/points.html
- ❑ Hours: Wednesday-Friday, 1:00pm-5:00pm. Saturday, 11:00am-5:00pm.
- ❑ Admission: FREE

Several stations available for families and groups to explore. The Naturalists' Center displays the natural history of local attractions giving you the opportunity to explore different aspects of widely recognized sites such as the Virginia Tech Duck Pond, Cascades Recreation Area, Appalachian Trail, and the New River. Mini-exhibits include: Virginia Save Our Streams Program, VTMNH Saturday Science, Virginia's rock and fossil, and artwork from Virginia Tech students. In The Kid's Niche there are several hands-on displays allowing you to observe and appreciate natural objects including snake skins and feathers. They also provide art supplies for making leaf rubbings and stenciling an assortment of animals. Bring your creativity and your thinking cap to this self-guided campus walk.

RED HILL-PATRICK HENRY NATIONAL MEMORIAL
1250 Red Hill Road (SR 40 east), Brookneal 24528

- ❑ Phone: (434) 376-2044, Web: www.redhill.org
- ❑ Hours: Daily 9:00am-5:00pm, Sunday 1:00-5:00pm (April-October). Daily closing at 4:00pm (November-May).
- ❑ Admission: $6.00 adult, $2.00 child.

Red Hill is the last home and resting place of Patrick Henry. Begin your tour with an orientation videotape. The museum houses the largest collection of Patrick Henry memorabilia in the world. Patrick Henry called Red Hill "one of the garden spots of the world". Of his many homes, this was said to be his favorite, with many of his 17 children being born and married here. Henry's grave, law office, coachman's cabin, stable, kitchen and gardens can be seen.

OCCONEECHEE STATE PARK

Clarksville - *1192 Occoneechee Park Road (US 58 east near the US 15 intersection), 23927. Phone: (434) 374-2210.* **Web:** *www.dcr.virginia.gov/parks/occoneec.htm. Admission: $2.00-$3.00 per vehicle. Miscellaneous: Campsites, picnicking, an amphitheater and boat launching ramps.* Named for Native Americans who lived in the area for hundreds of years, Occoneechee is located on the Kerr Reservoir, better known as Buggs Island Lake. The visitor center, with displays designed by the Virginia Museum of Natural History, introduces you to Native American culture and the indigenous Occoneechee people. A one-mile interpretive trail takes visitors to the terraced gardens of the Old Plantation grounds. The park also features a 15-mile multi-purpose trail for hiking, biking and horseback riding.

DANVILLE SCIENCE CENTER

Danville - *677 Craghead Street (Crossing of the Dan), 24541. Phone: (434) 791-5160.* **Web:** *www.dsc.smv.org. Hours: Monday-Saturday, 9:30am-5:00pm, Sunday from 1-5:00pm. Closed Thanksgiving and Christmas. Admission: $5.00 adult, $4.00 student, senior (60+) and child (ages 4+).* A satellite of the Science Museum of Virginia, the Danville Science Center is housed in Danville's renovated Victorian train station. The Science Center is loaded with hands-on exhibits that encourage you and your family to unlock the secrets of how things work. Push a button to make sparks fly. Build a crystal. Enjoy interactive exhibits in Light and Vision, Earth Science and more. In the spring, they have a seasonal Butterfly Station. See the Butterflies and look for cocoons, mix nectar and map a Monarch's migration. The awesome Outdoor Sound exhibit is another popular attraction.

WOMACK MUSEUM OF NATURAL HISTORY

Danville - *1008 S. Main Street on Neathery Lane (Danville Community College Campus), 24541. Phone: (434) 797-8498. Web: www.dcc.vccs.edu/aboutdcc/museum.htm. Hours: Tuesday-Sunday from 2:00-5:00pm. Admission: FREE.* The museum collection includes mounted animals, native birds, reptiles, amphibians and insects as well as Indian artifacts, fossils and minerals. There is everything from a Bengal tiger and huge nine-foot Polar bear to a tiny lizard, all displayed in their natural habitats. Twelve dioramas house part of the bird collection in their natural habitat. There is an exhibition bee hive that accommodates approximately 60,000 honey bees during the winter months.

BLUE RIDGE INSTITUTE & FARM MUSEUM

PO Box 1000, Rte. 40 (off Rte. 220 to Rte. 40)

Ferrum 24088

- ❑   Phone: (540) 365-4416, **Web: www.blueridgeinstitute.org**
- ❑   Hours: Walk-in visitors Saturdays 10:00am-5:00pm, Sundays 1:00-5:00pm, (mid-May to mid-August) Group tours are available by reservation any day April-October. Gallery open year-round.
- ❑   Admission: $4.00 adult, $3.00 senior (60+) and child (6-14). Gallery is FREE.

The Blue Ridge Farm Museum reflects the day-to-day lifestyle of prosperous German-American farmsteaders in the Blue Ridge in the year 1800. Visitors may find costumed interpreters preparing meals over the open hearth, baking bread in an outdoor bake oven, blacksmithing, or carrying out other household and farm chores of the period. Walk around the gardens and the farm buildings, heirloom vegetables and historic breeds of sheep, chicken, horses, pigs, and cattle speak to the region's agricultural heritage. Ask them about their special participatory programs when visitors can don Institute costumes and take part in farm activities or try their hands at vintage crafts.

SAILOR'S CREEK BATTLEFIELD HISTORIC STATE PARK

Green Bay - *Rte. 2, Box 70 (SR 307 north to Rte. 617 north), 23942. Web: www.dcr.virginia.gov/parks/sailorcr.htm. Phone: (434) 392-3435.* Nearly a quarter of Lee's army (more than 7,700 men) was killed, wounded or captured (even eight generals were captured) including one of Lee's sons. Lee surrendered his army three days later at Appomattox Court House. Costumed volunteers re-enact this battle near the historic Hillsman House, which served as a field hospital for northern and southern soldiers (summertime). Various interpretive programs are held throughout the year. Motorists traveling along Lee's Retreat can learn more about the battle by tuning their radios to AM 1610. FREE Admission.

TWIN LAKES STATE PARK

Green Bay - *Rte. 2, Box 70 (US 360 west to SR 613), 23942. Web: www.dcr.virginia.gov/parks/twinlake.htm. Phone: (434) 392-3435. Admission: $2.00-$3.00 per car. Fee waived for overnight guests.* This historical park offers a full array of cultural, environmental and recreational activities. Through historic photographs and interpretive signs, visitors to the Cedar Crest Conference Center can learn of the park's history. Twin Lakes was developed in 1950 as Prince Edward State Park for Negroes, a segregated separate, but equal facility. Prince Edward and Goodwin Lake merged and formed this new facility in 1986. You'll find a full service campground, group camping facilities and climate controlled cabins. Enjoy swimming, fishing and lakefront picnicking at Goodwin Lake. Hikers, mountain bikers and equestrians can take advantage of a multi-use trail developed in conjunction with Prince Edward State Forest.

BOOKER T. WASHINGTON NATIONAL MONUMENT

12130 Booker T. Washington Highway (US 220 south to Rocky Mount, then north on SR 122), **Hardy** 24101

- ❑ Phone: (540) 721-2094, **Web: www.nps.gov/bowa**
- ❑ Hours: Year-round daily from 9:00am-5:00pm except New Years, Christmas, and Thanksgiving.
- ❑ Admission: FREE

The monument commemorates Booker T. Washington's first 9 years of childhood slavery. Begin your self-guided tour with the audio-visual program titled "Longing to Learn" (a slide show about Mr. Washington's life with old time slave, gospel songs woven throughout the show). Here, you will learn that Mr. Washington left the Burroughs farm in 1865 at age 9, as a poor and uneducated newly freed slave. When he returned for a visit in 1908, he was a college president (he worked his way through college and later founded his own college) and influential political figure. Outside, follow the Farm Trail through the reconstructed farm buildings, crops and animals. Demonstrations of farm life in Civil War Virginia help bring to life the setting of Washington's childhood as a slave valued at $400. Kids noticed that the cabin he lived in didn't have a floor (only earth) and no glass in the windows. He ate cornbread and pork mostly. Why did he love molasses and ginger cakes? Getting into school (one day) would be like "getting into heaven". "Education and work must go hand in hand" he said. We love places like this that give you a glimpse of the life (and humble beginnings) of an everyday American hero.

SMITH MOUNTAIN LAKE STATE PARK

1235 State Park Rd (North shore of the lake in Bedford Cty. US 460 to SR 122 S to Rte. 608 east to Rte. 626 S), **Huddleston** 24104

- ❑ Phone: (434) 297-6066
  Web: www.dcr.virginia.gov/parks/smithmtn.htm
- ❑ Hours: Daily 8:00am-Dusk.
- ❑ Admission: $3.00-$4.00 per vehicle. Fee waived for overnight guests.

Smith Mountain Lake State Park (*cont.*)

❑   Tours: Virginia Dare Paddlewheeler sightseeing cruises (540) 297-7100.

❑   Miscellaneous: The Smith Mountain Dam Visitor Center is open daily 10:00am-6:00pm; call (540) 985-2587.

Located on the second-largest freshwater body in the state, this park is not just for water enthusiasts. In addition to water-related activities including swimming, paddle boat rentals, a boat ramp and a universally accessible fishing pier, families can also enjoy miles of hiking trails, picnicking, a visitor center, amphitheater and many special programs (Night hikes, hay rides, canoe trips, twilight programs, Junior Rangers). Primitive camping is available and they also have one three-bedroom cabin and 19 two-bedroom cabins. Both campsites and cabins have been upgraded with modern improvements recently.

AMAZEMENT SQUARE, THE RIGHTMIRE CHILDREN'S MUSEUM

27 Ninth Street (corner of Jefferson and ninth Streets along the riverfront, downtown), **Lynchburg** 24504

❑   Phone: (434) 845-1888, **Web: www.amazementsquare.com**

❑   Hours: Sunday and summer Mondays 1:00-5:00pm. Tuesday-Saturday 10:00am-5:00pm.

❑   Admission: $6.00 (age 2+). $1.00 admission on 4th Wednesday Family Fun Night.

❑   Miscellaneous: Big Red Barn's - farmland environment for preschoolers. Great gift shop out front.

The central exhibit of the museum is a meandering three-story interactive tangle of pathways, tunnels, stairs and a glass elevator called the Amazement Tower. Here's some of the best exhibit areas: On The James - Take the helm and row a virtual tour boat "bateaux"; work locks and dams (scale model size); create a rainstorm or watch the river flood. Once Upon a Building - sit in the "Architects Office" and design (using puzzles) a dream home or explore architecture using a computer drafting program (Jefferson influences); work as a team by manipulating a hydraulic crane to create a building or house; here the kids can also make a stained-glass object. Indian Island - explore a Monacan Hogan and ancient village; excavate for artifacts; Science Gallery and Your Amazing Body - explore electricity by making circuits and learn about gravity, walk-thru a heart or push a lung; virtual sports will test your physical fitness. Kaleidoscope - families can step inside a see-through room and paint it (The Paint Box - take off your shoes and enter the box...you won't believe the end result!) or jam with friends in the soundproof studio with electric and rhythm instruments from around the world; act out stories in the theater or make art projects to take home in imagination studio. One promise...in order to participate here, you will make new friends. Most of these exhibits are unique from most other children's museums that we've seen. Well done!

LYNCHBURG SYMPHONY ORCHESTRA

Lynchburg - *621 Court Street, 24504. Phone: (434) 845-6604.* **Web:** *www.lynchburgva.com/symphony.* Classical music during the seven concert season, including two for young people and a free outdoor concert with fireworks for the community.

PIEDMONT ARTS ASSOCIATION

Martinsville - *215 Starling Avenue, 24112. Phone: (276) 632-3221.* **Web:** *www.piedmontarts.org. Hours: Tuesday-Friday 10:00am-5:00pm, Saturdays 10:00am-3:00pm, Sundays 1:30-4:30pm (closed Sundays in the summer). Admission: FREE. Miscellaneous: Discovery Days once a month for small fee designed for parent and child (school-aged) as partners in creativity. Also Summer Workshops available.* Here's the spot for The Arts in Henry County...artistic performers, visiting artists and a rotating exhibitions gallery. The kids will gravitate to the Discovery Room where young visitors can create all types of art, inspired by the art in the museum around them. To engage your kids in the gallery pieces, be sure to ask for the Treasure Hunt page when you arrive. Look for Palette the Discovery Dog's paw print for clues and write the number of your answer in the space. Great way to keep the kids interested, having fun, but also learning about art.

VIRGINIA MUSEUM OF NATURAL HISTORY

1001 Douglas Avenue (corner of Rte. 220/58)

Martinsville 24112

- ❑ Phone: (276) 666-8600, **Web: www.vmnh.net**
- ❑ Hours: Monday-Saturday 10:00am-5:00pm. Sunday 1:00-5:00pm. Closed Thanksgiving, Christmas, New Years.
- ❑ Admission: $5.00 adult, $4.00 senior & youth (12-18), $3.00 child (3-11).
- ❑ Miscellaneous: Summer Programs include Special Saturdays and Summer week-long camps.

Discover the natural wonders of Virginia through permanent and traveling exhibits. Enter the "Age of Reptiles" when dinosaurs roamed the earth...find robotic scale models of these creatures and actual dino tracks. Once the dinosaurs died out, the mammals began to flourish as seen in "Age of Mammals". Touch fossil redwood that looks like wood but feels like stone. Meet "Clawd" the giant sloth (half bear...half something else). Finish the Nature Nook with dinosaur puzzles, coloring, videos, and computer games. Visitors can look for features of the ocean floor in Sea Life on a giant map, touch fossils that are millions of years old, and see whale fossils found in Virginia. There is a slide show presentation that highlights fossil excavations at the Carmel Church Quarry in Caroline County, Virginia. The Rock Hall of Fame allows lots of hands-on looks and touches of rocks from Virginia and around the world. How do we use rocks in everyday life today? (hint: jewelry or concrete?). Where do geodes come from? See the regionally famous Fairy Stones! If you ask good questions of a roaming scientist, they might take you downstairs for a peak at their working lab and show you current projects.

MARTINSVILLE SPEEDWAY

Martinsville - *US 220 (One mile north of the intersection of the US 220/58 Bypass and US 220 Business), 24115. Phone: (276) 956-3151 or (877) 722-3849. www.martinsvillespeedway.com. Admission: Family Section has several sections of backstretch tickets to be sold on race morning as unreserved seats to families* *with child. The family seating will allow parents to bring a child (6-12) to the race for $5.00 per child. Adult tickets in the family unreserved area will be $40.00. Child under age six gets in FREE to the family section. To watch time trials is $15.00 adult and FREE for child under 12.* Sponsors four major NASCAR races each year.

MABRY MILL

Blue Ridge Parkway, Milepost 176 (US 58 and Blue Ridge Pkwy)

Meadows of Dan 24120

- ❑ Phone: (276) 952-2947
- ❑ Hours: Gristmill area open 9:00am-5:00pm (May-October). Restaurant open 8:00am-7:00pm.
- ❑ Admission: FREE
- ❑ Miscellaneous: The Mill Restaurant serves breakfast all day plus yummy sandwiches and desserts. Please try the pancakes or corn cakes made from the mill ground corn meal.

Operated by E.B. Mabry from 1910 to 1935, this mill is one of the most photographed and artistically painted sites around the world. A trail takes you to the gristmill, sawmill, and blacksmith shop where old-time skills are demonstrated in the summer. Friday-Sunday special shows and "good ole time music" on Sunday.

STAUNTON RIVER BATTLEFIELD STATE PARK

1035 Fort Hill Trail (Rte. 92 to Clover to Rte. 600, turn left, and then turn right on Rte. 855), **Randolph** 23962

- ❑ Phone: (434) 454-4312
  Web: www.dcr.virginia.gov/parks/srbbsp.htm
- ❑ Hours: The Visitor Center is now open Wednesday- Saturday, 9:00am-4:30pm and Sunday, 1:00-4:30pm. The battlefield and self-guided trails are open daily from 8:00 am to Dusk.
- ❑ Admission: FREE

This park is a 300-acre Civil War historic site on which a rag tag group of Confederate old men and young boys beat the odds…and held off an assault by 5000 Union calvary on a bridge of strategic

importance to General Lee's army (that under siege in Petersburg).
The 1800 square-feet visitor center displays the history of the area
as well as on electric energy. It also has a ¼ mile nature walking
trail and two wildlife observation towers overlooking a wetland
enhancement project built for waterfowl and other wildlife.

ARTVENTURE/ ART MUSEUM OF WESTERN VIRGINIA

(Center in the Square, currently. Late 2007 will be in new facility at
Salem Avenue, between Market & Williamson), **Roanoke** 24011

- ❏ Phone: (540) 342-5760, **Web: www.artmuseumroanoke.org**
- ❏ Hours: Tuesday-Saturday Noon-4:30pm.
- ❏ Admission: ArtVenture center is $3.00 per person (age 3+) or
  $7.00 per family of four.

The fun-filled space of ArtVenture features multiple stations
directly linked to objects from the Art Museum's permanent
collection. The newer, hands-on, interactive gallery is designed
especially for kids to have a personal experience with art and fun.
The following descriptions of different areas will also give you an
idea of what's displayed in the main part of the art museum: Make
An Impression - in a Japanese shrine, visitors will make 3-color
relief prints by pressing three stamps into a template (just like
Japanese, large block stamp art). History in the Making -
Pocahontas storytelling and individual interpretation. Visual Vibes
- connects auditory sensations with the visual world by creating
vibration-musical sounds out of a famous painting (draw what you
hear - what does it sound like?). Circus Days - this circus-wagon
themed exhibition engages kids in make-believe circus play,
puppetry and dress up. Please Have a Seat - inspired by the "oops!"
chair, visitors complete chair puzzles and create their own designs
on a velcro wall. Vital Symbols - with modeling clay, you are
invited to create your own personalized clay animals, drawing
ideas from West African headpieces. Familiar Faces - self-image is
transformed to Expressionistic, Cubistic or Impressionistic styles.
Look at Me - see through glass easels allow artists to paint an
expressive portrait of a partner that may be turned into take-home
prints...this was our favorite spot for the whole family! History in

the Making - listen to Pocahontas and her tribe while viewing pictures of different artists' versions of her. The exhibits in the main museum showcase significant works of art from cultures around the world with a special emphasis on American art and the artistic expressions of the Blue Ridge Mountains. Wow, what fun and learning can be had here! Please include it in your family plans as often as possible.

HISTORY MUSEUM OF WESTERN VIRGINIA

One Market Square, SE (Center in the Square), **Roanoke** 24011

- ❏ Phone: (540) 342-5770 **Web: www.history-museum.org**
- ❏ Hours: Tuesday-Friday 10:00am-4:00pm, Saturday 10:00am-5:00pm, Sunday 1:00-5:00pm.
- ❏ Admission: $3.00 adult, $2.00 senior (60+) and child (6-17). (FREE Friday afternoons once a month). A ticket to the Link Museum is also a ticket to the History Museum and Historical Society.
- ❏ Miscellaneous: The O. Winston Link Museum (**www.linkmuseum.org**) in Downtown Roanoke is the only in America dedicated to a single photographer – is housed in the former N&W Passenger Station. Link's photo's of the last days of steam locomotion along the Norfolk and Western Railway take a nostalgic look back to 1950s rural life – to the world of drive-in theaters and old country stores along the rail lines.

Did you know that during the time of Lewis and Clark's expedition, the counties were larger, some extending all the way to the Mississippi? The museum spans the 10,000 year history of Western Virginia with an exhibit entitled "A Crossroads of History" that traces the history of mankind in the area from prehistoric to recent times. Here's a sampling of what you can find: a wigwam aside Indian pottery and beads (Rawrenoke: meant "string of shell beads" - were very valuable for trading); a 1781 land grant deed signed by Jefferson; Civil War surgical implements and walking sticks; the Victorian Boom Age late 1800's buggy and parlor room and an area where you can try you hand at making the best sailor's knots.

MILL MOUNTAIN THEATRE

Roanoke - _One Market Square, 24011. Phone: (540) 342-5740 or (800) 317-6455. Web: www.millmountain.org. Performances: Tuesday-Thursday & Sunday evenings at 7:30pm. Saturday & Sunday Matinees at 2:00pm. Friday & Saturday evenings at 8:00pm. Admission: Tickets: Between $15.00 and $30.00 for Main Stage and $10-$15.00 for Waldron Stage. Preview performances $12.00. $2.00 discount (except on Thursday, Friday and Saturday evenings) for student and senior._ Regional professional live year-round theatre offering dramas, musicals, children's plays, comedies, and family productions like "Miss Nelson is Missing" or "A Wonderful Life".

SCIENCE MUSEUM OF WESTERN VIRGINIA

One Market Square, downtown (4th & 5th floors near City Market)

Roanoke 24011

❑   Phone: (540) 342-5718, **Web: www.smwv.org**

❑   Hours: Tuesday-Saturday 10:00am-5:00pm. Sunday 1:00-5:00pm. Closed winter holidays.

❑   Admission: Exhibits only: $8.00 adult, $7.00 senior (60+), $6.00 child (3-12). MegaDome only: $5.00 adult, $4.50 senior, $4.00 child. Save $1.00-$2.00 on combos. One Friday each month, a local company sponsors FREE Friday which includes FREE admission to the museum's permanent exhibits. Parking free on weekends.

❑   Miscellaneous: Planetarium and MegaDome Theatre (programs vary from geography to nature).

Their mission is to "ignite and nurture life-long learning" through hands-on that encourage touching, twisting, spinning, pulling and turning. In Science Arcade, explore light, color and sound by interacting with games (make lightning come to you, create color from gas like neon). At Weather Gallery, televise your own forecast on their ChromaKey green screen, view the eye of the hurricane or a tornado! Get personal - Body Tech, only one of three exhibits in the country that focuses on the science behind medicine (see how blood flows, muscles connect, and the senses react). This is the best example of plaque and hardening of the arteries you'll find...you can even see a real healthy (and hardened) artery. At Mindplay, see illusions that will "tickle" your brain. Come surf the big waves in our SuperNet Gallery! Hardbottom Reef Tank and Chesapeake Bay Touch Tank (pet a horseshoe crab or sea urchin). Moms, Dads & Grandparents will explore this right along with the kids - so much to do (not just see) that many visits are required. Very, very well done!

TO THE RESCUE MUSEUM

Roanoke - *4428 Electric Road (Tanglewood Mall, second level), 24014. Phone: (540) 776-0364. Web: http://naemt.org/ttrescue/. Hours: Tuesday-Saturday Noon-9:00pm, Sunday 1:00-6:00pm. Admission: $2.00 adult, $1.00 child.* Visitors can: report an actual car accident, ride to the rescue in a real crash truck; be a 911 Emergency dispatcher; see a film of dramatic live rescues; hear alarm sounds from yesterday to today; examine the equipment used to train EMTs and Paramedics; and discover who comes to the rescue and why.

VIRGINIA'S EXPLORE PARK / BLUE RIDGE PARKWAY VISITOR'S CENTER

Blue Ridge Parkway, Milepost 115 (accessible from Rutrough Road), **Roanoke** 24014

❑   Phone: (540) 427-1800 or (800) 842-9163
    Web: www.explorepark.org
❑   Hours: Weekends only in April. Wednesday-Saturday 10:00am-
    5:00pm, Sunday Noon-5:00pm (May-October).
❑   Admission: $9.00 adult, $7.00 senior (55+), $5.00 child (4-15).
    FREE weekend wagon rides.
❑   Miscellaneous: Brugh Tavern restaurant serving (daily except
    Mondays) lunch and dinner (kid's menu) in a frontier setting.
    Mountain biking and hiking trails, fishing, canoeing and
    kayaking in the Roanoke River. Trading Company Gift Shop
    with items crafted by park interpreters.

The diverse park offers visitors the opportunity to stroll through history "outside the ordinary". The history area has costumed interpreters who depict life in western Virginia in 1671 with an Indian Village; in 1740 with a frontier settler's cabin; and in 1800's with a restored Roanoke county farmstead, gristmill, blacksmith's shop (he draws the children into demonstrations). In the 1860's school you're seated and taught in a pre-Civil War one-room schoolhouse. Great overview (for young and old) of all the folks who journeyed through and settled along the Blue Ridge Parkway land.

VIRGINIA MUSEUM OF TRANSPORTATION

303 Norfolk Avenue (I-581 exit 5, located in restored railway station next to Norfolk Southern mainline, downtown), **Roanoke** 24016

- ❑   Phone: (540) 342-5670   **Web: www.vmt.org**
- ❑   Hours: Monday-Friday 11:00am-4:00pm, Saturday 10:00am-5:00pm, Sunday Noon-5:00pm. Closed Mondays in January and February. Closed major holidays.
- ❑   Admission: $7.40 adult, $6.40 senior (60+), $5.25 child (3-11).
- ❑   Miscellaneous: A great gift shop with many "Thomas the Tank Engine" ™ items.

Come face to face with vintage electric locomotives, classic diesels and steam giants (the No. 611 is mighty!). Climb aboard a caboose, a railway post office car, and a No. 17, 1934 Dodge school bus. On Main Street, view early autos, freight trucks, fire engines, carriages and air travel. Learn basic principles of the development of transportation through hands-on exhibits that kids can touch, turn, drive, spin, and climb on (ex. Your muscles acting as steam pistons pushing wheels). Kids might also like the multi-level O-gauge model train layout (see who can spot the train first) or the model circus display or the giant Jupiter Rocket parked outside the museum. But mostly, the museum is about the American worker who built the roads, laid the track and built the trains, cars and carriages...the people behind transportation. Meet some of them personally in the railyard (where they are restoring other trains). Create your own safety art (coloring and dress up transportation safety area). Pretend you're in a modern coal mine shaft seeing mineshaft transport machines at work.

GEORGE WASHINGTON & JEFFERSON NATIONAL FORESTS

5162 Valleypointe Parkway, **Roanoke** 24019

❑ Phone: (540) 265-5100 or (888) 265-0019, **www.fs.fed.us/r8/gwj/**
❑ Hours: 24 hours a day.
❑ Admission: FREE. Beaches are $3.00-$8.00 per car.
❑ Miscellaneous: Camping, picnicking, hunting, fishing, hiking (almost 1100 miles of trails including 273 miles of Appalachian Trail), horseback riding, swimming, cross-country skiing.

Highlights include:

Falls of Little Stony, Clinch Ranger District, Wise (540-328-2931). Trail, trout stream, the Gorge (steep sides with large rock outcrops and rock ledges often towering hundreds of feet overhead), and the Views of three waterfalls. **Elizabeth Furnace** (log cabin center/Edinburg 540-984-4101). **Massanutten Storybook Trail**; **Bark Camp Lake Recreation Area** (Wise 540-328-2981); **Guest River Gorge Trail**, **High Knob Recreation Area** (tower observation). **Bear Tree Recreation Area**; **The Virginia Creeper Trail**; **Mount Rogers Scenic Byway**, highest point in state with trail to the top. Also trails thru pine forests, 60 mile segment of Appalachian trail, cross- skiing, Virginia Highlands Horse Trail. (Marion 540-783-5196); **Stony Fork** (Wytheville 540-228-5551); **Cascades Recreation Area** (66 foot cascades waterfall/Blacksburg 540-552-4641); **Dragon's Truth** (spires of quartzite on top of mountain, looks like teeth/New Castle 540-864-5195); **Fenwick Mines** (old miner town); **Roaring Run Furnace**; **Highlands Scenic Tour** (20 mile scenic auto loop including Falling Spring Waterfall and Humpback Bridge - the nation's only surviving arched single-span covered bridge, Covington 540-962-2214); **Lake Moomaw** (540) 962-2214; **Hidden Valley** (Hot Springs 540-839-2521); **Apple Orchard Falls** (200 foot falls/Natural Bridge 540-291-2188); **Crabtree Falls** - hike two miles to the top of the highest waterfall east of the Mississippi River (540) 291-2188; **Sherando Lake**. **Augusta Springs Wetlands Trail** (Staunton 540-885-8028); **Confederate Breastworks**; **Brandywine Lake** (Bridgewater 540-828-2591).

For updates & travel games, visit: **www.KidsLoveTravel.com**

MILL MOUNTAIN ZOO

Roanoke - *PO Box 13484 (on top of Mill Mountain, off the Blue Ridge Parkway and next to the famous Roanoke Star), 24034. Phone: (540) 343-3241. Web: www.mmzoo.org. Hours: Daily 10:00am-5:00pm. Closed Christmas. Extended hours in summer weekends until 8:00pm. Admission: $7.12 adult, $4.75 child (2-12). ZooChoo Rides are $1.50. Miscellaneous: Many special events and educational programs throughout the year. Picnic facilities, a wildflower garden, ZooChoo train rides, outdoor concession/café and gift shop.* This zoo has exhibits of 55 or more species of mammals, birds and reptiles. Animals found here include a Siberian Tiger, Snow Leopards, Red Pandas, Japanese Macaques, Bald Eagles, Fishing Cat, Clouded Leopard and Porcupine.

ROANOKE STAR

Roanoke - *(on top of Mill Mountain, next to the zoo. Follow signs from downtown or off BR Pkwy Milepost 120), 24034. Web: www.visitroanokeva.com.* This attraction is sure to make the kids' mouths drop wide open. See the world's largest man-made star! Erected in 1949 as a symbol of the progressive spirit of Roanoke, it towers nearly 100' high above Mill Mountain. This *huge* structure can be seen at night for over 60 miles.

DIXIE CAVERNS

Roanoke (Salem) - *5753 West Main Street (I-81 exit 132), 24153. Phone: (540) 380-2085, Web: www.dixiecaverns.com. Hours: Daily 9:30am-5:00pm (October-April) and daily 9:30am-6:00pm (May-September). Admission: $7.50 adult, $4.50 child (5-12).* Experienced guides take you "up" into the mountain and then "down" underground - look for formations shaped like a wedding bell, turkey wings or a magic mirror.

SALEM AVALANCHE BASEBALL

Roanoke (Salem) - *1004 Texas Street, Salem Memorial Stadium (From I-81, take exit 141 (Route 419) towards Salem. Follow 419 through two stop lights. Bear right onto Texas Street (Alt. 460), 24153. Phone: (540) 389-3333. Web :www.salemavalanche.com. Season: (April-August). Game times are generally 7:00pm and*

Sunday at 2:00pm or 6:00pm. Admission: General $4.00-$7.00. Senior Citizens and child (12 and under) receive $1.00 off the regular ticket price on box and reserved seating. The Salem Avalanche is a Class "A" Minor League Professional Baseball Team and an affiliate of the Houston Astros. The Avalanche play at a new, 10 million dollar state-of-the-art facility with sky boxes, picnic areas and hot tub. It is the finest minor league facility in America with a breathtaking view of the Blue Ridge Mountains.

STAUNTON RIVER STATE PARK

Scottsburg - *1170 Staunton Trail (US 360 to Rte. 344), 24589. Web: www.dcr.virginia.gov/parks/staunton.htm. Phone: (434) 572-4623. Admission: $2.00-$3.00 per vehicle. Fee is waived for overnight guests.* With woods by the acres, broad meadows and a lengthy shoreline on Buggs Island Lake (800-524-4347) there is much to offer. Freshwater fishing plus swimming and wading pools, camping and cabins, tennis courts, a children's playground, a boat launch, riverfront picnicking in shelters, miles of hiking trails, a multi-use trails open to hikers, bikers and equestrian riders are all well used.

SOUTH BOSTON SPEEDWAY

South Boston - *1188 James Hagood Hwy, 24592. Phone: (434) 572-4947 or (877) 440-1540 tickets. www.southbostonspeedway.com. Season: Saturday night racing opens every March. Admission: ~$10.00 (age 10+). Pit tours are $15.00 each. Special events around $30.00.* During its history, the speedway has been the site of a number of NASCAR Grand National (now Winston Cup) events, with the likes of Richard Petty taking Grand National wins at the oval. Known as America's Hometown Track, South Boston Speedway puts on a great show, with competitions among some of the best Late Model Stock car drivers around.

SOUTH HILL MODEL RAILROAD MUSEUM

South Hill - *201 S. Mecklenburg Avenue (South Hill Chamber offices), 23970. Phone: (434) 447-4547 or (800) 524-4347. Hours: Daily 9:00am-4:00pm.* The Museum is located in the renovated railroad depot downtown and features two operating HO Scale

For updates & travel games, visit: **www.KidsLoveTravel.com**

model railroad displays. The WBA (Wiggle Bump & Agony) is a "just for fun" railroad and features four tracks traveling through tunnels and over and under bridges in the imaginary towns along the track. The focal point of the museum is the replica of the Atlantic & Danville Railroad which ran through South Hill. The museum scale layout features many buildings and scenes meticulously recreated as they looked during the 1950's. It encompasses the route from Lawrenceville to Clarksville, Virginia and also features scenes from LaCrosse, Union Level, South Hill, Boydton, and the John H. Kerr Dam.

VIRGINIA S. EVANS DOLL MUSEUM

South Hill - *201 S. Mecklenburg Avenue (South Hill Chamber offices), 23970. Phone: (434) 447-4547 or (800) 524-4347. Hours: Daily 9:00am-4:00pm.* This Museum features exhibits of more than 500 dolls, some dating back to the 1860's, and represents the lifelong passion of Virginia Evans, a former South Hill school teacher. The collection includes both familiar and exotic dolls from around the world. From the famous Madame Alexander, China Head and German Bisque dolls to Kewpie dolls of the 1920's and the Campbell Soup kids and Tiny Tears dolls form the 1950's, this collection offers something for everyone. Your kids won't want to miss an exhibit of Authentic Period doll house furniture made from thin cardboard, fabrics and straight pins by Jack Lumpkin, age 10, in 1933.

FAIRY STONE STATE PARK

Route 2 Box 723, 907 Fairystone Lake Drive (Rte. 57 from Bassett or from Blue Ridge Pkwy.via Rte. 58, 8 or 57), **Stuart** 24171

❑ Phone: (276) 930-2424 or (800) 933-PARK
   Web: www.dcr.virginia.gov/parks/fairyst.htm
❑ Admission: $3.00-$4.00 per vehicle. Parking fee is waived for overnight guests. Additional swimming fee for day use (summer).
❑ Miscellaneous: 168 acre lake, climate controlled cabins, campgrounds, hiking trails, beach swimming and concessions, row boats, canoes, paddle boats, hydro bikes, picnicking and two playgrounds (including one in the water - Very Nice!), with weekend bluegrass concerts, and daily planned talks, walks, or tours.

Fairy Stone State Park (*cont.*)

Home of the lucky fairy stones (staurdites) - Story: Fairies (or angels) dance playfully around springs until they heard news that Jesus Christ had died. The saddened fairy tears fell onto the rocks and formed crosses made from stones. Many famous people have visited the park (including Presidents) and have made a stone into earrings, bracelets or pocket pieces, carried or worn for luck or blessings. Don't forget to stop by the park office to purchase fairystones (just a couple of dollars) or look for the Hunt Site (next to the gas station - look for signs - 3 miles southeast of the park entrance on Rte 57). If you stay overnight, the cabins are charmingly rustic with electric but with no telephone or TV. Bring along board games and good books to read for evening entertainment by the fire (wood available on site for a small fee), or out on the back porch. Also, be sure to bring a flashlight…it sure gets dark out at night in the woods! If you come during the summer, the water playground has wonderful, soft-sided floating logs, lily pads, frogs and turtles that kids can slide and climb on. A very family friendly park.

WOOD BROTHERS RACING

Stuart - *21 Performance Drive (US 58), 24171. Phone: (276) 694-2121. Web: www.woodbrothersracing.com. Hours: Museum: Weekdays 8:30am-Noon & 1:00-5:00pm. Also open Saturdays of Winston Cup Martinsville races. Admission: FREE. Miscellaneous: Racing gift shop.* One of the most successful racing teams in NASCAR history, Stuart's Wood Brothers have won races on every major track in the country. Their Race Shop and Museum contains memorabilia spanning 50 years of racing. They have a variety of trophies, helmets, uniforms, etc. from drivers like Pearson, AJ Foyt and Dale Jarrett. Also several classic race cars are displayed.

BLUE RIDGE PARKWAY

2551 Mountain View Road Vinton Ranger Station

Vinton 24179

❑ Phone: (540) 857-2458, **Web: www.BlueRidgeParkway.org**

❑ Hours: Activities run from (mid-June to October). Campgrounds, concessions and lodges open (May-October). The parkway closes by section during severe snow and icy conditions.

❑ Admission: FREE for parkway to drive. Some sites have minimal fee.

❑ Miscellaneous: Camping, hiking, fishing, bicycling, picnicking.

The Parkway runs parallel to I-81 and begins in Waynesboro at Milepost 0, and ends in Cherokee, NC. It connects the Shenandoah National Park (Skyline Drive) to the Great Smoky Mountains National Park. The speed limit is 45 MPH and the drive warrants "taking your time" to see the seasonal foliage. Look especially for these mile marker sites:

❑ Hogback Overlook (mile 21)

❑ Logging RR exhibit (mile 34.4)

❑ Humpback Rocks (mile 8.4) has Visitors Center, pioneer mountain farm exhibit.

❑ Fallingwater Cascades National Scenic Trail is a 1.5-2.5 mile hiking loop.

❑ Cave Mountain Lake Recreation Area (Natural Bridge area) has lake swimming, beach, hiking, picnicking and camping. Small vehicle admission. (540) 291-2188.

❑ James River Restored Canal Lock at US 501, James River Visitors Center in Big Island (586-4357). Battery Creek Lock #7 was part of the James River and Kanawha Canal System. May-October.

❑ Peaks of Otter Area (mile 84) has a Visitors Center, historical farm, trails, picnicking and camping. Mile 86 in Bedford is where the Johnson Farm is demonstrating southern mountain interpretive farming demos. Accessible from Peaks of Otter by trail. (August-November, 540-586-3707).

❑ Rocky Knob (mile 169) has picnicking, camping, Visitor Center, trails and cabins.

Blue Ridge Parkway (*cont.*)

- ❑ Mabry Mill (mile 176.1)
- ❑ Meadows of Dan town has an old general store and Nancy's Fudge (800) EAT-FUDGE. Call ahead and request a "chocolate talk" and candy making video presentation.
- ❑ Groundhog Mountain Overlook (mile 188.8) is a high point with 360 degree view and observation tower.
- ❑ Puckett Cabin (mile 189.9) the home of Grandma Puckett, the storied local midwife who helped birth 1000 babies.

SUGGESTED LODGING AND DINING

CLARION INN ROANOKE AIRPORT. **Roanoke**. 3315 Ordway Drive (I-581 exit 3). (540) 362-4500. Their indoor/outdoor (seasonally) pool combo is clean and warm (with whirlpool, too). They have picnic areas and volleyball and tennis courts. Their Food Court has family-friendly made-to-order and cafeteria-style food. In the suburbs with easy access to museums downtown.

Chapter 5
South East Area

Our Favorites...

* Chesapeake Bay Bridge & Tunnel - Cape Charles
* Chincoteague Island Ponies - Chincoteague
* Virginia Air & Space Center - Hampton
* Jamestown, Williamsburg, Yorktown
* Virginia Living Museum - Newport News
* Nauticus & Naval Boat Tours - Norfolk
* Rowena's Jams & Cake Factory - Norfolk
* Pamplin Historical Park - Petersburg
* Center for Virginia History - Richmond
* Richmond Raft Company - Richmond
* Virginia Aquarium - Virginia Beach

Pioneer Dressup - Yorktown

CHESAPEAKE BAY BRIDGE TUNNEL

PO Box 111 (Rte. 13 between Hampton Roads and Eastern shore)

Cape Charles 23310

❑   Phone: (757) 624-3511 or (757) 331-2960, **Web: www.cbbt.com**
❑   Admission: Toll for cars is $12.00, one way. Return trip within 24 hours, $5.00.
❑   Miscellaneous: Annual bridge walks. Visit website for details.

At 17.6 miles long, it carries US 13 across the mouth of the Chesapeake Bay using bridges, tunnels (underwater!) and 4 man-made islands. The route has wonderful panoramic views and the southernmost island has a fishing pier, a gift shop and a restaurant. (A great place to stop and take a break!) This is quite a unique experience! An interesting note: This bridge/tunnel must be completely inspected for safety every 5 years. Well, it takes about 5 years to complete an inspection…so it's a never ending job!

KIPTOPEKE STATE PARK

Cape Charles - *3540 Kiptopeke Drive (Eastern Shore, 3 miles north of Chesapeake Bay Bridge Tunnel on US 13, then west on SR 704), 23310. Web: www.dcr.virginia.gov/parks/kiptopek.htm. Phone: (757) 331-2267. Admission: $3.00-$4.00 per car. No parking fee for camping and cabin guests, up to two vehicles. Miscellaneous: Full-service and tent campsites, a boat ramp, a seasonal 24-hour accessible fishing pier, picnic areas, hiking trails, and a guarded swimming area and playground.* Kiptopeke offers recreational access to the Chesapeake Bay along with an opportunity to explore a unique habitat featuring a flyway for migratory birds, rarely seen animals & a coastal dune environment.

BERKELEY PLANTATION

Charles City - *12602 Harrison Landing Road (off SR 5 west), 23030. Web: www.berkeleyplantation.com. Phone: (804) 829-6018. Hours: Daily 9:00am-5:00pm. Last tour at 4:30pm. Admission: $10.50 adult, $7.00 student (13-16), $5.50 child (6-12).* This is the site of the first official Thanksgiving in 1619. It is also the ancestral home of two U.S. Presidents: Benjamin Harrison V, a signer of the Declaration of Independence and William Henry

Harrison, ninth President. "Taps" was composed here in 1862 during the Civil War. Knowledgeable and enthusiastic guides in period costumes conduct tours of the original 1726 mansion, furnished with a grand collection of 18th century antiques. The tour includes an audio-visual program and museum.

SHERWOOD FOREST PLANTATION

Charles City - *14501 John Tyler Hwy. (I-295 south to exit #22A heading east on SR 5 for 10 miles), 23030. Phone: (804) 829-5377. Web: www.sherwoodforest.org. Hours: Open daily 9:00am-5:00pm, except Thanksgiving and Christmas. Admission: $5.00 adult, $3.00 child. Miscellaneous: The mansion is not open to public tours except for special arrangements.* This house was the home of the 10th President, John Tyler (1841-1845) and the Tyler family since 1842. It is known to be the longest frame house in America and the tour features mid-19th century plantation life. Ten points of interest are included in the self-guided tour of the grounds and original out-buildings. Look for the ancient tree plantings (1850 ginkgo), the ballroom, the milk house and the restored slave house on tour.

SHIRLEY PLANTATION

501 Shirley Plantation Road (I-295 south to exit #22A heading east on SR 5 for 10 miles), **Charles City** 23030

- ❑ Phone: (800) 232-1613, **Web: www.shirleyplantation.com**
- ❑ Hours: Daily 9:00am-5:00pm. Last tour at 4:45pm. Grounds close at 6pm. Closed Thanksgiving and Christmas Days.
- ❑ Admission: $10.50 adult, $9.50 senior (60+) and military, $7.00 student (6-18).

Shirley was founded six years after the settlers arrived at Jamestown in 1607 to establish the first permanent English Colony in the New World. It was granted to Edward Hill I in 1660. The famous square-rigged, flying staircase rises three stories with no visible means of support and is the only one of its kind in America. During the Revolution, this plantation served as a supply center for the Continental Army. During the Civil War, Shirley survived two Campaigns. Ann Hill Carter, mother of Robert E. Lee, was born and raised at Shirley (she married Henry "Light-Horse Harry" Lee in the parlor). Outbuildings include a large two-story kitchen house, laundry house, and two L-shaped barns, one with the ice cellar beneath it, stable, smokehouse and root cellar. Archeological excavations are ongoing seasonally.

HENRICUS HISTORICAL PARK

Chesterfield - *251 Henricus Park Road, 601 Coxendale Road, 23832. Phone: (804) 706-1340. Web: www.henricus.org. Hours: Tuesday-Sunday 10:00am-5:00pm (March-December). Admission: FREE. Average $6.00 fee for some events. Miscellaneous: Visitors Center and Museum Store.* See history come alive at the second successful English settlement in the New World. Henricus was home to Pocahontas, the beginnings of the early plantations and the first English hospital in America. Witness history come alive through costumed interpreters. Enjoy nature hikes, birding and fishing at the Dutch Gap Conservation Area.

POCAHONTAS STATE PARK

Chesterfield - *10301 State Park Road (I-95 to SR 288 north, then SR 10 east to Rte. 655 west), 23832. Phone: (804) 796-4255. Web: www.dcr.virginia.gov/parks/pocahont.htm. Admission: $3.00-4.00 per vehicle.* Located 20 miles from downtown Richmond, this park has pool swimming, boating, bicycling, camping and group cabins. The Civilian Conservation Corps Museum is dedicated to the Depression-era volunteers who helped to build the state's park system. Algonquin Ecology Camp is available for overnight group camps as is the Heritage Center and the new amphitheater on a sloping hillside. There's also hiking and bridle trails.

ASSATEAGUE EXPLORER

(Departs daily from the dock at East Side Marina, on Chincoteague, just NE of the Pony Swim area), **Chincoteague** 23336

- ❑ Phone: (757) 990-1795 or (866) PONY SWIM
  Web: www.assateagueisland.com/explorer.htm
- ❑ Admission: Rates: Pony Express or Birdwatching Nature Tours - $30.00, child (4-11) and senior 30% off.

Assateague Explorer (*cont.*)

❑   Schedule: Pony Express Nature Tours: several times daily. Circle
(Chincoteague) Island Nature Tour: 2-3 times daily. Check out
the area map of expeditions on the website. Reservations are
recommended.

Assateague visitors often drive to the island and say, "Where are
the wild ponies?" The National Park Service has placed miles of
fence along the roadways to keep the wild horses away from roads
and back in their natural habitat. About 95% of the wild ponies are
found far away from the roads and these pony sighting trips take
you to these productive areas. Assateague Island has several
remote areas where you can consistently discover wild ponies on
your vacation and the Pony Express tour makes seeing ponies easy.
Your boat captain and guide is a commercial fisherman and native
of Chincoteague Island. The boat is specifically designed to go
where most other boats can not go. You will voyage into secluded
wildlife refuge areas and learn about wild ponies and their
behavior as you cruise up close to wild ponies. Get your best view
of Assateague's lighthouse and have a great chance of seeing bald
eagles, dolphin & other wildlife along miles of the refuge. This is
an action-packed adventure and recommended for families who
want to experience tons of wild ponies. The boat is large and stable
with a quick and shallow water running capability.

ASSATEAGUE ISLAND NATIONAL SEASHORE/ CHINCOTEAGUE WILDLIFE REFUGE

8586 Beach Road (Toms Cove Visitor Center)

Chincoteague 23336

❑   Phone: (757) 336-6122, **Web: www.nps.gov/asis/home.htm**
❑   Hours: Daily 5:00am-10:00pm (May-September). 6:00am-
8:00pm (April, October). 6:00am-6:00pm (rest of year). Tram
departures daily at 10:30am and 5:00pm (summer) and
Wednesday, Saturday and Sunday at various times (April, May,
September, October). Cruises depart daily at 1:00, 5:00 and
7:00pm (summer), by appointment (rest of year).

For updates & travel games, visit: **www.KidsLoveTravel.com**

❑   Admission: $10.00-$15.00 per vehicle for one week. Tram &
    Cruises start at $8.00 (age 5+).

❑   Miscellaneous: Tom's Cove Hook Area (southern end of
    Assateague) has a beach area open (mid-March - August). Pets
    are prohibited in the entire Virginia portion of Assateague Island,
    even in your car.

One in a chain of barrier islands along the Atlantic coast with
many species of migratory birds like snow geese, great blue
herons, balk eagles and osprey.   The Refuge is famous for
birdwatching due in part to its prime location along the Atlantic
Flyway which makes it a vital resting and feeding area for
hundreds of different kinds of migratory birds. The refuge is
located on the Virginia end of Assateague Island and is one of the
most popular in the United States. Many visitors choose to bike
along the bike paths while others enjoy the miles of Assateague
and Chincoteague coastline by taking wildlife voyages by boat.
Wild Ponies, horseshoe crabs, shellfish, waterfowl and a great
variety of birds can be found while you explore the natural features
of this unique ecosystem. Each November, the refuge sponsors a
program known as Waterfowl Week so that visitors may observe
and learn more about wintering waterfowl. Several paved trails of
wildlife viewing are open to walkers and bikers during the day and
automobiles after 3:00pm to dusk. Camping at Assateague Island
National Seashore is permitted only on the Maryland side of
Assateague. National Park Service provides bayside and oceanside
campsite year round. Assateague State Park is also located on the
Maryland side of Assateague and provides over 300 campsites.
Backcountry camping is also available for campers who wish to
backpack or paddle the island. No camping is available on the
Virginia side of Assateague. Look to the commercial campgrounds
on Chincoteague Island if you are visiting the Virginia side of
Assateague Island.

CAPTAIN BARRY'S BACK BAY CRUISES

(Capt Barry's boat is docked), off Main Street in the Landmark Plaza, **Chincoteague** 23336

❑ Phone: (757) 336-6508, **Web: www.captainbarry.bigstep.com**
❑ Admission: $40.00 per person for ½ day excursions. $20.00 for Half-Back Cruise or Birding Cruise (early am)
❑ Tours: 2 Half-Day Trips: Daily, departs 9:00am - returns 1:00pm. Departs 2:00pm - returns 6:00pm. Reservations necessary.
❑ Miscellaneous: No prior experience on the water is necessary. Free drinks and snacks provided.

Back Bay Cruises as well as Half-Back cruises (½ the time, $20.00 per person price) and a Birding Tour. Choose your tour based on age of kids and interest in nature. Participants can get their hands dirty and their feet wet as they identify aquatic animals and plants. Catch Crabs by pulling pots, looking for jelly fish, learning about clams and oysters, how they are caught and grown, learning inter-tidal biology, navigation, weather forecasting, bird identification, netting, beach combing for shells, hearing about our history (hear tales about pirates, smugglers and movie stars), swimming, sunbathing, photography, or just hanging out.

CHINCOTEAGUE PONY CENTRE

6417 Carriage Drive (Turn Left at the Light (by the Bridge), Turn Right on Maddox Blvd., Then Right on Chicken City Rd. (at the light), **Chincoteague** 23336

❑ Phone: (757) 336-2776
  Web: www.chincoteague.com/ponycentre/
❑ Hours: Monday-Saturday 9:00am-10:00pm (seasonal summer hours, hours vary in winter). Pony rides in the morning and afternoon. Pony Show 8:00pm Daily (except Sunday).
❑ Miscellaneous: Gift Shop. Find "Misty" related items & souvenirs.

The Pony Centre is dedicated to the showcase of the beautiful and talented Chincoteague Pony, from the time it is a young foal to the time of full maturity gentled to ride. Offers riding lessons and pony rides daily on Chincoteague Ponies as well as a Special Pony Show. Displays focusing on Misty, Marguerite Henry (author of

Misty of Chincoteague), the island itself, and various carriages add to the Centre. Live Chincoteague ponies, both descendents of Misty and ones bought from the Chincoteague Fire Company at Pony Penning are in stalls ready to meet the public. A film on Chincoteague and its ponies, runs continuously in the video room of the Centre. A special children's corner rounds out the area. Have your photo taken on or with a Chincoteague Pony at the Pony Shows nightly.

OYSTER & MARITIME MUSEUM

Chincoteague - *7125 Maddox Blvd. (north on Main, then east on Maddox to right before the bridge to Assateague), 23336. Phone: (757) 336-6117.* **Web:** *www.chincoteague.com/omm/. Hours: Daily 10:00am-5:00pm (Memorial-Labor Day). Saturday 10:00am-4:00pm, Sunday, Noon-4:00pm (March-May, September-November). Admission: $1.00-3.00 per person.* The only one of its kind in the US, they feature live marine exhibits (fresh live oysters, clams, and fish from the nearby waters), shell specimens (touchables), historical maritime artifacts and most uniquely, tools from the seafood industry. Did you know that Native Americans were the first oysterman? Young kids will have their eyes wide open looking at the giant clam, huge first-order Fresnel lens from the Assateague lighthouse. Oyster memorabilia here and there and everywhere in this area. Watch a 4 minute oyster processing video - amazing that this is still a manual process. Guess what the most popular dish they serve at local restaurants is?

NASA VISITOR CENTER

Chincoteague (Wallops Island) - *Wallops Flight Facility (US 13 to SR 175 west next to the Main Base of NASA), 23337. Phone: (757) 824-2298.* **Web:** *www.wff.nasa.gov. Hours: Thursday-Monday 10:00am-4:00pm (March-June, September-November). Daily (July 4-Labor Day). Admission: FREE.* See many spacecraft and flight articles and exhibits on America's space flight program, movies and video presentations. They showcase the world of past, present and future flights. Best to visit during a special program like Model Rocket Launch (first Saturday of each month at 1:00pm), Puppet Shows (weekends at 11:00am), or daily "Space Ace" Activities.

TURNER SCULPTURE

PO Box 128 US 13

Eastern Shore (Onley) 23418

- ❑   Phone: (757) 787-2818, **Web: www.turnersculpture.com**
- ❑   Hours: Call ahead for best viewing hours as they change monthly.
- ❑   Admission: FREE
- ❑   Miscellaneous: Gift gallery with items for sale. (Although the least expensive fine art sculptures are around $50.00)

You've probably seen a lot of Turner sculptures in your travels to the White House, Chicago's Botanical Garden, Philadelphia (and Chicago, Salisbury, New York, North Carolina) Zoo, and the Virginia Marine Science Museum. Most admirers of the art appreciate nature's creatures because the Turners (father & son) capture snapshots of it (especially waterfowl). The process of making these works is fascinating for children. First, the mold is fabricated around the original clay model. Step two is the wax casting followed by dipping a ceramic mold around the wax cast. Next, the wax is removed and 2000 degree molten bronze is poured into the hollow mold. The ceramic mold is then removed, the bronze is cooled and the pieces are welded together. Finally, artists apply patina for detail and color. Hopefully, you'll get to meet the artists or maybe be fortunate enough to see the pouring stage where the men wear "spacesuits" that are heat and fire retardant.

SALT MARSH TOURS

Eastern Shore (Willis Wharf) - *(Departing the Picturesque Village of Willis Wharf), 23486. Phone: (757) 442-4246. **Web:** www.saltmarshtours.com. Admission: $30.00 per person. Tours: They schedule tours in all seasons by reservation only. Minimum 2 people, maximum 6 people. Marsh Tours take about two hours (no toilet facilities). Miscellaneous: Habitat Studies, Barrier Island Trips, Clamming Trips (half day trips). Bring insect repellent and sunscreen.* Enjoy a Boat Tour of the Eastern Shore's peaceful and unspoiled seaside Marshes and Creeks. On the East Coast of

Virginia's Eastern Shore between the barrier islands and the mainland is the largest unspoiled saltmarsh estuary in North America. The saltmarshes along the Atlantic Flyway provides resting/feeding ground for migratory birds in both spring and fall. They are also home to many resident species year round.

CAPE HENRY LIGHTHOUSES

Fort Story - *583 Atlantic Avenue (east of US 13 via US 60, then northeast on SR 305), 23459. Phone: (757) 422-9421. Web: www.apva.org/apva/cape_henry.php. Hours: Daily 10:00am-4:00pm. Closed Thanksgiving and early December - early January. Admission: $2.00-$3.00.* Cape Henry Lighthouse is the first lighthouse structure authorized, fully completed, and lighted by the newly organized Federal Government. It is an octagonal stone structure, faced with hewn or hammer-dressed stone. The oil-burning lamps of the Cape Henry Lighthouse were first lighted late in October, 1792. The light at Cape Henry burned with regularity in years to come. Climb the many stairs, once you reach the summit, enjoy a panoramic view of the Atlantic Ocean and the Chesapeake Bay. Across the dune line, you'll find the new Cape Henry Lighthouse, built in 1881. It's the tallest iron-encased lighthouse in the country. Adjacent to the lighthouses is a replica of the First Landing Cross, planted by the first settlers to give thanks for a safe voyage after arriving here in 1607.

GLOUCESTER POINT BEACH PARK AND VIMS WETLANDS

Gloucester Point – *1208 - 1255 Greate Road, 23062. Web: www.gloucesterva.info/pr/parks/gpb.htm. Phone: (804) 642-9474 or (804) 684-7000 (aquarium). Hours: Beach: Seasonally, dawn to dusk. Aquarium: open seasonally for marsh walk tours and events. Admission: FREE. Miscellaneous: Boat Ramps, Fishing Pier, Charcoal Grills, horseshoes, Playground, and Volleyball courts.* Gloucester Point Beach Park is located on the bank of the York River. This park offers a large, shady, and grassy Park area with picnic areas and a shelter. The swimming area and sandy beach are perfect for sunbathing, wading, and beach fun! The Beach House has a concession stand, restrooms, and outdoor shower. The

Aquarium and Visitor Center offers visitors opportunities to observe marine life and learn about VIMS scientists' current research. Self guided exhibits include current issues in marine research, eight aquaria ranging in size from 50 to 3,000 gallons, and life-sized models of marine mammals and fishes.

AIR POWER PARK

Hampton - *413 West Mercury Blvd. (I-64 exit 263B), 23666. Phone: (757) 727-1163. Hours: Daily 9:00am-4:30pm. Closed Thanksgiving, Christmas and New Years. Admission: FREE. Miscellaneous: Playground area and picnic facilities.* Start your visit viewing the model airplane collection, wind tunnel exhibit and Freedom Shrine. Learn about early space exploration and aircraft testing. At the back of the center you enter the outdoor park. You will see jet planes, missiles, rockets and space artifacts as you walk your own self-guided park tour.

BLUEBIRD GAP FARM

Hampton - *60 Pine Chapel Road, 23666. Phone: (757) 727-6739. Hours: Open year-round: Wednesday-Sunday, 9:00am-5:00pm. Closed Thanksgiving, Christmas Day and New Year's Day. Also closed Wednesday when a major holiday falls on a Monday or Tuesday. Miscellaneous: Picnic facilities, playground.* Bluebird Gap Farm offers an exciting adventure and educational experience in an urban environment. Designed to resemble a working farm, this 60-acre site is home to bobcats, cows, horses, sheep, goats, mountain lions and other domesticated and wild animals familiar to traditional Virginia farmers.

COUSTEAU SOCIETY

710 Settlers Landing Road (near the Air & Space Museum)

Hampton 23666

❑   Phone: (757) 722-9300 or (800) 441-4395
     Web: www.cousteausociety.org
❑   Hours: Wednesday-Friday 10:00am-4:00pm, Saturday 11:00am-4:00pm, Sunday Noon-3:00pm. Closed Thanksgiving and Christmas-time.

For updates & travel games, visit: **www.KidsLoveTravel.com**

❏   Admission: FREE

Visitors to the gallery can enjoy the Cousteau Society's world-renowned underwater photography, view models of the famous Cousteau research vessels Calypso and Alcyone, look at past and present exploration diving equipment, and travel through history with artifacts from Cousteau expeditions such as a decompression chamber, a mini-sub, and a jeep with dents in the side from a rhinoceros charge. You can even view a hovercraft in which guests can sit and have their photograph taken. Underwater footage of the famed explorer's confrontation with sharks is displayed on monitors above the same shark cage in which he was enclosed.

HAMPTON HISTORY MUSEUM

Hampton - *120 Old Hampton Lane (downtown), 23666. Phone: (757) 727-1610 or (800) 800-2202. Web: www.hamptoncvb.com. Hours: Monday-Saturday 10:00am-5:00pm. Admission: $5.00.* The museum interprets Hampton's past spanning from its inhabitance by the Kecoughtan Indians through the 20th century. Learn about folks like Captain John Smith, Blackbeard the pirate, Booker T. Washington and astronauts. Part of an old tavern and a replica of a pirate's skeleton that was unearthed during Hampton's waterfront renovation are highlights. See the full-scale reproductions of the USS Monitor's gun turret and a portion of the CSS Virginia's (Merrimack) casemate.

LANGLEY SPEEDWAY

Hampton - *3165 N. Armistead Avenue (I-64 exit 262), 23666. Phone: (757) 865-1100. Web: www.langley-speedway.com. Hours: Each Saturday gates open at 4:00pm, qualifying at 5:00pm and racing beginning at 7:00pm. Admission: $10.00 adult, $5.00 child (6-12). Family Night - 2 adult/2 Kids get in for $25.00. Miscellaneous: Extreme Sports Wednesday is lots of fun events with 1 On 1 Drags, time attacks and burn out competitions ($8.00 general admission).* Featuring Pure Stock, Super-Mini Trucks, Legends, Baby Grands, Super Street Series, NASCAR ShorTrack Series Grand Stock and NASCAR Weekly Racing Series Late Model Stock Car Division racing.

SANDY BOTTOM NATURE PARK

Hampton - *1255 Big Bethel Road (I-64 to Hampton Roads Center Pkwy exit 26A), 23666. Web: www.hampton.va.us/sandybottom. Phone: (757) 825-4657. Hours: Open year-round: Daily sunrise to sunset. The nature center is open from 9:00am-5:00pm (May-September) and 9:00am-3:30pm (October-April). Admission: FREE, fees for rentals.* This 456-acre recreational facility features two lakes, wetlands areas, trails for hiking and biking, fishing, non-motorized boating, picnic areas, children's playground, a campground, tent cabins for rent and a beautiful nature center with creature displays. Call about special nature programs.

BUCKROE BEACH

Hampton - *(I-64 exit 268, Mallory Street to Pembroke Ave., turn right), 23669. Phone: (757) 727-6347. Hours: Open year-round: Daily. Summer season runs Memorial Day through Labor Day, daylight hours. Admission: FREE. Small parking fee.* Enjoy the wide, clean beach and gentle surf of this Chesapeake Bay beach. Lifeguards on duty during the summer season. Picnic shelters available. The park pavilion is the site of big band concerts and an outdoor movie series during the summer.

MISS HAMPTON II HARBOR CRUISES

764 Settlers Landing Road (purchase tickets at the Harbor Cruises office located at the bottom of the Radisson Parking Garage)

Hampton 23669

❏   Phone: (757) 722-9102 or (888) 757-2628
     Web: www.misshamptoncruises.com/misshampton.htm
❏   Admission: $18.00 adult, $16.00 senior & Military, $9.00 child (6-12)
❏   Tours: Tour Time: Daily, 10:00am. Approximately 3 hours. (April-October). Daily, 10:00am & 2:00pm (Memorial Day-Labor Day).

The double-decked tour boat offers daily narrated cruises of the Hampton Roads harbor and Chesapeake Bay. Get a taste of seafaring culture as you take to the water to see local fishing boats, mighty commercial cargo ships, Blackbeard's Point, Old Point

Comfort, Fort Wool and the awesome gray fleet at ↳
largest naval installation, Norfolk Naval Base. When
permits, passengers can disembark at Fort Wool for a guideo
of the island fortress. Cruises to view the Ghost Fleet located ↳
the James River are also offered in spring & fall.

VIRGINIA AIR & SPACE CENTER / HAMPTON ROADS HISTORY CENTER

600 Settlers Landing Road (I-64 exit 267)

Hampton 23669

- ❑ Phone: (757) 727-0900 or (800) 296-0800, **Web: www.vasc.org**
- ❑ Hours: Monday-Wednesday 10:00am-5:00pm, Thursday-Sunday
  10:00am-7:00pm ((Memorial Day to Labor Day). 10:00-5:00pm
  daily rest of year. IMAX daytime and evening shows. Closed
  only Thanksgiving and Christmas.
- ❑ Admission: $8.75 adult, $7.75 senior (65+), $6.75 child (3-11).
  Extra $5.00-$6.00 for IMAX Theatre. Great combo packages
  with Hampton area museums.
- ❑ Miscellaneous: IMAX presentations are related to space travel.
  The famous 1920 restored Hampton Carousel (757) 727-6381 is
  next door and gives old-fashioned rides.

The official visitor center for NASA Langley Research facilities,
this place houses flight and space artifacts, hands-on exhibits (like
Fly Sticky Feet or walk inside the Eye of a Tornado) and historical
displays. See a real moon rock (collected during the Apollo 17
mission); see the Apollo 12 Command Module that journeyed to
the moon and back; and a replica of the Lunar Orbiter, which
mapped the moon's surface for future landings. The kids can
actually be an Astronaut-for-a-Minute (see what you'd look like in
the "suit") or Launch-a-Rocket where they learn about the stages of
preparation for a launch and then, send a model rocket shooting up
into the clouds. Feeling silly? Take a spin on the Space Ball to feel
what it's like to be weightless or try on wings to feel the lift that
makes flight possible in Up, Up & Away. The 94 foot high ceiling
is full of hanging military aircraft and NASA spacecraft (one
aircraft was actually struck by lightning 700 times in research!).

The new Adventures in Flight gallery takes visitors on an aviation adventure when they "wing walk" on a Jenny bi-plane, see a replica 1903 Wright Flyer, explore a DC-9 passenger jet, ride in a WWII bomber, become an air traffic controller, sit in the cockpit of an F/A-22 fighter jet, or pilot an airplane. Lots of "Wows" from the kids here!

CASEMATE MUSEUM AT FORT MONROE

Hampton (Fort Monroe) - *PO Box 51341 (off I-64 to Bernard Road), 23651. Phone: (757) 788-3391. Hours: Daily, 10:30am-4:30pm. Closed Thanksgiving, Christmas Day and New Year's Day. Admission: FREE.* The largest stone fort ever built in the U.S., Fort Monroe is headquarters for the U.S. Army Training and Doctrine Command. Within the historic fort's stone walls is the Museum, which chronicles the history of the fort and the Coast Artillery Corps. During the Civil War, Fort Monroe was a Union-held bastion in the center of a Confederate state. In the museum's Civil War area, learn how Freedom's Fortress helped shelter thousands of slave refugees and see the cell where Confederate President Jefferson Davis was imprisoned.

AMERICAN THEATRE (THE)

Hampton (Phoebus) - *125 E. Mellen Street, 23663. Phone: (757) 722-2787.* **Web: www.theamericantheatre.com.** Home of the Hampton Arts Commission's Great Performers Series and especially, the Family Fun Series (Rumpelstiltskin, Pocahontas).

CITY POINT OPEN AIR MUSEUM WALKING TOUR

City Point (Hopewell) Historic District (begins on Cedar Lane at St. John's Church, exit 9 or 15, follow signs), **Hopewell** 23860

❑   Phone: (800) 541-2461 or (800) 863-8687
       Web: www.historichopewell.org/museum.html
❑   Hours: Most buildings that you can tour are at the beginning of the tour and close by 4:30pm. Most open at 10:00am (April-October).

❑ Admission: Tour is FREE. Small admission for inside tours of some buildings, if desired.

❑ Miscellaneous: Union fort breastworks and Weston Manor are nearby, as is Sears Mail Order Houses.

This self-guided tour (brochures available at the Visitors Info Center, exit 9 off I-295) captures the people and events of City Point during the Civil War. Walk down the same streets that Union Generals Grant, Sheridan, and Sherman or President Lincoln did and stop to read insights at 25 wayside exhibits. Of interest to kids along the tour are the St. John's Episcopal Church (505 Cedar Lane, where black and whites were baptized prior to the Civil War and the Union army used the church temporarily as a signal station, a Union stockade, and a place of worship - open to view most weekday mornings; Appomattox Manor (currently being renovated by NPS); City Point Early History Museum at St. Dennis Chapel (exhibits show visitors the 10,000 plus year history of old City Point). At certain sites, children can explore the interior of a Civil War hospital tent, or have photos taken with life size figures of a wounded soldier, President Lincoln, or an Appomattox Indian. Without a visit to some buildings, the kids might find the tour a little boring.

WESTON MANOR

Hopewell - *(Weston Lane & 21st Avenue), 23860. Phone: (804) 458-4682. Web: www.historichopewell.org/index.html. Hours: Monday-Saturday 10:00am-4:30pm, Sunday 1:00-4:30pm (April-October). Admission: $4.00 adult, $3.50 senior (65+), FREE child under 12.* Weston was owned by the Eppes family of City Point, originally presented as a wedding gift. Heirs linage includes ties to the Appomattox Plantation and Pocahontas. During the Civil War, Weston was the residence of 12 year old Emma Wood and her family. Later, she wrote a journal of her wartime experiences. Be sure to listen for stories about little Emma's adventures, occupation by Union Troops, and post-war tall tales.

SPCA PETTING ZOO

Newport News - *523 J. Clyde Morris Blvd. (I-64 exit 258A), 23601. Web: www.peninsulaspca.com/zoo.html. Phone: (757) 595-1399. Hours: Monday-Friday 10:00am-5:00pm, Saturday 10:00am-4:30pm, Sunday Noon-5:00pm. (Weather Permitting). Admission: $3.00 adult, $1.00 child (3-12).* The petting zoo has an exotic area with a tiger, lion, jaguar, mountain lions, otters, kangaroo, badgers, crocodiles, alligators, etc. Small children enjoy the opportunity to pet the farm animals and get a closer look at a llama, as well as ducks, turkeys, geese, sheep and goats.

VIRGINIA LIVING MUSEUM

524 J. Clyde Morris Blvd. (I-64 exit 258A)

Newport News 23601

❑ Phone: (757) 595-1900, **Web: www.valivingmuseum.org**

❑ Hours: Daily 9:00am-6:00pm (Summers). Monday-Saturday 9:00am-5:00pm, Sunday Noon-5:00pm (rest of year). Closed all major winter holidays.

❑ Admission: $11.00 adult, $8.00 child (3-12) - Museum. Planetarium shows daily are $3.00 extra or save $1.00 if get combo rates. Minimum age restrictions for planetarium shows.

❑ Miscellaneous: Summertime weekend safaris & Adventure Clubs.

The new museum building's living exhibits showcase Virginia's natural history from the mountains to the sea. Explore the underwater realm of the Chesapeake Bay and the underground world of a limestone cave. Follow the trail along a wooded lakeside boardwalk where you visit raccoons, bobcats, foxes (specifically Virginia's red fox), otters and beavers in their natural habitats. You'll find a meadow, bald eagles, endangered red fox, beautiful blue heron (searching for food in the wetlands/swamp aviary) and native wildflower gardens. Indoors at the Touch Tank, meet (and maybe touch) sea stars (with tube feet), horseshoe crabs and other marine life common to the Chesapeake Bay. Visitors can open the jaw of a pit viper model, watch a frog jump, create a chorus of nighttime sounds and do a virtual dissection of a frog. Walk through the James River (with a giant ocean aquarium), an indoor songbird aviary, and a nocturnal animal exhibit featuring bats, flying squirrels, screech owls (surreal!) tree frogs and other creatures of the night. In the springtime thru early summer, you can see many bugs and butterflies all native to the Eastern Coast Plains. When you arrive, check the listings for live animal & sky shows. Step up to the observatory and view the sky through a 14-inch telescope. We heard lots and lots of "Look...look..., mom and dad!"- here.

NEWPORT NEWS PARK

Newport News - *13564 Jefferson Avenue (I-64 exit 250B), 23602.* **Web: www.nnparks.com**. *Phone: (757) 888-3333 or (800) 203-8322. Hours: Daily, year-round. Park open dawn-dusk. Admission: FREE, fees for campsites.* This 8,000 acre park with two fresh water reservoirs is one of the largest municipal parks east of the Mississippi. Features: aeromodel flying field, 5-star archery range, bicycle rental, disc golf, freshwater fishing, boat ramp, boat rental, 180-site campground, Civil War battle site, golf course, horse show arena, interpretive programs, wildlife rehabilitation center, picnic shelters, playground, restrooms, stage, ropes and initiatives course, Tourist Information Center, 30 miles of hiking trails, 5-mile mountain bike trail, and 5.3 mile bikeway. Picnic shelters are available. Campground is a 180-site full-service campground located in a natural wooded setting adjacent to the Lee Hall Reservoir.

ENDVIEW PLANTATION

Newport News - *362 Yorktown Road (I-64 exit 247), 23603. Phone: (757) 887-1862.* **Web: www.endview.org**. *Hours: Monday-Saturday 10:00am-4:00pm, Sunday 1:00-5:00pm. Closed Tuesdays year-round. Closed winter Wednesdays. Admission: $6.00 adult, $5.00 senior (62+), $4.00 child (7-18). Miscellaneous: Visit nearby Lee Hall Mansion for additional glimpse at plantation life. 163 Yorktown Road. (757) 888-3371. Especially good for re-enactments and seasonal open houses (see Seasonal and Special Events).* Endview was used as a resting place or campground in September 1781 by 3000 Virginia militia en route to Yorktown and the climatic revolutionary War battle.

During the War of 1812, it was a campground for members of the Virginia Militia. By the outbreak of the Civil War, Endview had passed to the Curtis family and was the home of confederate Captain Humphrey Harwood Curtis. First Confederate, and then Union forces used the home and its grounds as a hospital during the 1862 campaign.

MARINERS' MUSEUM

100 Museum Drive (I-64 exit 258A), **Newport News** 23606

❑ Phone: (757) 596-2222 or (800) 581-SAIL
   Web: www.mariner.org

❑ Hours: Daily 10:00am-5:00pm except Thanksgiving and Christmas.

❑ Admission: $8.00 adult, $6.00 child (6-17). Age 5 and under FREE. Admission coupon on website.

❑ Miscellaneous: 550 acre park with picnicking and a walking trail with fishing. Coming in spring 2007, the USS MONITOR CENTER: Visitors walk along a recreated gun deck of a classic wooden warship where they learn about technological advances in naval warfare and design that led them to the creation of the first true ironclad warships. Come aboard the Monitor... Smell the gunpowder. Feel the excitement of being responsible for the most revolutionary piece of military weaponry of the day. Experience what it was like to do something no one had ever done before: guide tons of metal through an armada of wooden ships that cannot hope to compete with your might!

Capture the spirit of seafaring adventures by following Captain Cook and Captain John Smith's maps of the Age of Exploration. Discover artifacts from the wreck of the USS Monitor (anchor, signal light, propeller, and engine - seen in restoring tanks). Take a journey in an African canoe or a Jazz Age runabout in the International Small Craft Center; or examine the small details of the Crabtree miniature ships display. Catch a wink from the colorful figureheads (mermaids to polar bears) from the great Age of Sail. Study the US Navy and examine life on the water in the Chesapeake Bay gallery. Meet historical interpreters portraying a female pirate, an 18th century sea captain, and a crewman from the

Civil War ironclad Monitor. Learn boat-building techniques from the master craftsmen of the Wooden boat School. The giant Cape Charles lighthouse lamp greets you and many audio stations allow you to visit with some of the watermen. Kids will also be attracted to many of the miniature dioramas and the giant buoy.

PENINSULA FINE ARTS CENTER

Newport News - *101 Museum Drive (I-64 exit 258A, across from Mariner's Museum), 23606. Web: www.pfac-va.org. Phone: (757) 596-8175. Hours: Monday-Saturday 10:00am-5:00pm, Sunday 1:00-5:00pm and most Thursdays and Tuesdays open late until 8:30pm. Admission: $5.00 adult, $4.00 senior, student, military $3.00 child (4-15). Miscellaneous: Children's Art Adventures or Sunday Fundays. Occasional Parent's Night Out with daycare for kids while parents are entertained.* See some of the best in contemporary and fine art with exhibits changing every two months - some local or historical in nature. Do you like sculpture, paintings and photography? How about creating art on your own? The Hands On For Kids area is where kids put on a smock and paint, draw, color or make sculpture at Rocky's Diner, play games in the attic or paint in the studio. They can also put on a puppet show or fingerpaint with sound (something really different).

HUNTINGTON PARK / VIRGINIA WAR MUSEUM

9285 Warwick Blvd. (I-64 exit 263A or 258A),

Newport News 23607

❑   Phone: (757) 247-8523 or 886-7912
      Web: www.warmuseum.org or www.newport-news.va.us/parks
❑   Hours: Monday-Saturday 9:00am-5:00pm, Sunday 1:00-5:00pm.
❑   Admission: $2.00 adult, $1.00 senior (65+), military, child (6-15)

HUNTINGTON PARK Features: Ballfields, basketball, Tennis Center, public beach with swimming (attendants Memorial Day - Labor Day), picnic shelters, large playground area "Fort Fun" (a 13,000 sq. foot climbing hide-and-seek area), public boat ramp and children's fishing pier.

WAR MUSEUM: The museum interprets American military history from 1775 to the present. Its collection of over 60,000 artifacts includes uniforms, insignias, vehicles, weapons and one of the nation's greatest collections of propaganda posters. See a 10x10 foot section of the Berlin Wall, one of General Colin Powell's Desert Storm uniforms, an 1883 brass Gatling Gun and a portion of the outer wall from Dachau Concentration Camp. The newest exhibit, Marches Towards Freedom, traces the role of African-Americans in the United States military, beginning with the Revolutionary War.

U.S. ARMY TRANSPORTATION MUSEUM

Bldg. 300, Besson Hall, Washington Blvd. (I-64 exit 250A to Rte. 105), **Newport News (Fort Eustis)** 23604

❑   Phone: (757) 878-1115

   Web: www.transchool.eustis.army.mil/museum/museum.html

❑   Hours: Tuesday-Sunday 9:00am-4:30pm. Closed Federal holidays.

❑   Admission: FREE

Most kids probably don't think of Army transportation as being the key to victory. Inside, the exhibits lead you from early mule-drawn wagons to modern HUMMVEEs. Models, dioramas of typical war scenes and films explain transportation technology and its contributions to the growth of our nation. Look for the "jeep that flies" or the "truck that walks" or the "ships that fly" or the "flying saucer". Outside, the Marine Park displays DUKWs and a tugboat; the Cargo Yard has many trucks including the newest Tactical Vehicles; the Aviation Pavilion exhibits aircraft from the Korean War to present including parachute and vertical take off/landing airplanes; and the Rail Yard includes many locomotives, box cars and cabooses used in several wars. Hovercraft, Skycraft, "Destruction", and the Cybernetic Walking Machine are some of the most popular vehicles.

NORFOLK SPORTS

NORFOLK TIDES BASEBALL - www.norfolktides.com. (757) 622-2222. (follow I-264 west, exit 11A-Brambleton Ave-left at Park Ave.) AAA affiliate of the New York Mets. "Rip Tide," the large and fuzzy blue mascot roams the stands to entertain visitors in Harbor Park. Major League style stadium with full service restaurant. Season: (April thru Labor Day weekend).

NORFOLK ADMIRALS HOCKEY - www.norfolkadmirals.com or (757) 640-1212. Affiliate for the Chicago Blackhawks.

ELIZABETH RIVER FERRY

HRT, PO Box 2096 (departs from the Waterside Marketplace)

Norfolk 23501

❑   Phone: (757) 640-6300, **Web: www.hrtransit.org**

❑   Hours: Year-round, leaves every 30 minutes from each port. Monday-Friday 7:00am-midnight (summers). Weekends 10:00am-midnight (summer). Reduced schedule during rest of year.

❑   Admission: $1.00 per person.

Enjoy the panoramic harbor view from the Elizabeth River Ferry while traveling between downtown Norfolk and Portsmouth by paddlewheel boat. If you've ever been caught in congested traffic between these two cities, you know this mode is a welcome alternative during peak rush hours or as a leisurely way to park and enjoy both city's attractions.

NORFOLK EXPLORERS TROLLEY TOUR

Norfolk - *HRT PO Box 2096 (departs from the front side of the Waterside), 23501. Phone: (757) 222-6000. Hours: Call for tour times. (Summer). FREE service.* A fleet of eight electric buses provides shuttle service to all the attractions in downtown Norfolk. Norfolk visitors may board and enjoy the renowned Chrysler Museum of Art, the financial district, the MacArthur Memorial and more. It also passes by trendy restaurants and shops in the Ghent District. Passengers may get on and off the trolley at each location until ready to catch the return trolley to the Waterside.

VIRGINIA SYMPHONY / VIRGINIA YOUTH SYMPHONY ORCHESTRA

Norfolk - *880 North Military Hwy. (Norfolk's Chrysler Hall-performances), 23502.* **Web:** *www.virginiasymphony.org.* Phone: *(757) 466-3060, (757) 892-6366 box office or (757) 640-7541 (youth symphony). Concerts: (Fall to mid-Summer).*

Miscellaneous: The Virginia Symphony encourages parents to bring their children to the Peanut Butter & Jam Family Concert Series, which is open to children of all ages; but all other concerts are restricted to children age 6+. The symphony performs over 140 concerts annually including Classical Masterworks, Pops, Mozart & More. They offer Young People's Concerts in conjunction with area schools and a popular Peanut Butter & Jam Series for families. Youth Symphony performs occasionally throughout the city and at special events.

VIRGINIA ZOO

3500 Granby Street (I-264 west to downtown Waterside exit to St. Paul's Blvd to Monticello Ave), **Norfolk** 23504

❑   Phone: (757) 441-5227, **Web: www.virginiazoo.org**
❑   Hours: Daily 10:00am-5:00pm. Closed New Year's Day, Thanksgiving, Christmas Eve & Christmas Day. Seasonal hours may apply.
❑   Admission: $6.00 adult, $5.00 senior, $4.00 child (2-11).
❑   Miscellaneous: Café, Safari shop, concessions.

Close to the entrance is Farmland, the Primates Exhibit and the Nocturnal Animals Exhibit. One direction leads you to the Waterfowl Pond and the Botanical Observatory Gardens. Another direction wanders past the Large Animals Exhibit and the Tiger Exhibit where the popular Siberian Tigers are (born from cubs here at zoo). Farthest back from the entrance are the Okavango Delta exhibits of African animals set in unobstructed naturalistic settings similar to the largest inland delta in the world. Children love the Prairie Dogs - new at the zoo. The interactive habitat has underground tunnels and viewing bubbles allowing kids to safely come nose-to-nose with playful prairie dogs.

NAVAL STATION NORFOLK

Norfolk - *9079 Hampton Blvd. (all tours depart from the Naval Tour and Information Center), 23505. Phone: (757) 444-7955.* **Web:** *www.norfolkvisitor.com/norfolknavy. Hours: Call for tour times. During heightened national security or US battle times, no tours are offered. Admission: $5.00 adult, Half Price senior(60+) & child (3-11).* Home port to more than 75 ships and 100 aircraft of the Atlantic Fleet - this is the world's largest naval installation. The bus tour is 45 minutes long and narrated by naval personnel. It passes by submarines, destroyers, cruisers, amphibious assault ships, aircraft carriers and an airfield. Along the way, you'll also pass by historic homes from the 1907 Jamestown Exposition.

AMERICAN ROVER TALL SHIP CRUISES

(departs at the Marina at the Waterside)

Norfolk 23510

- ❑ Phone: (757) 627-7245, **Web: www.americanrover.com**
- ❑ Admission: Tickets may be purchased at the blue gazebo on the dock. $15.00 adult, $10.00 child-under 12 (2 hour) and $22.00 adult, $12.00 child (3 hour)
- ❑ Tours: Daily 3:00pm (mid-April thru October). 11:00am Saturdays (spring and fall). 11:00am Wednesday-Sunday (summer). 6:00pm sunset Wednesday-Sunday (spring and fall). 6:30pm sunset 3 hr. (daily, summer).

At 135 feet in length, she is the "largest three-masted topsail passenger schooner under U.S. flag," and is fully Coast Guard inspected for your safety. Venture into the smooth waters of Hampton Roads' historical harbor and rich maritime heritage. Sail by giant merchant and navy ships, tugs, fishermen, yachts, or, lend a hand at the sails, take a try at the helm, roam the decks, or relax, as the Captain points out the highlights around you. Live Entertainment available during certain cruises (try for the folk singers - sailing tunes).

CHRYSLER MUSEUM OF ART

245 West Olney Road (at Mowbray Arch), **Norfolk** 23510

❑ Phone: (757) 664-6200, **Web: www.chrysler.org**

❑ Hours: Thursday-Saturday, 10:00am-5:00pm. Wednesday, 10:00am-9:00pm (Wednesdays only - admission by voluntary contribution). Sunday, 1:00-5:00pm. All facilities closed Mondays, Tuesdays, and major holidays.

❑ Admission: $7.00 general, $5.00 student, senior, teachers, military; FREE child (age 18 and under). Wednesdays by voluntary contribution. Admission discount coupon online.

❑ Miscellaneous: Restaurant. Museum Shop.

Maybe pretend your family is on safari to explore the artistic interpretation of animals in the Chrysler Museum of Art's collections. Then, follow a theme such as Costumes (Explore the ways that people expressed their wealth, social status, individuality, and practical needs throughout the ages by the clothes they wore); Glass Art; Ancient Egypt/China: students discover the influence of Chinese porcelain and design on decorative arts in the Western world. They are taught the "recipe" that the Chinese discovered for making porcelain and some of the techniques involved in applying the colors and designs; or Sculpture: Three-dimensional art dating from ancient times to the 20th century. Family Programs include Sunday Surprises; Chrysler Creates (make n' take) and Tickle My Ears: Story and Art at the Chrysler.

MACARTHUR MEMORIAL

City Hall Avenue, MacArthur Square (I-264, exit 10, head west)

Norfolk 23510

❑ Phone: (757) 441-2965, **Web: www.macarthurmemorial.org**

❑ Hours: Monday-Saturday 10:00am-5:00pm, Sunday 11:00am-5:00pm. Closed New Years, Thanksgiving, and Christmas.

❑ Admission: FREE

❑ Miscellaneous: A 24 minute film on MacArthur's life is shown in the theatre. Gift shop displays 1950 Chrysler Imperial limousine which he used from 1950 to end of his life.

For updates & travel games, visit: **www.KidsLoveTravel.com**

General Douglas MacArthur was one of the most colorful and controversial men in American history. The General's final resting place is where he lies surrounded by nine separate galleries arranged in two levels, each portraying the principal periods of the General's life in murals and displays of awards, gifts, maps, photos and models. The memorial's goal is to renew your faith in those American values of Duty, Honor, Country.

NAUTICUS & NATIONAL MARITIME CENTER

One Waterside Drive (I-264 west, Waterside Drive exit)

Norfolk 23510

❑   Phone: (757) 664-1000 or (800) 664-1080
Web: www.thenmc.org
❑   Hours: Daily 10:00am-6:00pm (Memorial Day-Labor Day). Tuesday-Saturday 10:00am-5:00pm, Sunday Noon-5:00pm (Rest of Year). Closed winter holidays. Weekends only in January.
❑   Admission: $9.95 adult, $8.95 senior and military, $7.50 student (4-12). Combo packages available.

Journey through the world's oceans at the large maritime science and technology center that explores the power of the sea. Stand on the actual bridge of the USS Preble and scan the Elizabeth River through a real periscope. Kids can do lots of hands-on like chart and steer across treacherous waters, drill an oil well, or design a ship (can take the plans home to build in the backyard!). At the AEGIS Battle Simulated Theatre, you can sit in a command control room and help make decisions in battle - try not to mess it up or your ship will blow up! Watch "The Living Sea" in the giant screen theatre and then (since you're in the mood), touch live sharks (small ones!) and horseshoe crabs in the touch tanks. Now forecast the weather, predict hurricanes and warn ships of potential dangers via The Weather Channel. Be sure to try your hand at a game "Design Chamber: Battleship X", see the lifestyle exhibit "City at Sea", or enjoy a virtual tour of the battleship with very high tech BattleScopes. The theatre presents: "The Last Battleship". Our favorite photo op was the kids in a real shark cage being eyed by a great white shark. So-o-o-o real! On the same premises are several other related museums: Hampton Roads Naval Museum (naval history and why Hampton Roads became the largest naval base); or experience the pride of exploring the Wisconsin mighty military vessel that earned five battle stars during WWII and more recently Desert Storm. Once aboard, docents and exhibits, and a video on board invite you in. See giant chains (for the anchors) and guns (large enough to propel a shell the weight of a Volkswagen over 26 miles!).

VICTORY ROVER

One Waterside Drive (depart from Nauticus Docks)

Norfolk 23510

❑ Phone: (757) 627-7406, **Web: www.navalbasecruise.com**
❑ Admission: $10.00-$15.00 per person.
❑ Tours: 2 Hour Narrated Naval Base Cruises Depart Daily.
11:00am & 2:00pm, (Early April - Memorial Day Weekend).
11:00am, 2:00pm and 5:30pm (Memorial Day Weekend - Labor Day). 11:00am & 2:00pm. (Labor Day - Late October). 2:00pm Cruise, Tuesday-Sunday (November & December).

Your Front Row Seat to the Naval Fleet. Enjoy an entertaining commentary along the way aboard this Navy-themed vessel. See the sight of Aircraft Carriers, Nuclear Submarines, Guided Missile Cruisers, and all of the other ships that form the World's most powerful Armada. On board, guests can also enjoy plenty of comfortable seating, clean restrooms, air-conditioned enclosed deck, open air upper deck, snack bar and souvenir shop.

VIRGINIA STAGE COMPANY

Norfolk - *110 E Tazewell St (Housed in the Wells Theatre), 23514. Phone: (757) 627-1234. **Web: www.vastage.com**. Admission: $10.00-$30.00. Miscellaneous: At 1919 Monticello Ave, nearby is the home of the world's original ice cream cone making machine - Doumar's (757) 627-4163.* Six major productions each season as well as children's educational theater programs. Best for a holiday treat of the annual "A Christmas Carol".

ROWENA'S JAM & JELLY FACTORY TOUR

758 West 22nd Street, **Norfolk** 23517

- ❑   Phone: (800) 980-CAKE, **Web: www.rowenas.com**
- ❑   Admission: FREE
- ❑   Tours: January 15 – October 15, by reservation.
- ❑   Miscellaneous: Wheelchair and stroller accessible. Have tea or lunch in their tea room.

Smell the delicious aroma from the minute you walk in the door and adorn your paper hat...ready for the tour. Your guide, Miss Ann, first reads to you from the book "Rowena & the Wonderful Jam & Jelly Factory". Now you know the child's version of the magical cake and jam factory behind the pretty painted door (it reminds you of walking through the door in "Alice in Wonderland"). Meet Mr. Jellyfords Jam III (the co-star of the storybook) and explore the factory's kitchens with their giant whisks, steam kettles, and baking ovens (62 cakes can bake at one time). Notice the Ribbon Chart - each flavor of cake has a different color bow. Walk through the warehouse, refrigerators and freezers and finally the Tea Room...where young ladies can dress up before tea! Now, wander through the gift shop for tastings of every flavor of jams and pound cakes that are produced in the gourmet food production factory that you just saw. The sweetest smelling, most delightful food tour!

NORFOLK BOTANICAL GARDEN

6700 Azalea Garden Road (I-64 exit 279B-Norfolk Airport)

Norfolk 23518

- ❑   Phone: (757) 441-5830
       Web: www.norfolkbotanicalgarden.org
- ❑   Hours: Daily 9:00am-7:00pm (mid-April to mid-October) and daily 9:00am-5:00pm (mid-October to mid-April). Guided train and boat tours 10:00am-4:00pm daily, weather permitting.
- ❑   Admission: $6.00 adult, $5.00 senior, $4.00-$5.00 youth (4-18). Admission includes a complimentary tram tour. $2.00-$3.00 extra for boat tour.

Norfolk Botanical Garden (*cont.*)

❑   Miscellaneous: Visitor Center with maps, interpretive exhibit,
      orientation video and gift shop. Garden House Café.

Discover one of the largest collections of azaleas, camellias, roses
and rhododendrons on the East Coast. This is the only botanical
garden in the country offering tours by boat or trackless train.
Kids will probably like the Butterfly Garden, Japanese Garden,
Colonial Herb Garden and the lakes and Friendship Pond. Parents
like the 12 miles of pedestrian pathways to walk, skip and stroller
on. New in 2006: World of Wonders Children's Garden: a three-
acre garden dedicated to families and children. Located in the heart
of Norfolk Botanical Garden, WOW brings the world of plants to
our back door, literally creating a museum without walls. After
spilling out of an underground tunnel, kids can splash their way
around the world! Through fountains, bubblers, foggers and jet
sprays, they will explore the oceans and other major waterways on
Earth. In Discovery Peak – The Trade Route is lined with a low
wall for climbing and playing. Along the way, kids will find plants
from different continents and interactive displays to teach them
where plants originate and what products we get from them. Don't
forget the water spray fountain and a dirt factory!

PAMPLIN HISTORICAL PARK & THE NATIONAL MUSEUM OF THE CIVIL WAR SOLDIER

6125 Boydton Plank Road (I-85 exit 63A), **Petersburg** 23803

❑   Phone: (804) 861-2408 or (877) PAMPLIN
      Web: www.pamplinpark.org
❑   Hours: Daily 9:00am-5:00pm except Thanksgiving, Christmas,
      and New Years Day. Summer hours extended until 6:00pm.
❑   Admission: $13.50 adult, $12.00 senior, $7.50 child (6-11).
❑   Miscellaneous: Hardtack and Coffee Café offer deli sandwiches,
      salads (named The Sergeant, The Picket Line or The Colonel),
      and kid's meals. Gift shop- The Civil War Store.

Pamplin Historical Park delivers a fresh approach to historical
museums by combining a blend of new technology and old-

fashioned storytelling that immerses visitors in the war and the day-to-day lives of very common soldiers.

❑ <u>THE NATIONAL MUSEUM OF THE CIVIL WAR SOLDIER</u> - inside, you're greeted by 13 Civil War soldier's photographs, any one you can choose to be a soldier comrade to accompany you through the museum by "voice" (using a loaned MP3 explaining exhibits). (Children & Parents - we recommend to choose Private Delavan S. Miller, the youngest soldier). Your soldier/guide (by MP3) takes you to "A soldier's Life" which is the room packed full of artifacts and models and soldiers in army regimen. "Pack Your Knapsack" is where a sergeant tells you how to pick items essential to carry but not weighing more than 16 pounds - it's hard to discard a pot and pan and just bring "light-weight" tin cups, blankets, etc. The "Trial by Fire" display reveals sounds of the war: martial music, marching feet tramping, cannon fire, ground trembling, and PRAY that you don't get shot - Mommy did with a powerful puff of air to the chest! Ending at "A test Of Faith", where names of those who survived or were discharged or POW's is revealed - what was the fate of your chosen "soldier comrade"? This museum is fantastic!

❑ <u>TUDOR HALL PLANTATION</u> - down a short path to the 1812 house that reflects both civilian and military history. One side of the house is furnished as a family would have known it. The other side is outfitted to suit the needs of a Confederate general and his staff.

❑ <u>MILITARY ENCAMPMENT AND FORTIFICATIONS EXHIBIT</u> - a scale, authentic-looking scene of daily costumed programs where visitors mingle with soldiers as they spend a typical day in camp, cooking, cleaning equipment or mending clothes and playing games. Listen for the cannon blast every now and then...or learn soldier lingo. What artillery do you use as the enemy gets closer?

❑ <u>BREAKTHROUGH THEATER</u> - Multi-media show on the breakthrough battle presented in surround sound with bullets whizzing past and the ground shaking from artillery fire.

Pamplin Historical Park & The National Museum Of The Civil
War Soldier (*cont.*)

❑   BREAKTHROUGH TRAIL - winds through the battlefield of
       April 2nd, 1865 where General Grant's Union army broke thru the
       Confederate lines, ending the 10 month Petersburg Campaign and
       setting in motion the events leading to Lee's surrender at
       Appomattox one week later. Audio waysides tell of the fighting
       and personalities involved.

Plan on a 3-4 hour minimum stay to fully immerse your family in
the battlefield experience. This place helps the kids really feel like a
Civil War soldier! Our family's favorite Civil War museum, by far!

PETERSBURG NATIONAL BATTLEFIELD

1539 Hickory Hill Road (I-295 south to Rte. 36/Fort Lee exit

Petersburg 23803

❑   Phone: (804) 732-3531 & (804) 458-9504 & (804) 265-8244
       Web: www.nps.gov/pete/
❑   Hours: Grounds open from 8:00am-dusk. Grant's Hdqts. (City
       Point) /Appomattox Manor/ Eastern Front/ Five Forks Battlefield
       open and staffed year-round 9:00am - 5:00pm. Poplar Grove
       Cemetery staffed on weekends June-August from 9:00am-
       5:00pm. Notice: Petersburg National Battlefield is closed on
       Thanksgiving Day, Christmas Day and New Year's Day.
❑   Admission: September-May: $3.00/adult with a $5.00/car
       maximum.
❑   Miscellaneous: Biking, hiking, auto tour and horseback riding.

Can you imagine spending almost ten months of the Civil War
fighting in one area? Why were the soldiers here for so long?
How did they pass their days? What was it like living in the
trenches around Petersburg? Learn why Petersburg, Virginia,
became the setting for the longest siege in American history when
General Ulysses S. Grant failed to capture Richmond in the spring
of 1864. Grant settled in to subdue the Confederacy by
surrounding Petersburg and cutting off General Robert E. Lee's
supply lines into Petersburg and Richmond. On April 2, 1865,

nine-and-one-half months after the siege began, Lee evacuated Petersburg. Begin your tour at the park entrance Visitor Center viewing exhibits about the Petersburg campaign, an audiovisual map presentation, battlefield relics, maps, etc. The 4-mile self-guided Tour begins at this point, with some areas reserved for "walk-on" sites only. The Siege Line Tour picks up where the initial tour ends and leads to park areas south and west of Petersburg. An audiotape of the 35+ mile driving tour is available. Summertime is especially fun because costumed interpreters depict army life during the siege.

U.S. QUARTERMASTER MUSEUM

Petersburg (Fort Lee) - *(just inside main gate of Fort Lee), 23801. Web: www.qmmuseum.lee.army.mil. Phone: (804) 734-4203. Hours: Tuesday-Friday 10:00am-5:00pm, Saturday and Sunday 11:00am-5:00pm. Closed Monday, Thanksgiving, Christmas and New Years Day. Admission: FREE.* This supply center was founded only two days after the Army itself in 1775. The Quartermaster is responsible for almost every service function in the Army: food, clothing, transportation, aerial supply, petroleum supply and mortuary services. See the wagon supply vehicle used from the 1890s to WWII. When autos replaced horse-drawn vehicles, the Quartermaster Corps developed the jeep, which became one of the most famous of all military vehicles. They have a jeep used by General George S. Patton, Jr. in WWII. You'll also see a kitchen which could be pulled directly onto the battlefield providing hot meals to soldiers in WWI.

POKEY SMOKEY STEAM LOCOMOTIVE

Portsmouth - *140 City Park Avenue (Portsmouth City Park), 23701. Phone: (757) 465-2937 or (757) 465-2935. Hours: Saturday and Sunday 11:00am-5:00pm. (April-October). Admission: Small fee.* A 93-acre beautifully landscaped park along the Western Branch of the Elizabeth River Park features boat ramps, tennis courts, and the Pokey Smokey. The Pokey Smokey, an authentic 19th century reproduction of coal-fired steam locomotive, travels through Portsmouth City Park.

CARRIE B HARBOR TOURS

6 Crawford Parkway (depart from Portsmouth Visitor Info Center-I-264 west exit 7B or Waterside Drive, exit 9, Norfolk)

Portsmouth 23704

- ❑   Phone: (757) 393-4735, **Web: www.portsva.com**
- ❑   Admission: $16.00 adult, child half price (under 12)
- ❑   Tours: 2 ½ hour tours depart Portsmouth 10 minutes after departures from Norfolk at 11:00am, 2:00pm & 6:00pm (sunset cruise, unless chartered). (May - mid-October)

The cruises set sail seven days a week, rain or shine (April to mid-October) and no reservations are necessary. The climate-controlled replica 19th century Mississippi paddlewheel river boat passes mighty warships and chugging tugboats. As the captain narrates the history of historic harbors, the nation's first naval shipyard and floating dry docks - you'll have lots to look at and can even eat a snack while on board. The afternoon (2 ½ hour) tours also go to the site of the battle between the famous Monitor and the Merrimac, and the nation's largest naval base (get up close to the huge gray ladies of the Atlantic fleet, including destroyers, nuclear-powered submarines and aircraft carriers). Most fascinating: Supply Ships - They glide up next to a battleship and send supplies underwater! Drydocks - To see a boat nearly 1000' long raised (there is a secret) from the water is amazing! "Cranky" cranes - are always loading and unloading containers somewhere, Aircraft Carriers - The one we saw was nearly 1000' feet long, had 4 ½ acres of deck space, a barber shop…and was the home to 6000 crew! Pseudo Submarine Decoys - sonar boats that pickup war missiles, Nauticus & USS Wisconsin - You can pass by and see from the water (see separate listing). Excellent narration. Great way for youth to get the feel of the naval shipyard without being overwhelmed.

CHILDREN'S MUSEUM OF VIRGINIA

221 High Street (I-264 exit 7 or I-664 south exit 9 - downtown, Olde
Towne), **Portsmouth** 23704

❑   Phone: (757) 393-8393, **Web: www.childrensmuseumva.com**
❑   Hours: Tuesday-Saturday 9:00am-5:00pm, Sunday 11:00am-
      5:00pm. Closed winter holidays. Open summer Mondays.
❑   Admission: $6.00 general (age 2+) or part of money saving Key
      Pass.
❑   Miscellaneous: Planetarium

Two floors packed with over 90 hands-on displays to stimulate
imagination through science (physics of Bubbles - you can even be
"inside" a giant one), art (check out the Harmonograph drawing
area), music (giant musical instruments like drums and guitars),
communications, culture and technology (climb inside a giant
computer-have you ever clicked a computer mouse bigger than
you?). See four wonderful, working toy train collections, pretend
grocery store, ride a "waterbed raft", climb into the cab of a fire
engine or bus (with dress up clothes), hard hat stack up area,
electrifying weird, and funny science in motion.

LIGHTSHIP MUSEUM

420 High Street (I-264 exit 9 to downtown/old towne at the foot of
London St on the waterfront), **Portsmouth** 23704

❑   Phone: (757) 393-8741, **Web: www.portsnavalmuseums.com**
❑   Hours: Tuesday-Saturday 10:00am-5:00pm, Sunday 1:00-
      5:00pm. Open Mondays also in summer.
❑   Admission: $3.00 general (includes both Naval & Lightship
      admission).

Lightships were built to help mariners avoid dangerous shoals and
enter the harbor safely.   Sometimes, a land lighthouse wasn't
visible, so, lights were instead fixed to masts of ships that anchored
for months in strategic locations off the coastline. Your family can
actually board the vessel and see the most important object aboard
- the lantern.   The Fresnel lens had to be strong enough to be seen
for 12 miles or more. You'll also see the galley/dining hall, the
efficiently designed captain's quarters and crew's bunks.

NAVAL SHIPYARD MUSEUM

Portsmouth - *High Street Landing in Olde Towne (I-264 exit 7), 23704. Web: www.portsnavalmuseums.com. Phone: (757) 393-8591. Hours: Tuesday-Saturday 10:00am-5:00pm, Sunday 1-5:00pm. Open on Mondays during the summer and occasional observed Monday holidays. Admission: $3.00 for both museums (Naval & Lightship included in one fee).* Established in 1949 within the nation's oldest shipyard, on the Elizabeth River. Visitors will experience a steady stream of vessels from pleasure craft to carriers, and a collection of antique cannons. Inside, you'll see many ship models and uniforms. Many historic ships (the first ironclad, first battleship and first aircraft carrier) were built here.

VIRGINIA SPORTS HALL OF FAME

Portsmouth - *206 High Street (borders Olde Towne Portsmouth), 23705. Web: www.virginiasportshalloffame.com. Phone: (757) 393-8031. Hours: Tuesday-Saturday 9:00am-5:00pm, Sunday 11:00am-5:00pm. Open Mondays in summer. Open until 7:00pm on Fridays & Saturdays. Admission: $6.00 per person (age 5+).* This Hall of Fame honors sports heroes from the state. The Hall of Honor reflects the awards and prestige bestowed on sports greats. The theatre has a dynamic multi-media presentation on the history of Virginia sports. At Campus Champions, visitors will feel as though they have stepped into a team's locker room because 38 open lockers allow schools to feature their programs. In Game Time, you can try basketball, football, baseball and soccer activities - then try a NASCAR simulator - while interactive displays evaluate skills crucial to athletic performance (Health & Fitness body mechanics displays).

CANAL WALK

Visitor Center at Hillcrest & Riverside Drive (Tredegar Iron Works to 12th St. and James River and Kanawha from 12th to Triple Crossing), **Richmond** 23219

❑   Phone: (804) 648-6549

    Web: www.richmondriverfront.com/canalwalk.shtml

❑   Hours: Daily sunrise to sunset.

For updates & travel games, visit: **www.KidsLoveTravel.com**

❑   Admission: FREE. Charge for boat rentals or guided tours by boat.

❑   Miscellaneous: To rent a boat or schedule a guide boat tour dial (804) 788-9989.

Enjoy a leisurely walk along the restored Kanawha and Haxall canals, with History Medallions pointing out the rich history of Richmond's waterfront. Or take a guided boat tour on the restored Kanawha Canal, originally designed by George Washington. First envisioned in 1774, these canals were to be part of a continuous transportation route from the Atlantic Ocean to the Mississippi River. Boats are also available for group rentals & self-guided tours.

CIVIL WAR VISITOR CENTER AT TREDEGAR IRON WORKS: serves as the gift shop and information center for the War aspects of the James River. Three floors of exhibits and artifacts are on display. Orientation film is shown every half hour. **www.nps.gov/rich/**

FEDERAL RESERVE MONEY MUSEUM

Richmond - *701 East Byrd Street (Federal Reserve Bank), 23219. Phone: (804) 697-8110. Web: www.rich.frb.org/econed/museum. Hours: Monday-Friday 9:30am-3:30pm with advance notice. Admission: FREE.* A self-guided tour exhibits forms of currency, rare bills (even $100,000 bills!) and gold and silver bars (a favorite of the kids). A great virtual tour of the museum with a view of the gold bar is available on the website. 500 items depict the history of currency including such items as compressed tea bricks which could be spent or brewed or an actual coin of the Kingdom of Lydia, the birthplace of coinage.

MAGGIE L. WALKER NAT'L HISTORIC SITE

600 North 2nd Street, **Richmond** 23219

❑   Phone: (804) 771-2017, **Web: www.nps.gov/malw**

❑   Hours: Monday-Saturday 9:00am-5:00pm. Closed major winter holidays.

❑   Admission: FREE

❑   Tours: offered every half-hour.

Maggie L. Walker Nat'l historic site (*cont.*)

❏ Miscellaneous: The visitor's center has a short film presentation to begin your tour. The film speaks from Maggie's point of view talking to children.

The site honors Maggie Walker, a prominent businesswoman, who overcame social obstacles of her time - being physically impaired, black and a woman. She founded the St. Luke Penny Savings Bank, the first chartered bank in the country started by a woman, and became a success in the world of business and finance. Her home, next to the visitor center, has been completely restored to the 1930's appearance with many Walker family furnishings to view. The house has 28 rooms - rather large and ornate. She showed her wealth with a chauffeured limousine, diamond rings and many gold-leafed furnishings. She also was very generous and gave most extra money away. Learn how she helped fellow African-Americans "turn nickels into dollars". The main interpretive exhibits feature the story of her life. The exhibits include many historical photographs, a recreation of the St. Luke Penny Savings Bank teller window, displays of museum artifacts such as Mrs. Walker's dress and St. Luke regalia, and a child's personal St. Luke savings bank (like the ones she gave children in the area). The opening of the new exhibits changes the way visitors view Mrs. Walker's home. Previously, tours left the visitor center and angled across the courtyard entering the home from the rear porch. Now visitors will view the exhibits, then exit onto Leigh Street and enter Mrs. Walker's home from the front door just as invited guests would have arrived during her lifetime.

MUSEUM OF THE CONFEDERACY

1201 East Clay Street (downtown, 2 blocks north of Broad Street)

Richmond 23219

❏ Phone: (804) 649-1861 **Web: www.moc.org**
❏ Hours: Monday-Saturday 10:00am-5:00pm, Sunday Noon-5:00pm. Closed Major winter holidays.
❏ Admission (separate for each museum) $7.00 adult, $6.00 (61+ and military ID), $4.00 child (7-18). Combo tickets help you save

$2.00-4.00 on admission to both museums. Members, children under 7, and active duty military in uniform are free.

❑   Tours: Guided of the White House start in the basement and cover the first and second floors are daily and last about 40 minutes.

Located in the historic Court End district of downtown Richmond, the location consists of a massive museum and original White House of the Confederacy. Museum: 500 wartime flags, 250 uniform pieces and the personal belongings of many Confederate generals like Jefferson Davis, Robert E. Lee, J.E.B. Stuart and Stonewall Jackson. Displays on the lives of free and enslaved African Americans and the giant, 15 foot painting of "The Last Meeting of Lee and Jackson" are here also. White House: The executive mansion of President Jefferson Davis and his family during the Civil War. Children's Activities Days (hands-on activities, games with guide), Civil War encounters (costumed living historian will portray an "eyewitness" to various events), and day camps for kids, too.

RICHMOND RAFT COMPANY

4400 East Main Street (Headquarters and meeting place)

Richmond 23219

❑   Phone: (800) 222-RAFT, **Web: www.richmondraft.com**
❑   Tours: Family Outing trips last 4-5 hours. Saturday at 9:00am, Sunday at 2:00pm (June to Labor Day). Sundays only (May and Sept.-Oct). Other hours available for groups of 20 or more Admission: average $55.00 per person (includes equipment rental- raft, paddles, PFDs, slickers and snacks/beverages). Minimum age: must be at least 50 pounds for a floatation device to fit properly. Wear swimsuits and old cover-up clothes plus sandals that fit snug or old sneakers. Don't forget sunscreen!
❑   Miscellaneous: For teens and adults who want more adventure, they offer tours past the picnic grounds that immediately take you over rougher water and straight towards downtown skyscrapers. The Introduction tours may be too boring for adventurous teens and parents.

Richmond Raft Company (*cont.*)

The James River drops 105 feet over a seven-mile stretch in Richmond Virginia, creating class I - IV whitewater! Only Class I & II rapids appear along this leisurely intro to rafting trip (no nervous worrying parents). A great way to get a feel for whitewaters and have some family fun by allowing for time to raft, "surf", and swim the rapids (sometimes, all at once!). The guides are "family-friendly" and teach wonderful basic skills and safety. Ask for more history or more splash play on your tour. Look for osprey, beavers, large fish and maybe an eagle as you pass pony pasture, choo-choo trains and arched bridges. Guess how many arches in the bridge or splash attack a neighboring raft...it's how your family wants to create their fun. And, all this adventure in a metro downtown area on the James River...who would have thought?

RICHMOND SYMPHONY

Richmond - *300 W. Franklin Street (venue varies by production), 23219. Web: www.richmondsymphony.com. Phone: (804) 788-1212 Ticket office. Admission: $5.00-$15.00 for family style pops concerts.* Founded in 1957, the Richmond Symphony offers a variety of performances ranging from classical to pop. Kid Classics Family Concerts and Handel's Messiah each year.

SCIENCE MUSEUM OF VIRGINIA

2500 West Broad Street (off I-95 and I-64, exit #78 south towards Broad Street), Richmond 23219

❑ Phone: (804) 367-6552 or (800) 659-1727, **Web: www.smv.org**

❑ Hours: Monday-Saturday 9:30am-5:00pm, Friday-Saturday until 7:00pm, Sunday 11:30am-5:00pm. Closed Thanksgiving and Christmas.

❑ Admission: $10.00 adult, $9.00 senior (60+) and child (4-12). Reduced admission specials in the winter.

❑ Miscellaneous: Café (behind the museum in a cute railroad dining car #20) with sandwiches called: The Conductor, The Aluminaut, the DNA, The Incubator, or homemade ice cream.

For updates & travel games, visit: **www.KidsLoveTravel.com**

In a former 1919 train station, the museum offers 250 + hands-on exhibits and demonstrations plus major touring exhibits. Subjects covered include aerospace, astronomy, electricity, physical sciences, computers, crystals, biology, telecommunications, and an IMAX Dome. Bioscape - Life Sciences - Start at the "Very Small Gallery" (microscopic cells and DNA) to "my size" systems of the human body and the "Really Big Gallery" where we interconnect with Earth's systems. Look at dozens of cells, then start "Seeing Things". At FLASH, watch computer-controlled infrared, visual and magnetic sensors control model cars. Explore Newton's laws, gravity, momentum, potential and kinetic energy in whole-body experiences! Walk, bounce and leap in the reduced gravity of the moon. Float on air. Look for the Tabletop Science Sites and Demonstration Stations (different each day). Outside see restored trains and the giant Aluminaut Submarine (why aluminum?). Note: to take advantage of the many demonstrations and theatre science presentations, check the announcement board as you enter.

ST. JOHN'S CHURCH

2401 East Broad Street, **Richmond** 23219

❑   Phone: (804) 649-7938, **Web: www.historicstjohnschurch.org**
❑   Hours: Monday-Saturday 10:00am-4:00pm, Sunday 1:00-
       4:00pm. Closed New Years, Easter, Thanksgiving and
       Christmastime.
❑   Admission: $5.00 adult, $4.00 senior, $3.00 child (7-18).
❑   Tours: Guided tours, last tour leaves one half hour before closing.
❑   Miscellaneous: It is best to visit here after the children have
       studied the Revolutionary War. Then, they are very impressed.

Built in 1741 (the first church and largest building built in town), Patrick Henry delivered his famous "Liberty or Death" speech in favor of independence at this site. Reenactments of the Second Virginia Convention of 1775 are held Sundays at 2:00pm during the summer. Why did the convention meet in a church in Richmond? Why did they originally sit in the high-back pews...not for private naps, but to stay warm (there was no central heat). The costumed guide gives excerpts of the speech as it applies to the times.

VALENTINE MUSEUM-RICHMOND HISTORY CENTER

Richmond - *1015 East Clay Street, 23219. Phone: (804) 649-0711. Web: www.valentinemuseum.com.* Hours: *Tuesday-Saturday 10:00am-5:00pm, Sunday Noon-5:00pm. Admission: $7.00 adult, $6.00 senior/student (college), $4.00 child (7-12), $1.00 child (3-6).* "The Museum of the Life and History of Richmond" focuses on urban and social history, decorative arts, costumes and architecture. The National Landmark 1812 Wickham house is newly refurnished and offers mostly architectural history. Exhibitions Description: Settlement to Streetcar Suburbs: Richmond and its People; Creating History: The Valentine Family and Museum; Generations: The Wickham Family Collections; Signs of the Times: Neon Sign Collection. What types of tools might a 19th century artist use? Who was Valentine? How did an elegant Richmond home handle the heat before air conditioning? The self-guided Wickham House basement examines the slaves' private spheres. A timeline in the shape of a river highlights important events as it winds across the gallery floor.

VIRGINIA STATE CAPITOL & GOVERNOR'S MANSION

Capitol Square (9th & Grace Streets), **Richmond** 23219

❑   Phone: (804) 698-1788

      http://legis.state.va.us/CapitolTours/CapitolTours-Jamestown.htm

❑   Hours: Monday-Friday 9:00am-5:00pm, Saturday 10:00am-5:00pm, Sunday 1:00-5:00pm (rest of year).

❑   Admission: FREE

❑   Tours: Last tour leaves at 4:15pm. Governor's Mansion tours are Tuesday-Thursday 10:00am-noon & 2:00-4:00pm with reservations.

❑   Miscellaneous: Watch for construction updates as the major renovations are completed. Parking may be difficult to find.

The Capitol was designed by Thomas Jefferson and houses the second oldest legislative body in the western hemisphere. Highlights are: the Houdin statue of George Washington, the hidden interior dome, seen only from inside the building, and busts of the eight Virginia born presidents; the Old Senate Hall and the Old Hall of the House of Delegates, where Aaron Burr was tried for treason in 1807, Robert E. Lee received his commission as commander of the VA troops and the Confederate Congress met during the Civil War. If you have time, guided tours offer more insight into the state's governmental historical figures and stories. Look for the doorknobs throughout the building with the State Seal on them - how many can you count? The Governor's Mansion is the oldest continuously occupied governor's home (1814) in the country. You can view the Capitol grounds from the upstairs window. This tour is probably a little long for the young ones.

CENTER FOR VIRGINIA HISTORY / VIRGINIA HISTORICAL SOCIETY

428 North Boulevard (I-95 / I-64 East to Exit 78 (Boulevard). Turn right onto Boulevard (heading south) to the corner of Kensington)

Richmond 23220

❑   Phone: (804) 358-4901, **Web: www.vahistorical.org**
❑   Hours: Monday-Saturday 10:00am-5:00pm, Sunday 1:00-
5:00pm. Closed major holidays.
❑   Admission: $5.00 adult, $4.00 senior (54+) or $2.00 on Tuesdays,
$3.00 child & student.
❑   Miscellaneous: Museum Shop full of Virginia history items & crafts.

Any Virginian or anyone who wants an overview of the state's historical highlights needs to visit here (and more than once to get it all). You'll start at the main permanent exhibit "The Story of Virginia" orientation theatre. The film shown is an "easy to follow" path of state history. Now, move on to the first inhabitants (Powatan Indians) including a dugout canoe, a wooden musket, and Pocahontas portraits (even a piece of her hat). Move on from the settlers to the Conestoga Wagon display and the move out west (most Virginians who left went towards Ohio). As you progress past the early 1800's (see Revolutionary War stuff along the way), move to the Civil War gallery, and then it's on to the 1900's. Here you'll see an actual streetcar theatre and famous native Virginians (especially sports figures). Be sure the kids play in the Little Virginia's History Computer Game (hint: choose the easy game...the questions are still hard...) - You'll get a certificate printed with your name and test score.

CHILDREN'S MUSEUM OF RICHMOND

2626 West Broad Street (I-95/I-64 exit #78 south, adjacent to the Science Museum)

Richmond 23220

❑ Phone: (804) 474-CMOR or (877) 295-CMOR
   Web: www.c-mor.org
❑ Hours: Tuesday-Saturday 9:30am-5:00pm, Sunday Noon-5:00pm. Open summer and some holiday Mondays.
❑ Admission: $7.00 general (age 1+). Seniors pay $1.00 less. Daily science and nature craft times to hands-on make a craft experiments to take home.

Kids from 6 months to 12 years old will ask to go here often. Here's the highlights of what they like best: Our Great Outdoors - climb to treetops to look in an eagle's nest, big enough for five people; or, explore a limestone cave, or crawl on the James River. Tour de Tummy - lets you crawl through a "food tube" as you step into a gigantic mouth, cross over the tongue, then crawl through a digestive tube to experience a digestive system. How it Works includes: Inside/Outside House - where the plumbing and electrical systems are on the outside of the house. See the workings of clocks and ATM's too. Inventor's Laboratory - check out a discovery box and construct your own project (good area for the pre-teens). Little CMoR - a special area dedicated for creeping, crawling, tumbling - Preschoolers only. See the new WaterPlay area, too. The noticeable focus here is the crawling and climbing aspects - an educational playplace! Even parents can pose for a picture in the "mouth" or "spyder chair".

MAYMONT

2201 Shields Lake Drive (I-195 Maplewood exit, follow signs),

Richmond 23220

❑ Phone: (804) 358-7166, **Web: www.maymount.org**

❑ Hours: Exhibits: (Maymont House, Nature Center, Children's Farm Barn & Maymont Shop): Tuesday-Sunday, 12:00-5:00pm. Grounds, Gardens & Visitor Center: Daily, 10:00am - 5:00pm

❑ Admission: $4.00 suggested donation at Nature Center & Maymont House

❑ Miscellaneous: Tram, Carriage Rides (Noon-5:00pm) and Hayrides (weekends in summer, Noon-4:00 or 5:00pm) are $1.00-$3.00 fee per person per ride.

The 100 acre estate is home to the new Nature Center. Thirteen linked aquariums are home to playful river otters, many species of fish, turtles and other creatures. Interactive galleries include a replica of Richmond's flood wall, a weather station and a fish ladder. There are also exhibit areas to view bison, black bear, otters and hundreds of other animals. Also, explore the opulent Victorian mansion, gardens, wildlife exhibits and the children's Farm.

RICHMOND CULTURAL CONNECTION

Richmond - *Convention and Visitors Bureau, 23220. Phone: (804) 358-5511 or (888) RICHMOND. Hours: Shuttle Operates Weekends (June-September). Admission: $1.00 per person for shuttle. Ask for the Richmond Region Pass card with discounts to many sites and eateries around town.* The Richmond Cultural Connection transports you to many area attractions, historic sites and gardens, as well as unique shopping and dining areas in air-conditioned comfort. For only $1, you can ride and transfer all day, as many times as you like, and enjoy the many offerings of the city. Park your car and aboard at any of the stops along the routes. It's a great deal, convenient and easy.

RICHMOND INTERNATIONAL RACEWAY

Richmond - *602 E. Laburnum Avenue, 23220. Phone: (804) 345-7223 (RACE).* **Web: *www.rir.com***. A ¾ mile "D" shaped asphalt oval surrounded by the greatest number of seats of any VA sport complex. Twice annual admissions exceed 170,000 to NASCAR Busch Series and Nextel Cup series race weekends. Admission varies with event.

RICHMOND KICKERS SOCCER

Richmond - *2320 West Main Street (play at Univ. of Richmond Soccer Complex), 23220. Web: www.richmondkickers.com. Phone: (804) 644-5425. Season: (mid-April to mid-August). Admission: $6.00-$8.00.* The Richmond Kickers are a professional USL-Division 2 team.

THEATRE IV

Richmond - *114 West Broad Street (Empire Theatre - the oldest theater in Virginia), 23220. Web: www.theatreiv.com. Phone: (804) 344-8040. Admission: Regularly priced tickets are around $30.00.* Theatre IV presents two performance series: The Family Playhouse Series of plays, musicals and puppet shows for the entire family and the Broadway series with more mature themes. The Family Series includes favorites like: Charlie Brown, A Christmas Carol, The Secret Garden, and Beauty and the Beast.

VIRGINIA MUSEUM OF FINE ARTS

Richmond - *2800 Grove Avenue @ Blvd (I-195 Boulevard exit), 23221. Phone: (804) 340-1400. Web: www.vmfa.state.va.us. Hours: Wednesday-Sunday 11:00am-5:00pm. Admission: Donations. Miscellaneous: Cafeteria and gift shop.* This art museum focuses on collections of art nouveau, art deco, Himalayan, contemporary, impressionist and British sporting art. Children's Studios are designed to follow what your child is learning in school. The hands-on process makes new links between art and other experiences, and makes them all more meaningful to children. Family Open Houses bring the art in the galleries to life with related performances, storytelling, art activities, and more. They're free and open to all; no registration needed.

CHIMBORAZO MEDICAL MUSEUM

Richmond - *3215 East Broad Street (I-95: take exit 74C west then follow signs to Civil War Visitor Center located at 490 Tredegar Street), 23223. Web: www.nps.gov/rich/pphtml/facilities.html. Phone: (804) 226-1981. Hours: Daily 9:00am-5:00pm. Admission: FREE. Miscellaneous: A short film supplements the exhibits.* The museum stands on the eastern end of downtown Richmond, at the site of the Civil War's famous Chimborazo Hospital. Between 1861 and 1865 more than 75,000 Confederate soldiers received treatment at this spacious facility. The medical museum tells the story of those patients and the hospital and physicians that cared for them. Using artifacts, uniforms and documents the exhibits describe the state of medicine in 1860 and the care of wounded and sick soldiers on the battlefields and in the many large centralized Richmond hospitals like Chimborazo.

RICHMOND NATIONAL BATTLEFIELD PARK

Richmond - *3215 E. Broad Street (I-95: take exit 74C west then follow signs to Civil War Visitor Center located at 490 Tredegar Street), 23223. Phone: (804) 771-2145. Web: www.nps.gov/rich. Hours: Daily 9:00am-5:00pm. Admission: FREE.* Richmond Civil War Visitor Center provides orientation to Richmond's Civil War battlefields, as well as related historic sites and museums. Highlights focus on the 1862 Peninsula campaign and Grant's 1864 attack at Cold Harbor. View the park film and complete three activity sheets and you will receive a Junior Ranger badge.

THREE LAKES NATURE CENTER

Richmond - *400 Sausiluta Drive (off Wilkerson Road, east of Chamberlayne Avenue), 23227. Phone: (804) 501-8230 or (804) 262-4822. Web: www.co.henrico.va.us/rec/nature.htm. Hours: NOTICE: due to hurricanes, the center is undergoing massive renovations. Check website for updates and hours of operation. Admission: FREE.* Three Lake Nature Center and Aquarium brings together three worlds - air, land and water. A 50,000-gallon freshwater aquarium (largest in Central Virginia), wetland exhibits, aquatic animal/plant life, forest animals, etc. give you "Nature's" view of the world. Features also include a variety of exhibits designed to give the visitor hands-on knowledge of the plant and animal life of the area.

LEWIS GINTER BOTANICAL GARDEN

Richmond - *1800 Lakeside Avenue (I-95 North take Exit 80, the Lakeside Avenue exit), 23228. Phone: (804) 262-9887. Web: www.lewisginter.org. Hours: Daily 9:00am-5:00pm. Closed*

Thanksgiving, Christmas, and New Years. Admission: $9.00 adult, $8.00 senior (55+), $5.00 child (2-12). Miscellaneous: Gift shop and café (lunch). Lewis Ginter Botanical Garden brings you new horticultural displays each season. The more than 25 acres of gardens includes the Conservatory glass-domed showcase with exotic and tropical displays; an elegant Victorian-style garden; Asian Valley; the Island Garden, a wetland environment with a stunning display of pitcher plants, water irises and lotuses; a Children's Garden with colorful and interesting plants to attract butterflies and birds, a TreeHouse, Farm and Waterplay areas. Good to take a stroller along the winding paved paths.

RICHMOND BRAVES

Richmond - *3001 N. Boulevard (The Diamond), 23230. Phone: (804) 359-4444 or (800) 849-4627. Web: www.rbraves.com. Season: (April-September). Admission: General $4.00-$10.00.* The AAA Richmond Braves, top farm team to the Atlanta Braves. In addition to traditional seating, The Diamond features a 150-seat restaurant- The Diamond Bar & Grill – with a glass wall that affords an excellent view of the playing field from the first base side of the stadium. Kids 13 and under can join the Kids Club for chances to participate in part of home games and win prizes.

METRO RICHMOND ZOO

Richmond (Chesterfield) - *8300 Beaver Bridge Road, 23219. Phone: (804) 739-5666. Hours: Monday-Saturday 9:30am-5:00pm (March-November). Saturday only (December-February). Admission: $7.75 adult, $6.75 senior, $5.75 child (2-11).* Privately owned zoo featuring exotic animals such as endangered lemur, ostriches, giraffes, penguins, lions, tigers, chimpanzees and a new nocturnal exhibit featuring bats and sloth, and more than 200 monkeys are just some of the animals currently at the zoo.

CHESTERFIELD MUSEUMS

Richmond (Chesterfield) - *10011 Iron Bridge Road, 23832. Phone: (804) 748-1026. Web: www.chesterfieldhistory.com. Hours: Monday-Friday 10:00am-4:00pm, Sunday 1:00-4:00pm. Admission: $4.00 per person (all 3 sites).* Chesterfield Museum exhibits pre-historic fossils and Indian artifacts plus artifacts of history of Chesterfield County. Magnolia Grange plantation house (1822) and The Old Jail (1892) are also part of the historical complex.

PARAMOUNT'S KINGS DOMINION

1600 Theme Park Way (I-95 EXIT 98)

Richmond (Doswell) 23047

- ❑ Phone: (804) 876-5000, **Web: www.kingsdominion.com**
- ❑ Hours: Weekends (April-Memorial Day), Daily (Memorial Day-Labor Day), and Weekends (Labor Day - first few weekends in October). Generally opens at 10:00 or 10:30am and closes around 8:00-10:00pm.
- ❑ Admission: One-Day General Admission: $40.00+.

This 400-acre family theme park offers 12 coasters and tons of kiddie rides. Try the new Stunt Coaster. WaterWorks features 4-8 awesome slides, a Big Wave Bay wave pool, Surf City Splash Playhouse, Kiddie Kove, Lil' Barefoot Beach and Lazy Rider. But, kids are in charge at:

- ❑ NICKELODEON CENTRAL: Nickelodeon characters and Scooby Doo and SpongeBob welcome visitors.
- ❑ KIDZVILLE: Boulder Bumpers, Treasure Cave, Picnic Basket, Boo Boo's Tree Swing, Top Cats Turnpike-Alley Cat 500, Touche Turtle's Clipper, Taxi Jam Coaster, Ranger Smith's Jeep Tours, George Jetson's Space Port, Scooby-Doo Ghoster Coaster, an old-fashioned carousel, or Snagglepuss' Parachute School!

Many shows throughout the day vary from Country, to today's hits, to yesterday's favorites, to hot Latin Beats, or maybe Nicktoons Summer Jam songs from favorite Nick shows.

MEADOW FARM MUSEUM

3400 Mountain Road (I-95 exit 84 to I-295 west to Woodman Road South exit to Mountain Road), **Richmond (Glen Allen)** 23060

❑   Phone: (804) 501-5520

  Web: www.co.henrico.va.us/rec/mfarm.htm

❑   Hours: Tuesday-Sunday Noon-4:00pm (early March-early December). Weekends only (December, mid-January to early March). Closed many holidays.

❑   Admission: FREE. Small fee for some events. If you want to "visit" with living history farm hands, come on theme weekends.

Start your visit at the orientation center with everything from old wooden farm tools to hand-make paper dolls. Many of the displays are at a child's eye-level and short storyboards help to explain customs and traditions of the time. The story of the Sheppard family thru the seasons is a great video to watch at least once. Walk around the farm and see the cows, horses, sheep, pigs and fowl that are typical of the nineteenth century. Watch farmhands planting the crops every spring and many other chores including pickling, harvesting, or Dr. Sheppard preparing homemade medicine for his patients. Also outside on the farm, you'll find a barn, smokehouse, doctor's office and blacksmith. You might see the women churning butter and learn how you can make your own at home using one cup of heavy whipping cream-along with a marble-in a jar with tight fitting lid. Shake it hard for a while, pour off liquid and the solid part is sweet, creamy butter. Spread it on fresh bread for an authentic 19th century lunch!

VIRGINIA AVIATION MUSEUM

Richmond (Sandston) - *5701 Huntsman Road (Richmond International Airport), 23250. Phone: (804) 236-3622. **Web: www.smv.org/wvamhome.html**. Hours: Monday-Saturday 9:30am-5:00pm, Sunday, Noon-5:00pm. Closed Thanksgiving and Christmas. Admission: $6.00 adult, $5.00 senior (60+), $4.00 child (4-12).* This shrine to the "Golden Age of Aviation" enhances the Science Museum's aerospace exhibits with its extensive collection of vintage flying machines. You'll see Capt. Dick Merrill's 1930s open cockpit mail plane; a special exhibit on

Virginia's legendary Adm. Richard E. Byrd and his Stars and Stripes (the first American scientific research aircraft to fly in Antarctica); replicas of the Wright Brothers gliders; a World War I SPAD VII in mint condition; or, how about the cool spy plane, the SR-71 Blackbird. Learn which planes earned the nicknames: Rolls Royce, Cadillac and Flying Bathtub. Enjoy aviation films in the Benn Theater or stroll through the Virginia Aviation Hall of Fame.

ISLE OF WIGHT COUNTY MUSEUM

Smithfield - *103 Main Street, 23430. Phone: (757) 357-7459. Web: www.co.isle-of-wight.va.us/park_rec/museum.html. Hours: Tuesday-Saturday 10:00am-4:00pm, Sunday 1:00-5:00pm. Closed New Years, Thanksgiving and Christmas. Admission: FREE. Miscellaneous: In the same small town of Smithfield, there is the Old Brick Church (St. Luke's Church) said to be the oldest Gothic Church in America (757) 357-3367 (open almost same hours as county museum). In a circa 1900 country store, see prehistoric fossils, Native American and colonial artifacts, Civil War history thru the area, a miniature plantation house and the famous Smithfield Ham galleries. See the "World's Oldest Smithfield Ham" among this exhibit of historical ham memorabilia.*

GREAT DISMAL SWAMP NATIONAL WILDLIFE REFUGE

Suffolk - *PO Box 349 (I-664 to Rte. 58 west to Rte. 337 to Rte. 642, White Marsh Rd., follow signs), 23439. Phone: (757) 986-3705. Web: www.albemarle-nc.com/gates/gdsnwr/. Hours: The Washington Ditch and Jericho Lane entrances are open Daily 6:30am- 8:00pm (April 1-September 30) & 6:30am-5:00pm (October 1-March 31). Miscellaneous: Hiking, biking, photography, wildlife observation, fishing and boating. Portions of the Refuge may be closed to public use. A variety of unpaved roads provide opportunities for hiking and biking, with Washington Ditch Road the best suited for bicycle traffic. An interpretive boardwalk trail meanders almost a mile through a portion of the Swamp.* Located in southeastern Virginia and northeastern North Carolina, the Refuge consists of over 107,000 acres, with Lake Drummond, a 3,100 acre natural lake in the center of the Swamp. The Swamp supports a variety of mammals, including otter, bats, raccoon, mink, gray and red foxes, and gray squirrel. White-tailed deer are common, and black bear and bobcat also inhabit the area. Three species of poisonous snakes are found here (cottonmouth, canebrake rattler, and the more common copperhead) along with 18 non-poisonous species. Yellow-bellied and spotted turtles are commonly seen, and an additional 56 species of turtles, lizards, salamanders, frogs, and toads have been observed on the Refuge. Of the over 200 species of birds identified on the Refuge since its establishment, 96 of these species have been reported as nesting on or near the Refuge. Birding is best during spring migration from April to June. Two southern species, the Swainson's warbler and Wayne's warbler are more common in the Great Dismal than in other coastal locations. Other birds of interest are the wood duck, barred owl, pleated woodpecker, and prothonotary warbler.

CHIPPOKES PLANTATION STATE PARK

Surry - *695 Chippokes Park Road (access via SR 10 to Rte. 634), 23883.* **Web: *www.virginia.gov/parks/chippoke.htm*.** *Phone: (757) 294-3625. Hours: Mansion guided tours: Saturday 10:00am-4:00pm, Sunday 1:00-4:00pm (April-October). Grounds open daily (seasonally) along with Farm Museum self-guided tours. Admission: $2.00-$3.00 per vehicle. Miscellaneous: Children's playground, biking, hiking, swimming and picnicking.* This park offers a working farm for more than 370 years. Visitors may tour an antebellum mansion, stroll the gardens, or view a collection of antique farm and forestry equipment in the Farm and Forestry Museum. The park has a visitor center with a gift store, interpretive programs. A new campground and three overnight cottages allow visitors to spend the night on the historic grounds.

JAMESTOWN-SCOTLAND FERRY

Surry - *(Rte. 31 between James City and Surry counties), 23883. Phone: (800) VA-FERRY. Hours: Daily Every 20 minutes in the summer. Less often the rest of the year. Call for schedule each season. Admission: FREE.* Passenger vehicle ferry service, Surry County to Jamestown. Fun way to first look onto Jamestown with similar angle as the explorers.

SMITH'S FORT PLANTATION

Surry - *SR 31/641 Smith's Fort Lane (across the river from Jamestown, 2 miles from the ferry dock), 23883. Phone: (757) 294-3872. Web: www.apva.org/apva/smiths_fort.php. Hours: Tuesday-Saturday 10:00am-4:00pm, Sunday Noon-4:00pm (April-October). Weekends only in November. Admission: $7.00 adult, $5.00 senior (65+), $4.00 youth (ages 6-18 and college student).* Captain John Smith built a fort on land directly across from Jamestown as a refuge in event of a Indian attack. When John Rolfe married Pocahontas in 1614, the Indian chief Powhatan presented this land as part of her dowry. The house is furnished with early English and American furniture. A footpath leads to the original fort site. Neither Pocahontas, John Smith, nor John Rolfe ever permanently lived here, but they do weave much history of all three throughout the tour.

FIRST LANDING STATE PARK AND NATURAL AREA

2500 Shore Drive (US 60 at Cape Henry)

Virginia Beach 23451

❑   Phone: (757) 412-2316

   Web: www.dcr.virginia.gov/parks/1stland.htm

❑   Hours: Dawn-Dusk

❑   Admission: $3.00-$4.00 per vehicle. No parking fee for camping and cabin guests, up to two vehicles.

In April of 1607, some 100 English settlers landed here and established the first government in English America before heading up the James River to establish Jamestown. Along with its historical significance, the park offers recreational activities to explore lagoons, large cypress trees and rare plants and critters. 19 plus miles of hiking trails wind through the natural area. Climate controlled cabins, campsites, picnic areas, a swimming beach, boat ramps and a bicycle trail are offered too. The Chesapeake Bay Center - showcases a historical exhibition of the first landing of settlers in 1607, aquariums, environmental exhibits, classroom space, a wet lab and touch tank. It also has information, supplies, and equipment rentals so visitors can participate in programs such as sea kayaking in the Chesapeake bay. This is one of the most popular state parks in Virginia because of its significance and tourism location.

OCEAN BREEZE WATERPARK

849 General Booth Blvd. (1.5 miles south of the resort area, just past the Virginia Marine Science Museum)

Virginia Beach 23451

❑   Phone: (757) 422-4444 or (800) 678-WILD
     Web: www.oceanbreezewaterpark.com
❑   Hours: Park generally opens around 10:00am and closes between 5:00-8:00pm (longer hours when school's out) (Memorial Day-Labor Day).
❑   Admission: $15.00-$19.00 general (ages 3+); discounts for military families and half day or evening admission.
❑   Miscellaneous: Arcade, food court, locker rentals and a Caribbean grill restaurant.

Enjoy 19 acres of fun. Slither down your choice of 16 water slides, shoot the rapids on an inner tube, or sprawl on the spacious sundeck. Enjoy the waves in a million-gallon Runaway Bay Wave Pool, or enjoy the Paradise Pipeline water slide. For the more adventurous, try the Bahama Mamma speed slide. Or, for leisurely fun, Dive In Movies. Enjoy your favorite Disney movies while floating atop Runaway Bay.

OLD COAST GUARD STATION

Virginia Beach – *24th Street & Atlantic Avenue (just off the boardwalk), 23451. Web: www.oldcoastguardstation.com. Phone: (757) 422-1587. Hours: Monday-Saturday 10:00am-5:00pm, Sunday Noon-5:00pm (Day after Memorial Day-September). Closed Mondays rest of year. Closed major winter holidays. Admission: $1.00-$3.00 (ages 6+).* A restored 1903 lifesaving / Coast Guard station which traces life-saving and Guard services in history. The quaint museum is probably most noted for artifacts and displays about shipwrecks that have occurred off the coast. Don't leave without taking a peek through TOWERCAM, a roof-mounted video camera that zooms in on passing ships dotting the horizon (can also be viewed from home at: **www.vabeach.com**). The camera transmits its pictures to a television monitor, affording museum visitors the same view crewmen had from the tower nearly 100 years ago.

VIRGINIA AQUARIUM & MARINE SCIENCE MUSEUM

717 General Booth Blvd. (I-64 exit Rte. 44 east, get off on the Birdneck Road exit and head south),

Virginia Beach 23451

❑ Phone: (757) 425-FISH, **Web: www.VirginiaAquarium.com**

❑ Hours: Daily 9:00am-5:00pm. Summer season open until 7:00pm. Closed Thanksgiving and Christmas.

❑ Admission: $11.95 adult, $10.95 senior (62+), and $7.95 child (3-11). IMAX films are $6.50-$7.50 each or discounted if combo tickets purchased.

❑ Miscellaneous: IMAX films are shown several times daily with subjects of whales, dolphins, dinosaurs and nature. Some are 2D, some 3D. Call for schedule. The Osprey Café offers breakfast, lunch and snack items. There are two museum stores.

The marine museum takes visitors on a journey of water through four different habitats. You'll find "touch tanks" around seemingly every turn in this museum:

COASTAL RIVER ROOM - a freshwater habitat where birds and turtles roam free with a temperate-zone environment (you just have to see turtles "flirting" with each other…)

CHESAPEAKE BAY AQUARIUM - houses the largest collection of Chesapeake bay fish in the world, 30 species in all, so you're bound to see something new or different. Look for the fish with the human-like bucked teeth!

ATLANTIC OCEAN PAVILION - explore the depths of the open ocean with sharks, sea turtles, jellies, lobster and stingrays. Here is where you'll find the 300,000 gallon aquarium which re-creates the Norfolk Canyon. Look for the funny "follow the leader" schools of fish, watch sea turtle hatchlings, or interact at oceanographic exhibits. Understand simple exhibits like sand scapes and waves & water. Build-your-own hurricane and tong for oysters.

<u>OWLS CREEK MARSH PAVILION</u> - focuses on plants and animals in a salt marsh that is the last undeveloped salt marsh in Virginia with direct access to the ocean. Get there by walking the one-third mile long nature trail. In the pavilion, you'll love to watch the antics of a live river otter habitat with over and underwater viewing; an aviary and insect micro marsh; and a macro marsh display showcasing marsh animals at ten times their normal size. Don't miss the Secret Life of Owls Creek 9 minute film that introduces you to what appears to b a muddy, murky environment.

<u>BOAT TRIPS</u> (757) 437-BOAT (extra $5.00 to $25.00 per person with reservations). Highly recommended! Where do playful bottlenose dolphins go for summer vacation? Where do juvenile humpback whales winter? Virginia Beach is a regular visitation spot for these, and other marine animals. Seasonal boat trips lasting 30 minutes (Pontoon Cruises along Creek) to 2 hours are educational and eventful. Trips leave from Rudee Inlet Fishing Center (one mile down the road from the Museum) mornings and afternoons, and, while dolphin or whale sightings aren't guaranteed, you'll for sure see some historic landmarks and take samplings of ocean marine life collected, displayed in temporary tanks and then released back. All that watery excitement and you don't have to get wet. We saw over 60 dolphins on our early morning trip (July & August are the best months for dolphin). Even babies (that little fin is so-o-o cute!) and pods (groups) fishing. When in the area, please fit a boat trip into your plans. You'll find screams of excitement and education about "dolphin family groups" at the same time. It's also a great, relaxing way for parents to recover before beginning the next adventure.

VIRGINIA BEACH BOARDWALK

Virginia Beach – *1ˢᵗ thru 40ᵗʰ Streets, along Atlantic Avenue, 23451. Phone: (800) 822-3224. **Web:** www.vbfun.com.* Stretching from Rudee Inlet on the south end of the resort area up to 40ᵗʰ Street. Lifeguards are on duty from mid-May to mid September, 9:30am-6:00pm. Permanent restrooms are adjacent to the boardwalk at 17th, 24th, and 30th Streets and are open all year. They do not contain changing facilities. Foot showers are available along the oceanfront. Virginia Beach Amusement Park is on the Boardwalk at 15th Street. Full-scale rides include roller coasters, ferris wheels, games of chance and picnic tables. Near 11th Street is the Atlantic Wildfowl Heritage Museum (DeWitt cottage) 757-437-8432 or **www.owhm.org**. The museum displays art and artifacts documenting migratory wildfowl that pass. See wood carvings (some demos to watch, occasionally), interactive computer programs and a historical collection of decoys.

FALSE CAPE STATE PARK & BACK BAY NATIONAL WILDLIFE REFUGE

4001 Sandpiper Road (5 miles south of Sandbridge, no vehicular access), **Virginia Beach** 23457

❑ Phone: (757) 426-7128 or (757) 721-2412 or (800) 933-7275
   Web: www.dcr.virginia.gov/parks/falscape.htm

❑ Hours: Trials & Refuge: Daily, Dawn-Dusk. Visitor Stations: Monday-Friday 8:00am-4:00pm and Weekends 9:00am-4:00pm (April-September). Open again after the 1st week of October through the end of October.

❑ Admission: $4.00 per vehicle entrance fee. Tram fees: $6.00 adult, $4.00 child (under 18) and senior. FREE for child able to sit in parent's lap.

❑ Tours: Tram service is a 4 hour tour departing Tuesday, Thursday - Sunday from Little Island Park at 9:00am. Reservations needed (757) 498-BIRD.

This 4,321-acre area is a mile-wide barrier split between Back Bay and the Atlantic Ocean, in the extreme southeast corner of Virginia Beach. It has 6 miles of unspoiled beaches, 12 primitive campsites, and 9 miles of hiking / biking trails. Access is through Back Bay National Wildlife Refuge and is limited to hiking, biking, tram or boating. The park also features Wash Woods Center - an extensive environmental educational program and group overnight facility in one of the last undisturbed coastal environments on the East Coast. Tram rides (covered) travel through the refuge and State Park past unique beach, dune and marsh habitats. Catch glimpses of a variety of wildlife - maybe a white-tailed deer, red fox, otter, mink, etc. Summers are full of birds, Fall lures concentrations of waterfowl, shorebirds and raptors. A stopover at False Cape allows you to climb one of two observation towers located in the park entrance for bird watching.

OCEANA NAVAL AIR STATION

Virginia Beach - *Oceana Blvd. (only open to employees and tour vehicles), 23460. Web: www.nasoceana.navy.mil/Visitors.htm. Phone: (757) 433-3131. Tours: Available (Memorial Day through mid-September) pending closing to the public for national security or battle time. Tours (conducted by TRT Tours & Trolley system) depart 24th and Atlantic Avenue. $7.50 adult, $5.00 child & senior.* One of the Navy's four master jet bases, it is home to 19 aviation squadrons, including the F-14 Tomcat fighter planes and the A-6 Intruder medium attack bombers. Watch training sequences, too. There are two observation parks located near the runways to watch aircraft take-off and land. One is located on Oceana Boulevard at the POW/MIA memorial, and the other is off London Bridge road on the opposite side of the air station (blue circles).

AIRFIELD 4-H CENTER

Wakefield - *15189 Airfield Road (I-95 to Rte. 460), 23888. Phone: (757) 899-4901. Web: www.airfieldconference.com. Admission: Lodging ranges $15.00-$40.00 per person each night. Wildlife tours and Challenge Course are additional small fee. Most recreational facilities are included in lodging or group fees. Miscellaneous: Food catering available.* The Airfield Center is located on 113 scenic and wooded acres, surrounded by a 105 acre lake. Recreation facilities include: Olympic size outdoor swimming pool, Fishing on the lake (state license required), outdoor tennis courts, Campfire circle, Softball, Canoes, Nature trail, Paddle boats, Horseshoes, Basketball, and 100 stalls for horse show functions plus two rings with outdoor lighting. You can also sign up for Wildlife Tours: includes a unique variety of animals and the Challenge Course: a combination of obstacle course activities, coupled with individual and group initiatives. The Executive, Conference and Dorm lodges are nestled among the shores of Airfield Lake.

MILES B. CARPENTER MUSEUM COMPLEX

201 Hunter Street (Rte. 460 west near Rte. 40)

Waverly 23890

❑   Phone: (804) 834-3327 or (804) 834-2151
❑   Hours: Open Daily except Tuesday and Wednesday 2:00-5:00pm.
❑   Admission: FREE
❑   Miscellaneous: Herb Garden, Art Studio (sign up for programs with folk artists) and nature trail. See local folk art and visiting artists and exhibits too.

Located in a Victorian house, you'll see that Mr. Carpenter's whittled work is folksy and is best known for "the watermelon with a bite". This cute, small town museum complex is run by retired townsfolk who personally knew Mr. Carpenter (or worked in the peanut or woodworking industry). Begin in the Miles B. Carpenter Home and Museum. As you walk from room to room, you'll see many of Mr. Carpenter's whimsical wooden carvings. We found his animal and people figurines were the best. By taking a branch or limb from a tree, he formed snakes, birds, and funny looking people - just from some rough carving and paint. (The kids will certainly get some new ideas about crafting here!) Next, visit the first peanut museum in America. Here, you'll actually see how peanuts grow (really...did you know that they grew underground?) and are harvested (then & now). The original seeds came from Peru in 1830, but a hearty seed (the heart of the peanut) was grown until 1842 in Waverly? Finally, walk inside the Wood Products Museum and see different species of wood. What started as a sawmill eventually became Mr. Carpenter's famous workshop.

WATERCOUNTRY USA

176 Water Country Pkwy (off Rte. 50, follow signs)

Williamsburg 23147

❑   Phone: (757) 253-3350 or (800) 4ADVENTURE
    Web: www.watercountryusa.com
❑   Hours: Weekends (May, September). Daily (Memorial Weekend to Labor Day). Park opens at 10:00am (May to mid-September).

Watercountry USA (*cont.*)

- ❑   Admission: $32.00-$38.00 per person.
- ❑   Miscellaneous: Gift shops, food service, picnic pavilion, locker rental, bathhouse and free use of life vests and inner tubes. Red Cross swim lessons offered.

Water Country USA, the mid-Atlantic's largest family water play park, features the world's latest, greatest, state-of-the-art water rides and attractions, entertainment, shopping and restaurants - all set in a colorful 1950s and '60s surf theme. More than 1,000 lounge chairs are available throughout for parents to rest. Several pools are climate-controlled for comfort. They start with a classic Wave Pool but add an Aquatic Dive Show. There's the easygoin' Hubba Hubba Highway and wild Big Daddy Falls with plenty of flumes and tunnels in between. Other popular activities include the obstacle course, Adventure Isle. Also, slide over to the Tots area, superspeed Beach Blanket Slide, 4 person high speed toboggan, dark tunnel tube rides, sci-fi kids interactive area, whitewater rafting, 2 person flume ride, surf boggans, lazy river floating or the other classics - waterslides and twisty tubes.

HISTORIC AIR TOURS, INC.

Williamsburg - *102 Marclay Road (Jamestown Flight Center-Williamsburg-Jamestown Airport), 23185. Phone: (800) VA-BY-AIR.* **Web:** *www.historicairtours.com. Hours: Daytime, by reservation. Admission: $60.00 per person. Minimum two people.* See the historic sites and natural wonders of the Hampton Roads area from an entirely new vantage point. See Yorktown Battlefield, majestic James River plantations, historic Fort Monroe, Colonial Williamsburg, Jamestown Island, Norfolk Naval Shipyard and the World War II Ghost Fleet (what you see depends on which tour you take - three to choose from). The narrated flights allow you to see the scope and flow of the events which shaped the nation…a good way to visit the area, especially if you've already seen it by land a few times.

PRESIDENT'S PARK

Williamsburg - *201 Water Country Parkway (I-64 exit 242B), 23185. Phone: (757) 259-1121. Web: www.presidentspark.org. Hours: Daily 10:00am-8:00pm (April-August). Daily 10:00am-4:00pm (September-March). Closed Christmas and New Years. Admission: $9.75 adult, $8.75 senior (55+) and military, $6.50 student (6-17). Miscellaneous: Café, gift shop.* This fun park displays sculpted busts of each U.S. President, 10 times life size, set in a landscaped garden. Every giant sculpture includes facts about each President. In addition to showcasing Presidents, the park also follows American History featuring exhibits that recount 14 defining moments of the past. Visitors can take one of ten different tours of the grounds, such as the Civil Rights tour or the First Ladies tour. A close-up, light-hearted and patriotic way to study Presidents and significant changes in history.

BUSCH GARDENS WILLIAMSBURG

US 60 (I-64 exit 242A), **Williamsburg** 23187

- ❏ Phone: (757) 253-3350 or (800) 832-5665
  Web: www.buschgardens.com
- ❏ Hours: Park Opens at 10:00am, closing times vary seasonally between 6:00pm-11:00pm (peak season June-August with latest closing times daily). Open weekends only in late March, early April, September and October. See website for exact times.
- ❏ Admission: ~$45.00-$52.00 for general all inclusive admission. Combos with Water Country USA. Parking fee. Be sure to look for discounts offered by AAA or fast food restaurants.
- ❏ Miscellaneous: Every village has 1-3 gift shops with fancy and playful themed toys and gifts. Many larger rides have minimum height requirements of 48" or more. If your kids "don't measure up", no fear…there are kiddie versions of the adult rides for their enjoyment.

This action-packed European-themed park has 17th century charm with the technology and conveniences of the modern age. All the 50+ thrill or kiddie rides are based on the theme of the area you are journeying through. Here's the six European areas you'll visit: (by the way, parents, you'll love the well-maintained landscapes and clean facilities, not to mention, the yummy European-themed food concessions and restaurant food!)

- ❑ IRELAND, KILLARNEY - Corkscrew Hill (a white-knuckle, 4-D adventure ride through mythical Celtic lore of a land of giants where you become one of the main characters!); or "The Secrets of Castle O'Sullivan" musical show (look for the rainbow after the storm) or Sound Machine resident leprechaun roaming act; Grogans Grille and Pub serve Irish fare of corned beef, smashed potatoes, soda bread and Irish stew.

- ❑ SCOTLAND, HEATHERDOWNS - Loch Ness Monster steel roller coaster with interlocking loops; Highland Stables, home to the famous Clydesdales horses; Li'l Clydes kiddie ride.

- ❑ ENGLAND, BANBURY CROSS - Aeronaut Skyride is a scenic aerial tour of the park; Royal Preserve and Menagerie Petting Zoo offers guests viewing and contact with miniature breeds; the Globe Theatre has "Haunted Lighthouse" the twisted 4-D adventure film that puts guests in the middle of the action as they experience sprays of water or chilling wind.

- ❑ JACK HANNA'S WILD RESERVE - Greystone Tower viewing of gray wolves' unique habits; Lorikeet Glen where guests become perches as the brilliant birds land on arms, shoulders and heads; the zany antics in Pet Shenanigans; Eagle Canyon sanctuary for American balk eagles; and Reptiles education presentations.

- ❑ FRANCE, AQUITAINE - test drive classic European race cars through tunnels and across bridges at Le Mans Raceway; The Royal Palace Theatre showcases entertainment on selected summer evenings.

- ❑ NEW FRANCE, CANADA - Le Scoot log flume ride with a 50 foot vertical plunge; "American Jukebox" combines favorite Canadian dances and music from the 50's to today.

- ❑ GERMANY, OKTOBERFEST - Bavarian hamlet has the Big Bad Wolf, a suspended roller coaster and many cute, creative kiddie rides dot the village; "This is Oktoberfest" has a cast of musicians and dancers celebrating at Das Festhaus - guests may dance and sing along.

❑ GERMANY, RHINEFELD - cruise down the Rhine River to rides including Alpengeist inverted steel roller coaster, Land of Dragons magical play area designed for kiddies, Kinder Karussel antique merry-go-round, and Wilde Maus single car steel coaster with dips and turns; march along with "the Boogie Band" or catch fantasy and imaginary shows at the Land of Dragons area; many sweet treats are available here too. This will probably be the younger kids favorite play, climb, and crawl place.

❑ ITALY, FESTA ITALIA - home to the high-speed hypercoaster, Apollo's Chariot and several festive themed rides and games including Roman Rapids white-water raft journey through choppy waters, raging water falls and geysers.

❑ ITALY, SAN MARCO - tour the ruins of Mt. Vesuvius on Escape from Pompeii thrilling water ride with special effects; Da Vinci's Garden of Inventions features rides for children like the Cradle, the Flying Machine and the Battering Ram; "Holiday in Roma" features modern operatic and pop sounds in the daytime and Starlight Orchestra big band sounds in the evening.

COLONIAL WILLIAMSBURG
P O Box 1776, **Williamsburg** 23187

❑ Phone: (800) HISTORY or (757) 220-7645 or (757) 229-7193 for theme tours. **Web: www.colonialwilliamsburg.org**

❑ Hours: Daily 9:00am-5:00pm (may vary by season/special events).

❑ Admission: $34.00 adult, $17.00 child (6-17) Day Pass; Visiting for more than one day? Look into the FREEdom Pass (one year). Discounted tickets in winter.

❑ Miscellaneous: Start at the Visitors Center to get oriented, otherwise it will be a chaotic day. Make reservations for tavern meals and evening programs upon arrival. Evening programs, children's tours, and special events are particularly fun for repeat guests. School-aged kids and parents will like the 35 minute film "Williamsburg-The Story of a Patriot" to get "in the mood". Strollers welcome or can be rented on first come, first serve basis. Be sure to pick up the guide for families (a simple brochure to steer you in the right direction).

Colonial Williamsburg (*cont.*)

Explore a typical day in the life of an 18th century child blending English and Colonial cultures and soon, Revolution. Costumed (and sometimes, wigged) characters ply their trades and re-enact and interpret aspects of colonial life. Tour the Costume Design Center and Millinery to see the effort they put into authenticity (you can even rent costumes for the day!).

Discuss the day's chores, independence and freedom with "People of the Past" at the Capitol or get the highlights of the final days of the last royal governor at the Palace (lots of leisurely games - like lawn bowling and tops) - can be played on the side lawn. Be sure to try the Garden Maze while in this area as well. At the Wythe House, go around back to visit with the slave cook or visit the stable and laundry.

Many buildings house trades that kids can help with like: the Geddy Site (craft brass, bronze, silver and pewter), the Carpenter's Brickyard (help knead clay that is molded into bricks), the Fire Engine bucket brigade, or the daily household tasks at the Benjamin Powell Site (child's chores varied by season and time of day).

Song and Dance are heard and seen throughout the day with special storytelling, dance and music of African-Americans; 18th century dance by youth where, once demonstrated, kids can participate; Palace Green musicians; and the Fife & Drum Corps perform in parades and military programs in the summer.

Four taverns explore the connection between 18th century foodways and operation of eating establishments. Each tavern offers 18th century lunch and dinner menus served in authentic colonial surroundings (George Washington's favorite spot was the Campbell's Tavern). Check out an 18th century "time out" spot at the stockade (good photo ops) or step inside the courthouse for a mock trial.

If you have time, stop by the College of William and Mary - the second oldest college in the US with the oldest academic building in continuous use, the Wren Bldg. And the Brafferton Bldg., a former "Indian school". Programs on rural slave life interpretation occur often and are well done.

For updates & travel games, visit: **www.KidsLoveTravel.com**

Words of advice: First, be sure to plan on a full (9:00am-5:00pm) day. This is the only way to visit with the characters of the day and tour all the buildings that interest you. Second, as soon as the children are "involved", purchase or rent them hats (and maybe clothes) - you'll be amazed at how much more they learn "in character". Third, characters like "Martha Washington" (she invited us to "sit for a spell" and taught the children morals and manners plus gave us the "skinny" on Thomas Jefferson!) help. The house cooks also really give you the best interpretations on a kid's level and teach about the tasks of the day. We learned all about the meals of the day - midday being the largest, followed by leftovers at supper and breakfast the next day. Fourth, if you want to snack, purchase some tavern rolls (we renamed them pretzel rolls) and apple cider and eat like fellow colonists.

GREAT WOLF LODGE INDOOR WATERPARK RESORT

549 East Rochambeau Drive (I64, take the Lightfoot/Route 199 exit, 234 or 234(A). On Rte. 199, take the second Mooretown Road exit. At first light, turn left),

Williamsburg 23188

❏   Phone: (800) 905-WOLF, **Web:** www.greatwolflodge.com

The 301-suite destination, Great Wolf Lodge has an array of amenities including: a huge indoor Waterpark, an Arcade, Cub Club activity/crafts room, Spa, Fitness Room, the Camp Critter Bar & Grille, The Loose Moose Cottage gourmet buffet and food court, Claw Café confectionary and an animated Great Clock Tower to greet you. Attractions at the 84-degree indoor waterpark include eight waterslides, six pools and tipping bucket, but also boasts a giant indoor wave pool and new four-person raft ride. Seasonal Specials. Rates (include admission to waterpark) for lodging run $159-$300 per night depending on package.

YORK RIVER STATE PARK

Williamsburg - *5526 Riverview Road (I-64 to Croaker exit, north on SR 607 to SR 606), 23188. Phone: (757) 566-3036. Web: www.dcr.state.va.us/parks/yorkrive.htm. Admission: $2.00-$3.00 per vehicle. Miscellaneous: Visitors Center plus more than 20 miles of hiking, biking and equestrian trails allow visitors to explore a marsh up close. Boat ramp, fishing (fresh and saltwater), picnicking, and seasonal bike and boat rentals available.* This park is known for its rare and delicate environment where freshwater and saltwater meet to create a habitat rich in marine and plant life. Taskinas Creek and the surrounding marsh are designated as a Chesapeake Bay National Estuarine Research Reserve. Activities here focus on the history and preservation of the York River and its marshes.

JAMESTOWN SETTLEMENT

PO Box 1607 (I-64 exit 242A, between SR 31 and Colonial Pkwy)

Williamsburg (Jamestown) 23185

❑   Phone: (757) 253-4838 or (888) 593-4682
    Web: www.historyisfun.org

❑   Hours: 9:00am-5:00pm daily, until 6:00pm (mid-June to mid-August). Closed on New Years and Christmas.

❑   Admission: $11.75 adult, $5.75 child (6-12). Combo ticket with Yorktown Victory Center add only $2.00-$5.00.

❑   Miscellaneous: Jamestown was founded almost 400 years ago, and plans are underway for a GIGANTIC 400th Birthday Party in 2007!

Jamestown Settlement tells the story of Jamestown, America's first permanent English Colony, from its beginnings in Europe through the first century of its existence. The museum has two elements: an indoor theater and exhibits (they are very engaging and present wonderful historical facts and artifacts) which orient guests to the time and place recreated outside the center. Board the Discovery, Godspeed and Susan Constant, re-creations of the three ships that colonists navigated across the Atlantic during their four-month winter voyage to the New World. It's fun watching the kids try to imagine a journey (yet alone across the ocean) in these wonderful reproductions. Explore a re-created Powhatan Indian village and a re-created fort built by the Jamestown colonists. Costumed interpreters invite kids to climb into a sailor's bunk (or steer the rudder and help set sail); grind corn (then make cornbread pancakes or grind shells to make beads); make cordage (from hemp) in an Indian village; try on armor and play a game of Quoits in a colonial fort. Kids can also try their hand at 17th century map-making, navigation and ship design in the gallery hall. Our advice, plan to spend at least a half-day here.

JAMESTOWNE, THE ORIGINAL SITE

(I-64 exit 242A, Rte. 199 west to Colonial Pkwy or Rte. 31
via the Jamestown Ferry),

Williamsburg (Jamestown) 23185

- ❑ Phone: (757) 229-1733, **Web: www.nps.gov/colo/**
- ❑ Hours: 9:00am-5:00pm daily except Christmas and New Years.
- ❑ Admission: $8.00 adult (17+). Under 17 FREE. Weeklong pass. Jamestowne and Yorktown Combo pass is $10.00.

This is the actual original site of the first permanent English settlement in the New World. Guided programs are offered from the Visitor Center. Here you can see a film and view artifacts (look for the miniature village or layers of soil exhibits) or you can take a self-guided walking tour past statues of Pocahontas and John Smith, remains of the 1639 church tower, and brick outlines of the original town. You'll find interpreters at the 1607 James Fort site where they have a lab / excavation area. Your family can also take the 3 and 5-mile driving tour to explore natural features of the island and some of the industries attempted like glassblowing. The ruins of the original glass furnace of 1608 may be seen and nearby, glassblowing demos are given regularly by costumed craftsmen in a re-created period type glasshouse. The five mile Island Loop road winds through 1500 acres of woodland and marsh, looking much as it would have in the 1600s. The most popular attractions here for kids are their Colonial Junior Ranger, Young Settlers, or Pinch Pot Programs. Kids can make their own clay pinch pot (takes 20 minutes) daily in the summer. Use the same techniques as Pocahontas did as written by Captain John Smith in his journal (this is a wonderful, hand-made souvenir). Use your imagination here...Pocahontas and the Colonial settlers will probably appear in your dreams that night!

WATERMEN'S MUSEUM

309 Water Street (off SR 238 east)

Williamsburg (Yorktown) 23090

- ❑ Phone: (757) 887-2641, **Web: www.watermens.org**
- ❑ Hours: Tuesday-Saturday 10:00am-4:00pm, Sunday 1:00-4:00pm (April 1-Thanksgiving). Weekends only (Thanksgiving through Christmas).
- ❑ Admission: $4.00 adult, $1.00 student (grades K-12)

The museum tells the story of Virginia's working Watermen and their families who, for generations, have harvested the rivers and tributaries of the Chesapeake Bay for its abundant seafood year round. Indoor exhibits include models of workboats, tools of the trade, nautical artifacts, and paintings and photographs of life on the bay. Outdoor exhibits feature a 100 year old Poquoson 5-log canoe as well as other boats. Visitors can also tog for oysters.

YORKTOWN VICTORY CENTER

P O Box 1607 (I-64 to Exit 247. Turn left onto Route 143. Turn left at the first traffic light, onto Route 238)

Williamsburg (Yorktown) 23187

- ❑ Phone: (757) 253-4838 or (888) 593-4682
  Web: www.historyisfun.org/yorktown/yorktown.cfm
- ❑ Hours: Daily 9:00am-5:00pm, until 6:00pm in the summer.
- ❑ Admission: $8.25 adult, $4.00 child (6-12). Combo pricing with Jamestown Settlement add $4.00-$9.00.

Innovative exhibits and a film chronicle the Revolutionary era from the beginnings of colonial unrest to the emergence of the new nation (wonderful short stories - as seen through the eyes of ordinary men and women of the time). Outdoors, visitors can join a cannon crew, see the crews "kitchen in the dirt", and learn about 18th century medical care (ex. Blood letting) in a Continental Army encampment. Kids can water and weed the garden at a 1780s farm (or smell the cooking over the open-hearth). They can even try on 18th century clothing in "A Children's Kaleidoscope" discovery room indoors (games and schooling...the young ones will want to spend at least a half hour here!), or view an archeological excavation site. Did you know that the victory of the French & Indian War led to Colonial taxes to pay for the now England owned Canada debt? You'll fully understand this point of history by attending the orientation. Did you know there was more than one "tea party"? Why was the tea tax the "last straw"? Even slaves joined the militia for freedom.

YORKTOWN AND YORKTOWN BATTLEFIELD

(I-64 exit 242B, Rte. 199 east to Colonial Pkwy)

Williamsburg (Yorktown) 23690

- ❏ Phone: (757) 898-2410, **Web: www.nps.gov/colo**
- ❏ Hours: 9:00am-5:00pm daily except Christmas. Summer hours slightly longer.
- ❏ Admission: $5.00 adult (17+). FREE for those under 17. Combo pass with Jamestown is $10.00.

This is the site of the last major battle of the American Revolutionary War and the surrender of Lord Cornwallis to General George Washington in 1781 (Moore House open 1:00-5:00pm daily in summer and weekends in the spring and fall, is site of surrender negotiations and can be toured). Ranger guided programs are offered from the Visitor Center which has a short film presentation, a museum with George Washington's original field tents and a children's exhibit, a bookstore and great Battlefield overlook. The driving tour (cassette tapes of tour can be rented for $2.00 in the museum shop) includes the earthworks, Moore House and Surrender Field. On the Battlefield, kids can volunteer in the non-firing artillery demonstration. You can stop by the Nelson House (home of one of the signers of the Declaration of Independence open 10:00am-5:00pm (summer) and 1:00-4:30pm (rest of year) and chat with Thomas or Lucy Nelson. Note: In our opinion, the battlefield tour is too long for the young ones.

SUGGESTED LODGING AND DINING

EMBASSY SUITES – **Richmond**, 2925 Emerywood Pkwy., I-64 exit 183. (804) 672-8585 or **www.embassy-suites.com**. Each suite lets the family spread out with a separate living room with sofa bed, galley kitchen with wet bar, microwave, refrigerator and coffeemaker, two phones and two TVs. Your stay includes a complimentary full breakfast (cold and hot, made-to-order foods) plus an evening snack/beverage reception. The hotel also has a tropical atrium indoor pool and whirlpool. Ask about summer Nickelodeon Family Package.

HOPKINS AND BROTHERS STORE & RESTAURANT - **Eastern Shore (Onancock)**, 2 Market Street, waterfront. (757) 787-3100. One of the oldest general stores on the east coast, they still sell merchandise ranging from groceries and dry goods to locally made arts and crafts. Waterfront restaurant serves mostly seafood (locally caught) with a kids' menu.

KINGSMILL RESORT – **Williamsburg**, 1010 Kingsmill Road. Phone: (757) 253-1703 or (800) 832-5665 or **www.kingsmill.com**. Upon checking into one of their villa room (s), the kids can pick up a "kid's fun map" to all the activities they offer (especially in the summer). Kingsmill Kampers is for kids ages 5-12 (all day or half day) and Junior Kampers for preschoolers ages 3-4. Different sports are played, also crafts, cooking, reading, and meals provided for a fee. Some nights (especially weekends) they have "Kids Night Out" where parents can enjoy an evening out while the kids have supervised play like the Game Room, Beach Party, Pool Party, or Nite Golf (with glow in the dark balls). We also loved the Treasure Hunt around the property, pool games, poolside bingo on Sundays and they even offer complimentary golf, tennis and fishing clinics, for the young-uns. Great "family-friendly" eats at Regattas' Café and deli market. This great location is just a shuttle drive away from Busch Gardens, Water County, and Williamsburg. A great place also to settle in and enjoy top-notch sports facilities.

DUKE OF YORK MOTEL – Williamsburg, on the York River. (757) 898-3232 or **www.dukeofyorkmotel.com**. Here they have York Riverfront rooms and a beach or pool for swimming. Family friendly dining is also available on premises.

Chapter 6
South West Area

GILES

Radford

Pulaski
PULASKI

Hillsville
58

77 CARROLL

BLAND

Wytheville

WYTHE

77

Wythe

Pocahontas

GRAYSON

TAZEWELL

SMYTH

Marion

Tazewell

Tazewell

81

460

WASHINGTON

Abingdon

BUCHANAN

19

RUSSELL

DICKENSON

Bristol

23 Wise

SCOTT

Duffield

WISE

Big Stone
Gap

23

LEE

58

NW NE SE

SC

SW

Our Favorites...

* Trail of the Lonesome Pine - Big Stone Gap

* Natural Tunnel State Park - Duffield

* Pocahontas Mine & Museum - Pocahontas

* Farms - Tazewell

* Homeplace Mountain Farm - Weber City

* Numerous State Parks

...Hanging out at the cabin

BARTER THEATRE

Abingdon - *133 West Main Street (I-81 exit 17), 24210. Phone: (276) 628-3991. Web: www.bartertheatre.com. Performances: Wednesday-Thursday at 8:00pm, Friday-Saturday at 8:30pm with matinees Wednesday, Thursday, Saturday at 2:00pm and Sunday at 3:00pm. Admission: $20.00-$26.00. Reservations recommended.* Comedies, musicals, and dramas (like Snow White or the Christmas Show). "The State Theatre of Virginia" was founded in 1933 on the theory that drama could be bartered for food. During the Depression, the owner convinced several handfuls of Broadway actors that it was better to eat in Virginia than to starve in New York. Cash is now accepted replacing barters for tickets of milk, ham or poultry.

MORGAN MCCLURE MOTORSPORTS MUSEUM

Abingdon - *26460 Newbanks Road (I-81 exit 22), 24210. Phone: (888) 494-0404. Web: www.morgan-mcclure.com. Hours: Thursday & Friday, 9:00am-5:00pm, Saturday 10:00am-5:00pm.* Racing fans visiting the Abingdon area can see the building from the highway. The museum includes winning race cars, other racing related exhibits, a complete line of racing apparel and collectibles. There is also a viewing window that gives visitors a first-hand look as MMM prepares cars for upcoming NNCS events. Home of three-time Daytona 500 Champions.

WOLF CREEK INDIAN VILLAGE & MUSEUM

Rte. 1, Box 1530 (off I-77 exit 58, US 32 south)

Bastian 24314

- ❑ Phone: (276) 688-3438, **Web: www.indianvillage.org**
- ❑ Hours: Daily 9:00am-5:00pm. Closed New Years, Thanksgiving and Christmas.
- ❑ Admission: Both Museum and Village: $8.00 adult, $5.00 child (5-16), $30.00 Family (2 adult, 3 or more children).
- ❑ Miscellaneous: Nature trails, picnicking.

It was around the year 1215 that a group of Native Americans went in search of a new tribal home. Their journey led them to a valley nestled between two mountains (a natural protection from the harsh winter winds, a constant source of fresh water, and abundant collection of trees, game, nuts, herbs and clay, and fertile land to grow their crops). So nearly 100 primitive Indians constructed a barricaded circular village. Where they came from, where they went, and exactly who they were remains somewhat of a mystery. The recreated village is near the site of the original McCord archeological excavations. The Village has in costume re-enactors of the original crafts of the Eastern Woodland Indians. The museum has many artifacts and Indian related objects.

SOUTHWEST VIRGINIA MUSEUM

10 W. First Street North (West First St and Wood Ave, off US 23)

Big Stone Gap 24219

❏   Phone: (276) 523-1322

Web: www.dcr.state.va.us/parks/swvamus.htm

❏   Hours: Monday-Thursday 10:00am-4:00pm, Friday 9:00am-
      4:00pm, Saturday 10:00am-5:00pm, Sunday 1:00-5:00pm
      (Memorial Day-Labor Day). Closed Mondays (September-
      December, March-May). Closed Thanksgiving and Christmas.
❏   Admission: $2.00-$3.00 (age 6+).

By the mid-1700s, settlers looking for a fresh start were traveling south out of Pennsylvania and Maryland into the valley of Virginia. In 1775, Daniel Boone pushed the Wilderness Road through Cumberland Gap, opening the way west. Braving the unknown and constantly facing the threat of Indian attacks, pioneer settlers were almost totally dependent on the land, their own skills and the contents of their wagon for their every need. Displays of tools, household furnishings, quilts and early commerce tell the story of these hardy pioneers. The first floor of the museum features exhibits about the area's coal and iron ore deposits, part of the "boom and bust" eras here. Kids like the "Daniel Boone-like" artifacts.

TRAIL OF THE LONESOME PINE OUTDOOR DRAMA

Drawer 1976 (June Tolliver Playhouse)

Big Stone Gap 24219

- ❑ Phone: (276) 523-1235 or (800) 362-0149
  Web: www.naxs.com/trail
- ❑ Hours: Thursday-Saturday in July and August only. Curtain time 8:00pm.
- ❑ Admission: $12.00 adult, $10.00 senior and $8.00 child.
- ❑ Miscellaneous: Before the drama, you might visit the June Tolliver House and Craft Shop, where the heroine of "Lonesome Pine" actually lived while attending school. Also in town is the John Fox, Jr. Museum. Here, the author of "Lonesome Pine" wrote 15 novels and more than 500 short stories (small admission, open Wednesday-Sunday afternoons).

Staged on the historic site where the story was actually lived, the drama tells an exciting and tender love story of a beautiful Virginia mountain girl and a handsome young mining engineer from the East. It tells the story of the great boom in Southwest Virginia when the discovery of coal and iron ore forced the proud mountain people into making many drastic changes in their way of life. Witty and humorous characters intermingle with tragedy, suspense and folk music. The main characters draw you into the dilemmas that develop and the love that underlies. Try to participate as a member of the jury (volunteers are chosen from the audience). We really liked this quaint, wholesome and easy-to-follow story. Parents, they sneak in history, too.

BREAKS INTERSTATE PARK

PO Box 100 (off SR 80 on eastern edge of Cumberland Mountains)

Breaks 24607

- ❑ Phone: (276) 865-4413 or (800) 982-5122
  Web: www.breakspark.com
- ❑ Hours: Park: Daily 7:00am-dark. Visitor Center: Daily 10:00am-6:00pm (April-October).

Breaks Interstate Park *(cont.)*

❑   Admission: FREE
❑   Miscellaneous: Picnicking, hiking, boating, swimming, fishing
     (12 acre lake), boat rentals, horseback riding, biking. Lodge with
     58 rooms.

Aptly called the "Grand Canyon of the South", the Russell Fork of
the Big Sandy River has cut a "break" (1600 foot deep gorge)
through the surrounding mountain. A paved road leads from the
entrance to the canyon rim with many overlooks providing views
of palisades, rock formations, caves, springs and rhododendron in
bloom annually. The Visitors Center contains natural science and
historical displays and is the place to pick up maps of the park's
trails.

RALPH STANLEY MUSEUM AND TRADITIONAL MOUNTAIN MUSIC CENTER

Clintwood - *Chase House, 24228. Phone: (276) 926-5591. Web:
www.ralphstanleymuseum.com. Hours: Monday-Saturday 10:00am-
5:00pm, Sunday 1:00-5:00pm. Admission: $10.00-$12.00 per
person (age 6+).* The Ralph Stanley Museum and Traditional
Mountain Music Center features the life and music of the
legendary music performer. Recognized as a pioneer in traditional
Appalachian old-time music, Stanley has donated his extensive
collection of memorabilia – ranging from vintage instruments to
countless musical awards – to the museum. Located in a historic
Victorian home, the collection includes exhibits on Dr. Stanley, the
region's musical roots, and on popular successors like Ricky
Skaggs and Patty Loveless. A short film highlights the best of Dr.
Stanley's career. The facility is a resource center for students and
music fans to learn more about traditional American and
Appalachian music.

CLAYTOR LAKE STATE PARK

Dublin - *4400 State Park Road (off I-81 exit 101), 24084. Phone:
(540) 643-2500. Web: www.dcr.virginia.gov/parks/claytor.htm.
Hours: Daily 8:00am-4:30pm. Admission: $3.00-$4.00 per vehicle.*
Wooded hills and a sparkling lake provide an ideal setting for

boating, swimming, camping, hiking and picnicking, plus sport fishing. Cabins overlook the 4500 acre lake and the historic Howe House which features interactive exhibits describing the ecology of the lake and surrounding areas.

NATURAL TUNNEL STATE PARK

Rte. 3 Box 250 (US 23 then to Rte. 871)

Duffield 24244

❑   Phone: (434) 940-2674
     Web: www.dcr.virginia.gov/parks/naturalt.htm
❑   Hours: Daily 8:00am-dusk. Chairlift service begins around 10:00am.
❑   Admission: Small fee for the pool and chairlift. $2.00-$3.00 per vehicle to enter park grounds.
❑   Miscellaneous: Lighting of the Tunnel event begins the last Saturday in May through December in the evening (last Saturdays each month only). Showcases the beauty of the Tunnel through the magic of lights.

More than 850 feet long and as high as a 10 story building, Natural Tunnel was naturally carved through a limestone ridge over thousands of centuries. Other scenic features include the view of the steep stone walls and several pinnacles or "chimneys". Natural Tunnel State Park offers seven walking trails, the longest one being 1.1 miles long. These trails lead to the unique features of the park: the tunnel floor, Lover's Leap, Tunnel Hill and Gorge Ridge. Cove Ridge Center has limited overnight camping, picnicking, swimming pool, amphitheater and chairlift to the tunnel floor. It's an adventure slowly "floating" in your chairlift seat to the bottom platform (the way back up seems steeper!). Hear the sound of a train whistle? Don't be mistaken, trains still ride on the tracks of Natural Tunnel. On the platform, just outside the tunnel, there are informational kiosks.

WILDERNESS ROAD STATE PARK

Ewing - *Rte. 2, Box 115 (off US 58 at the intersection of rte. 923), 24248. Web: www.dcr.virginia.gov/parks/wildroad.htm. Phone: (276) 445-3065. Admission: $2.00-$3.00 per vehicle fee.* Open for picnicking and hiking, canoeing plus visitors can enjoy the 10 mile stretch of the Wilderness Road for additional hiking, biking, and equestrian trails. In the shadow of the Cumberland Gap along the old Wilderness Road, is the reconstructed Martin's Station. Consisting of several 18th century frontier cabins, outbuildings, and a stockaded fort, the property regularly holds living history demonstrations with blacksmithing, surveying, farming and militia musters. These activities, combined with the annual Raid on Martin's Station reenactment and the Trade Fair, bring the Wilderness Road era to life. Park open 8:00am-dusk; Visitors Center open 10:00am-5:00pm.

NEW RIVER TRAIL STATE PARK

Foster Falls - *(access points to the trail at Ivanhoe, Fries, Galax, Draper, Pulaski and Foster Falls), 24360. Phone: (276) 699-6778. Web: www.dcr.virginia.gov/parks/newriver.htm. Hours: Dawn-dusk. Admission: $2.00-$3.00 per car. Miscellaneous: New River Adventures (276) 699-1034 or www.newriveradventures.com.* The park parallels the scenic and historic New River for 39 miles and serves as a link to a number of other recreational areas. The gentle slope of the trail makes it great for visitors to hike, bike or ride horses. Horse, boat and bike rentals, a boat launch, camping, a concession stand, fishing and picnicking.

CARTER FAMILY FOLD MUSIC GATHERINGS

Hiltons - *Carter Family Fold & Museum (I-81 to Rte. 23 north to Hwy. 58 east to 709 to 614), 24258. Phone: (276) 386-6054. Web: www.fmp.com/orthey/carter.html. Hours: Shows are Saturdays from 7:30-11:00pm, year-round. Admission: $5.00 adult, $1.00 child (6-11).* The Carter Family Fold is a rustic, 1000 seat music "shed" offering traditional music every Saturday night. In keeping with the traditional music style, no electrical instruments are allowed (everything is acoustic). There's lots of dancing and fun for the entire family. Shows are family-oriented; no alcohol is permitted at concerts. The museum opens an hour prior to the show, and visitors can explore the role of the Carter family in the development of traditional bluegrass and country music.

HUNGRY MOTHER STATE PARK

Marion - *2854 Park Blvd. (I-81 exit 47 to Rte 11 to SR 16), 24354. Web: www.dcr.virginia.gov/parks/hungrymo.htm. Phone: (276) 781-7400. Admission: $2.00-$3.00 per car. Fees waived for overnight guests.* Named for a little Indian child's cry of "Hungry, Mother" legends. Today, the mountain he cried from is Molly's Knob. Beautiful woodlands and a placid 108 acre lake in the heart of the mountains. The park features a sandy beach with bathhouse, pleasure boats and boat launch, a fishing pier, campgrounds, cabins, a lake overlook restaurant, a new visitors center, a six bedroom guest lodge, hiking and biking trails and guided horseback trail rides.

GRAYSON HIGHLANDS STATE PARK

Mouth of Wilson - *829 Grayson Highland Lane (I-81 exit 45 to rte. 16 to US 58 west), 24363. Phone: (276) 579-7092. Web: www.dcr.virginia.gov/parks/graysonh.htm. Admission: $2.00-$3.00 per vehicle, except for overnight guests.* Located near Virginia's highest point, this park offers views of "Swiss" peaks more than 5,000 feet high. Facilities include a visitor center, campgrounds, hiking trails (lead to overlooks and waterfalls) and picnic areas. Scenic horse trails and a horse camping area with stables and parking for trailers.

BUSH MILL

Nickelsville - *Rte. 2, Box 117 (SR 680), 24271. Phone: (276) 479-2965. Web: www.mounet.com/~badd/mill.html.* The only restored operational mill in the region, Bush Mill was built between 1896 and 1897 and the original machinery in the mill is intact. Recently restored, the 1896 water-powered gristmill uses stones to grind grain into meal. Occasional demonstrations are offered, mostly spring and fall.

POCAHONTAS EXHIBITION MINE & MUSEUM
Centre Street, PO Box 128 (CR 644 to CR 659)
Pocahontas 24635

- ❑ Phone: (276) 945-2134
  Web: www.wvweb.com/www/pocahontas_mine
- ❑ Hours: Monday-Saturday 10:00am-5:00pm, Sunday Noon-6:00pm (late April-October).
- ❑ Admission: $6.00 adult, $3.50 child (6-12)
- ❑ Miscellaneous: Temperature in mine is 52 degrees year round, wear a light jacket.

Opened in 1882, this coal mine has a spectacular 13 foot tall coal seam. The Mine operated for 73 years and produced more than 44 million tons of coal (would fill a train 6000 miles long). The walking tour allows you to step into the mine; listen as guides explain the story of mining at Pocahontas No. 3 Coal, and learn how the hand-loading era slowly gave way to mechanization.

MUSEUM OF THE MIDDLE APPALACHIANS
123 Palmer Avenue, downtown, **Saltville** 24370

- ❑ Phone: (276) 496-3633, **Web: www.museum-mid-app.org**
- ❑ Hours: Tuesday-Saturday 10:00am-4:00pm. Sunday 1:00-4:00pm.
- ❑ Admission: FREE, donations accepted.
- ❑ Miscellaneous: "Kids Dig" sponsored each summer. Gift shop.

The Museum of the Middle Appalachians is a collection of the paleo-archeological findings from annual digs. The earliest visitors to Saltville were drawn by the saline springs and their need for salt. Excavations as early as 1882 have revealed prehistoric mammals. The Museum showcases five permanent displays: The Ice Age, Woodland Indians, The War Between the States, The Company Town and Rocks & Minerals of the Appalachian Area. The first salt mine in the country was here and the town also served as the main source of salt for the Confederacy. Exhibits also cover battles in the area, natural history and nearby excavations. Self-guided tour brochure available. Look for mascots Whooly and Salty around town.

For updates & travel games, visit: **www.KidsLoveTravel.com**

BURKE'S GARDEN / GARDEN MOUNTAIN FARM

Rte. 3, Box 784 (Rte. 623, Banks Ridge Road)

Tazewell 24651

❏   Phone: (276) 472-2512 or (276) 988-5091

Sometimes referred to as "God's Thumbprint", this mountain-ringed bowl is 10 miles in diameter and filled with some of the most fertile farmland in the state. The area, which is the highest mountain valley in Virginia, was designated a National and Virginia Rural Historical District. The community can be viewed from the Appalachian Trail or by car from state route 623. Visitors can bike on area roads, hike and hunt in nearby Jefferson National Forest. The most noteworthy working farm here features pastured poultry and environmentally friendly methods of production. Organically grown products can be purchased and tours are available.

HISTORIC CRAB ORCHARD MUSEUM

Tazewell - *(Rt. 19 & 460), 24651. Phone: (276) 988-6755. Web: www.craborchardmuseum.com. Hours: Monday-Saturday 9:00am-5:00pm. Open summer Sunday afternoons. Closed on Saturdays Christmas through March. Admission: $8.00 adult, $7.00 senior, $4.00 child (6-11).* Historic Crab Orchard Museum & Pioneer Park in Tazewell features Southwest Virginia from prehistoric times to the present. Kids can take a guided tour through the park's log buildings and learn how people lived during the pioneer days of the region. This pioneer park and museum focuses on the history of Southwest Virginia from prehistoric times to the present. Includes Native American artifacts from nearby Crab Orchard archeological site, exhibits on Revolutionary and Civil Wars, agricultural and mining, industries. Highway construction unearthed nearly all of the Native American artifacts seen in some of the exhibits. Sometimes, bluegrass bands perform on the porches, and folks picnic on the grounds on Saturdays.

THISTLE COVE FARM

Rte. 1, Box 351 (directions on website), **Tazewell** 24651

- ❏ Phone: (276) 988-4121, **Web: www.thistlecovefarm.com**
- ❏ Hours: By reservation or during special events.
- ❏ Admission: Small fee for tours per person or group rate.
- ❏ Tours: Educational farm tours to families, school groups, etc. have various themes mentioned below.

The Bennetts operate a working homestead and breed American Curly horses and have Romney and Shetland sheep, too. Mrs. Bennett spins, knits, weaves and felts the fiber from these animals. Different themed tours include: We Love to Fleece You, A Year on the Farm in 1 Day, ALBC Noah's Ark, The War Between the States and the Reconstruction Period and Ease into the Holidays (children may make a pot holder for Mom). Children especially like meeting and feeding the sheep, lambs and horses. Crafts for the children include weaving pot holders or making felt balls or planting sunflower seeds or braiding a friendship bracelet. While people visit the farm, they try to teach you about farming and why it's so vital to all our lives. Farmers supply the world with food and fiber.

HOMEPLACE MOUNTAIN FARM & MUSEUM

Wadlow Gap Road (Hwy. 93N - John B. Dennis By-Pass Hwy.58- Rte. 224), **Weber City** 24251

- ❏ Phone: (276) 386-2465 or (276) 386-6300
- ❏ Hours: 10:00am-5:00pm Monday-Saturday, 1:00-5:00pm Sunday (April-December)
- ❏ Admission: $3.00 adult, $2.00 child (age 5+)

The mountains of Southwest Virginia still echo voices of the first pioneer settlers. Watch a small boy pushing an old horse-drawn corn planter, or maybe an old-time mountain broom maker, or a sorghum miller or cider miller, or a quilter or furniture maker. Southern soldiers gather in mid-summer to do battle with Northern forces holding Moccasin Gap. They seek to create the feeling of an early pioneer mountain farmstead, including the everyday activities of everyday living. The Clinch Mountain Cultural Center contains primitive artifacts and interpretive displays to aid understanding of the Appalachia people.

BIG WALKER NATIONAL FOREST SCENIC BYWAY OVERLOOK

Wytheville - *8711 Stony Fork Road - Star Route (I-77 OR I-81 exit US-52, 12 miles North on Byway), 24382. Phone: (276) 228-4401, Web: www.scenicbeauty-va.com. Hours: Daily 10:00am-5:00pm (April-October).* The Overlook of the Big Walker National Forest Scenic Byway provides great views from the Scenic tower and swing bridge attraction. They offer craft/gift shop with locally made Appalachian Crafts, sweets and gifts. Located in the historic pass of the mountain where Molly Tynes made her famous midnight ride to warn Wytheville of impending Civil War raid by John Toland. Location of the short hiking trail to Monster Rock Overlook (15-20 minute hike.)

ROCK HOUSE MUSEUM & BOYD HOUSE

Tazewell Street, **Wytheville** 24382

- ❑ Phone: (276) 223-3330, **Web: http://museums.wytheville.org/**
- ❑ Hours: Tuesday-Friday 10:00am-4:00pm. Saturday, Noon-4:00pm (April-December)
- ❑ Admission: $3.00 adult, $1.50 child (age 6+) - each museum.
- ❑ Tours: 30 minute, guided tours of Rock House.

<u>ROCK HOUSE</u>: The home of Wytheville's first resident physician, the Rock House has played a significant role in Wytheville's and the county's history since its construction. Dr. John Haller served his community as a country doctor, county coroner, and delegate to the Virginia Legislature. The home has been used as an infirmary and school during the Civil War years and as a boarding house when Wytheville became a popular summer resort. As you walk through this home you will learn about Dr. Haller, his wife and children; his great granddaughter Fannie Gibboney, pioneer of women's independence; and great, great granddaughter Kathleen Campbell, the last family member to own the house.

<u>THOMAS BOYD MUSEUM</u>: Located in the Thomas J. Boyd Museum, the Discovery Corner offers ten interactive stations where students will learn math and science, as well as area history. Children get a "feel" for the past by actually touching artifacts to learn how they were used.

Chapter 7

Seasonal &
Special Events

JANUARY

NE – ROBERT E. LEE'S BIRTHDAY OPEN HOUSE – Stratford.
Stratford Hall Plantation. (804) 493-8038, (804) 493-8371. Refreshments are
served and prize drawing held. General Lee visits. FREE. (second Saturday
in January)

FEBRUARY

NE - GEORGE WASHINGTON'S BIRTHDAY CELEBRATION -
Alexandria. Mount Vernon. **www.mountvernon.org.** (703) 780-2000.
Visitors can celebrate the history of George Washington by visiting his
home and burial site. The traditional presidential wreath-laying ceremony
occurs at 10:00 am, followed by patriotic music and military performances
on the bowling green. Open house, Friendship Firehouse, Gadsby's
Tavern Museum, and a Birthday Parade around town. There's a
Revolutionary War Encampment at Fort Ward Park. Sample Washington's
favorite breakfast (hotcakes & butter & honey while they last). Admission:
Free. (February – weekday during President's week)

NE – SLAVE LIFE AT MT. VERNON TOUR & AFRICAN-AMERICAN
HERITAGE PROGRAMS - Alexandria. **www.mountvernon.org.** (703)
780-2000. In observance of Black History Month, Mount Vernon offers a
30 minute walking tour highlighting the lives of the slaves who built and
operated the plantation home of George and Martha Washington.
Following each tour, a wreath-laying and brief presentation occurs at the
Slave Memorial site. On Saturdays and Sundays only, on the Bowling
Green Lawn, is an interactive program of colonial slave music, singing
and story telling from slave history. Tours: Daily. Presentation: Saturday
& Sunday. Admission fee. (February – month long)

NE – CELEBRATE GEORGE WASHINGTON'S BIRTHDAY-
Fredericksburg. Ferry Farm. (540) 370-0732. **www.kenmore.org.**
Games, crafts, storytelling, and refreshments for children. This is the place
where he celebrated 14 of his childhood birthdays. Colonial re-enactors
and demos, a stone toss across the Rappahannock River and, of course,
birthday cake. Admission (February, President's Day)

NE – GEORGE WASHINGTON'S BIRTHDAY - Fredericksburg. Historic
Kenmore Plantation & Gardens. (540) 373-3381. The nation's first President
was a frequent visitor to the elegant, colonial mansion of his sister, Betty
Washington Lewis in Fredericksburg. Admission. Also, half price admission
tours of Hugh Mercer Apothecary, Rising Sun Tavern, Mary Washington House,
& James Monroe Museum. (February - weekday during President's week)

For updates & travel games, visit: **www.KidsLoveTravel.com**

NE – GEORGE WASHINGTON'S BIRTHDAY PARTY – Colonial Beach. Washington Birthplace. George Washington Birthplace National Monument. (804) 224-1732. Visitors can celebrate George Washington's birthday with special park ranger programs commemorating the event. Gingerbread and hot cider will be served in the log house. Admission: Free. (February – President's Day weekend)

SE – FEBRUARY FREEZE - Chesapeake Bay. Cape Charles Beach. (757) 331-2304. "Plunge" benefiting the Eastern Habitat for Humanity. Beach water plunge, bonfire and lunch. (February, third Saturday)

SE – HORSEBACK RIDE IN HONOR OF BLACK HISTORY MONTH - Portsmouth. (757) 465-1443, (757) 446-2487. The Buffalo Riders of Hampton Roads, an equestrian team founded in 1997 to honor the memory of the Buffalo Soldiers, celebrates Black History Month each year with a six-mile horseback ride through Portsmouth. The riders meet in Olde Towne Portsmouth at 9:30am. All riders welcome. (February, third Saturday)

SE – CELEBRATION OF PRESIDENTS - Williamsburg. Colonial Williamsburg. (800) HIS-TORY. **www.colonialwilliamsburg.org**. Three of our country's first four presidents were Virginians. Military salute, talk with re-enactors portraying Presidents. Admission. (February, third weekend)

MARCH

NE – ST. PATRICK'S DAY CELEBRATION & PARADE - Alexandria. (703) 237-2199. Fun Dog Show, Parade in Old Town. Admission: Free. (March, first weekend)

NEDC – NATION'S ST. PATRICK'S DAY PARADE -Washington, **DC**. (March, second weekend)

NW – VIRGINIA FESTIVAL OF THE BOOK - Charlottesville. (434) 924-3296. **www.vabook.org**. This annual public festival features authors and book-related professionals in more than 150 programs. Events held throughout the city and county. Most events are FREE. (late March, Wednesday – Sunday)

NW – HIGHLAND MAPLE FESTIVAL - Highland County, **Monterey**. (540) 468-2550 or **www.highlandcounty.org/events.htm**. Maple sugar, clogging, music, pancakes and syrup, fresh toast and maple donuts. History of maple syrup is found in their open-air museum. Free. Directions with map available plus watch for "Maple Sugar Tour" signs at: Eagle Sugar Camp, Puffenbarger's Sugar Orchard, Rexrode's Sugar Orchard, Southernmost Maple Products, Sugar Tree Country & Sugar House (800) 396-2445. (March, middle two weekends).

March (*cont.*)

NW – <u>JAMES MADISON BIRTHDAY CELEBRATION</u> - Montpelier.
Montpelier Station. **www.montpelier.org**. (540) 672-2728. This date
marks the anniversary of the birth of President James Madison. (March
16th)

**SC – <u>ST. PATRICK'S DAY PARADE & CELTIC FESTIVAL</u> -
Roanoke.** Downtown. (540) 853-2889 or **http://roanokespecialevents.org**.
This is the largest St. Patrick's Day celebration in western Virginia. The
parade features ten marching and bagpipe bands and many colorful
entries. Celtic Festival in the Historic Market includes Celtic bands,
dancers & Celtic vendors. (March 17th)

SE – <u>ANNUAL CIVIL WAR RE-ENACTMENT</u> - Newport News.
Endview Plantation. (757) 887-1862. **www.endview.org**. Visitors can
experience living history programs, battles each day, sutlers, ladies'
activities & house tours. Admission fee. (March, fourth weekend)

**SE – <u>WW I RE-ENACTMENT: SECOND BATTLE OF THE SOMMES</u>
- Newport News.** Virginia War Museum. Lee Hall Mansion. (757) 247-
8523 or **www.warmuseum.org**. WW I re-enactors portray life in the
trenches with barbed wire, craters, machine guns, cannons, etc.
Admission. (March, first weekend)

SE – <u>MILITARY THROUGH THE AGES</u> – Williamsburg. (757) 253-
4838 or **www.historyisfun.org**. Jamestown Settlement takes visitors
through military history with re-enactors demonstrating everything from
weaponry to military vehicles and equipment. This is one of the most
popular annual events in Virginia. Admission. (March, third weekend)

MARCH OR APRIL

EASTER

Sunrise Services or Easter egg hunts which include the Easter Bunny,
refreshments and other activities: (Easter weekend)

❑   **NE – Stratford.** Stratford Hall Plantation. (804) 493-8038 or
     www.stratfordhall.org. Free admission to the grounds.

❑   **NEDC – Washington.** White House, This annual tradition dates back to
     1878 and President Rutherford B. Hayes. Children ages 3 to 6 can frolic
     on the South Lawn searching for over 24,000 wooden eggs that have been
     hidden throughout the grounds. There is also an Easter celebration at the
     Ellipse including entertainment, music, storytelling and food giveaways
     for the whole family to enjoy. **www.whitehouse.gov/easter/**. FREE.

- ❏ **NW – Middletown.** Belle Grove. (540) 869-2028. **www.bellegrove.org**
- ❏ **NW – Millwood.** Historic Long Branch. (888) 558-5567 or **www.historiclongbranch.com**
- ❏ **NW - Natural Bridge** at 7:00am Easter Sunrise Service. (April)
- ❏ **NW – Staunton.** Easter Traditions - Frontier Culture Museum. (540) 332-7850). **www.frontiermuseum.org**. Explore some of the Easter traditions, such as Easter egg hiding and coloring. Admission fee. (April – first half of the month)
- ❏ **SC – Bedford.** Holy Land USA. (540) 586-2823. Wagons leave the parking lot promptly at 7:00am to go to the Garden Tomb. Special music and message. (Easter Day)
- ❏ **SE – Hampton.** Fort Monroe's Continental Park Easter Sunrise Service, (757) 727-2611.
- ❏ **SE – Portsmouth / Norfolk** - 7:30am by the Elizabeth River/ Oceanview Beach Park. (757) 441-2345. Free.
- ❏ **SE – Norfolk.** Spirit of Norfolk, **www.spiritcitycruises.com**. Easter Bunny Cruise. Celebrate Easter with a lunch cruise. This fun-filled cruise includes delicious and abundant kid friendly food, wonderful entertainment and a special appearance by the Easter Bunny. Kids will also enjoy an Easter egg hunt. Admission.
- ❏ **SE – Richmond.** Easter On Parade - Monument Avenue, between Davis and Allison Streets. (804) 643-2826 or **www.citycelebrations.org/easter/index.shtml**. This street festival on historic Monument Avenue is one of Richmond's favorite spring celebrations. Visitors enjoy live music, jugglers, clowns, kiddie rides, delicious food and first-rate people watching. (Easter Day)
- ❏ **SE – Richmond.** Family Easter At Maymont - Maymont. (804) 358-7166. **www.maymont.org**. This Richmond traditional event features activities for children – egg hunts, rolls, tosses, races, Giant Straw Maze, "Best Bonnet Contest", pony rides, live musical entertainment, puppet shows and craft activities. Admission: Free, with a nominal fee for some games.
- ❏ **SE - Virginia Beach.** Easter Eggstravaganza - 24th Street Park. (757) 491-SUNN. **www.vbfun.com**. This is the place to celebrate spring. Puppet shows, face painting, games, a moonwalk, and the Easter Bunny are some of the featured events. (Easter weekend)
- ❏ **SW – Damascus.** Easter In The Park - (276) 475-5261. More than 30 churches and the Damascus community present this event that takes visitors back 2000 years to the villages & cities of Palestine. Admission: Free. (Easter weekend)

APRIL

NE – GEORGE WASHINGTON'S FIRST INAUGURATION –
Colonial Beach. George Washington Birthplace National Monument.
(804) 224-1732. **www.nps.gov/gewa/**. George Washington took the oath
of office as the first president of the United States on April 30th, 1789.
Special ranger programs interpreting this event will be offered during the
day. Admission. (April-last Sunday)

NE – SCOTTISH BLOCK PARTY & COLONIAL CHILDREN'S
FESTIVAL - Fredericksburg. James Monroe Museum. (800) 678-4748,
(540) 654-1043. Scottish music and dancing, colonial crafts, and an open
house at the James Monroe Museum will honor the anniversary of the
birth of our nation's fifth president. (April-last Saturday)

NEDC – CHERRY BLOSSOM FESTIVAL - Washington, DC's annual
National Cherry Blossom Festival is a celebration of the coming of spring
and commemorates the gift of 3,000 cherry trees given to the U.S. by
Tokyo mayor, Yukio Ozaki in 1912. The two-week festival includes many
cultural, sporting and culinary events culminating with the Festival Parade
and DC's Sakura Matsuri Japanese Street Festival, presenting over 80
organizations highlighting Japanese performances, arts, crafts and food.
The Parade showcases entries from across the country and around the
world, including Ringling Bros. And Barnum & Bailey circus, lavish
floats, gigantic helium balloons, exciting international performance
groups, marching bands and celebrity guests. Also, The Smithsonian Kite
Festival on the grounds of the Washington Monument. Most events are
FREE. **www.nationalcherryblossomfestival.org**. (first two weeks of
April, beginning end of March)

NW – COMMEMORATION OF THE ANNIVERSARY OF THOMAS
JEFFERSON'S BIRTH - Charlottesville. **www.monticello.org**. (434)
984-9800. This outdoor ceremony is held at Jefferson's gravesite and
features fife & drum corps and wreath-laying by Jefferson - affiliated
groups. Admission: Free. (April 13th)

SC – CELTIC FESTIVAL - Big Island. Sedalia Center. (434) 299-5080.
Visitors can enjoy this Celtic celebration with games, Scottish foods,
beverages and music. Admission. (April-last Saturday)

SC – **APPALACHIAN FOLK FESTIVAL** - **Roanoke**. Virginia's Explore Park. (540) 427-1800. Heritage and lifestyle of Appalachian people with music, demonstrations by historic interpreters and re-enactors re-living native Americans. Storytelling, stone tool-making, crafts; 17th and 18th century woodworking, dyeing, fireplace cooking, quilting, herbal remedies, children's games. (April, last weekend)

SC – **BLUE RIDGE KITE FESTIVAL** – **Roanoke (Salem)**. (540) 387-0267. This show features free kites for children and an exhibition by the Richmond Air Force Kite Club. Free. (April, third Saturday)

SE – **VIRGINIA WATERFRONT INTERNATIONAL ARTS FESTIVAL** - **Hampton**. Hampton Roads. **www.virginiaartsfest.com**. (757) 664-6492. This 25-day festival showcases a diverse array of artists renowned in the fields of classical music, chamber music, dance, world music, opera, gospel music & family entertainment. (mid-April to mid-May)

SE – **ATLANTIC COAST KITE FLYING FESTIVAL** – **Virginia Beach** oceanfront, 17th Street Park. (800) 822-3224. April is National Kite Month, and what better way to celebrate the joys of kite flying than at this event at the Virginia Beach oceanfront! Appropriate for all ages, the Atlantic Coast Kite Festival combines several unique activities into a day-long festival held right on the beach. Featured activities include kite demonstrations and ballets, kite building, and lessons on flying all sorts of kites. Prizes will be awarded for kite building and kite flying skills!

MAY

NE – **MEMORIAL DAY** – **Arlington & Washington DC** Memorials. (800) 222-2294. Join in a formal ceremony honoring all the men and women who took up arms in defense of America and paid the ultimate price for our freedom. (May, Memorial Day)

NE – **RUNNING OF THE CAMPTOWN RACES** - **Ashland**. Graymont Park. **www.camptownraces.org**. (804) 752-6678. The Camptown Races are an opportunity to see thoroughbred flatrack horse racing in Virginia at its best. Pre-race activities include a Terrier race, a parade and a mounted drill team demonstration. Children will enjoy the Boot Scooters, clowns, jugglers, pony rides and games. Admission. (mid-May)

May (*cont.*)

NE – CIVIL WAR WALKING TOURS - Fredericksburg. George Washington's Ferry Farm. (11:00 am-1:00 pm). (540) 370-0732. www.kenmore.org. In honor of Memorial Day, special guided walking tours will be given by costumed interpreters. Tour the site where a temporary pontoon bridge crossed the Rappahannock in the Battle of Fredericksburg during the Civil War. Admission fee. (May)

NE – MEMORIAL DAY CEREMONY - Fredericksburg. Historic Masonic Cemetery & Confederate Cemetery. (800) 678-4748. This ceremony remembers the Revolutionary and Civil War veterans who are buried in the cemetery, as well as others from Fredericksburg's past. (May, Memorial Day)

NE – MOTHER'S DAY - Fredericksburg. Pageant, Mary Washington House. (800) 678-4748. George Washington's sentimental farewell to his mother as he left for his presidential inauguration in 1789 is dramatically re-created every 30 minutes. Admission.

NE – COLONIAL MARKET DAYS & CIVIL WAR LIVING HISTORY - Fredericksburg. Downtown Historic Fredericksburg. (800) 678-4748, (540) 371-4504. Visitors can join in on the celebration of the region's rich heritage, highlighting crafts, dress, music, and merchandise from the colonial era. Re-enactments of battles. Admission fee for Civil War Tours. (May, beginning mid-month for 10 days)

NE – GREEK FESTIVAL - Fredericksburg. National Guard Armory. (800) 678-4748, (540) 898-3260. www.fredericksburgva.com. This festival features Greek food, pastries, music, dancing and crafts. (May, Memorial Day weekend)

NW – MONACAN INDIAN POWWOW - Elon. (434) 946-0389. This American Indian Powwow features Indian Nations from across the United States as they perform dances, tell stories, and demonstrate historical crafts. Live buffalo and birds of prey will be on display. Admission fee. (May, third weekend)

NW – BATTLE OF NEW MARKET CEREMONY & FULL DRESS PARADE - New Market Battlefield. (540) 740-3101. This ceremony and parade honors the cadets that fought and died during the Civil War at the Battle of New Market. Admission. (mid-May)

NW – SOAP BOX DERBY - Waynesboro. www.brsoapbox.com. (540) 943-5569. One of the largest soap box derby events in the United States. (May, second Saturday)

NW – SHENANDOAH APPLE BLOSSOM FESTIVAL - Winchester. Downtown Winchester and Jim Barnett Park. (800) 230-2139, (540) 662-3863. **www.sabf.org**. The festival celebrates the advent of spring in the Shenandoah Valley and the blooming of apple trees. More than 30 events include dances, two parades, band competitions, Circus, coronation of Queen Shenandoah and various firefighters' events. (May-first week)

SC – ROANOKE FESTIVAL IN THE PARK - Roanoke. (540) 342-2640. **www.rev.net/festival**. The annual parade is part of the anniversary 10-day celebration of Roanoke Festival in the Park. Huge Macy-style balloons and costumed characters will be featured. Backyard circus, kids arts & crafts, storytelling, games and puppet parade. (May, Memorial Day weekend)

SC – STRAWBERRY FESTIVAL - Roanoke. Downtown. (540) 342-2028. Visitors can enjoy homemade strawberry shortcakes and sundaes, frozen fruit slushies, chocolate-dipped berries, plus live entertainment, children's activities & crafts. (May - first Friday)

SE – ANNUAL INTERNATIONAL MIGRATORY BIRD CELEBRATION - Chincoteague. Chincoteague National Wildlife Refuge. Eastern Shore National Wildlife Refuge. **www.chincoteaguechamber.com**. (757) 336-6161, (757) 336-6122. Attention is focused on bird migration during the spring when migrants may be seen throughout North America. Thousands of shore birds, numbering more than 20 different species, use Chincoteague National Wildlife Refuge and Fisherman Island to feed and rest during the spring migration before moving on to their final destination. Lighthouse and canoe trips are featured. (May, second weekend)

SE – AIR POWER OVER HAMPTON - Hampton. Langley Air Force Base. (757) 764-2018 or **www.langleyafbairshow.com**. Air show of Hampton Roads. Dozens of military and civilian aerial demonstrations, displays, vendors. Admission: Free. (May, second weekend)

SE – ANNUAL CHILDREN'S FESTIVAL OF FRIENDS - Newport News. Newport News Regional Park. (757) 926-8451. **www.newport-news.va.us/parks**. Children of all ages are the focus of this festival filled with hands-on activities, rides, food, exhibits, and entertainment. Admission fee. (May, first Saturday)

SE – MEMORIAL DAY REMEMBRANCE - Portsmouth. High Street Landing. (800) PORTS VA. The city's Memorial Day Parade is the nation's oldest. Memorial service, enactors and flag ceremony. FREE. (May, Memorial Day)

May (*cont.*)

SE – <u>ANNIVERSARY RE-ENACTMENT OF PATRICK HENRY'S FAMOUS "LIBERTY OR DEATH" SPEECH</u> - Richmond. St. John's Church. (804) 649-7938. Eleven actors recreate the 1775 Second Virginia Convention. (May 25th)

SE – <u>OLDEN DAYS FESTIVAL</u> - Smithfield. Downtown. (800) 365-9339, (757) 357-5182. **www.smithfield-virginia.com**. Visitors can see blacksmiths, colonial herbalists, kettle corn poppers and quilters perform their heritage craft. On Friday and Saturday night, visitors are introduced to Smithfield's more famous, and often infamous forefathers, as well as their eccentricities, during the lantern-lit guided Ghost Walks. Entertainment. Call for hours. (May, Memorial Day weekend)

SE – <u>JAMESTOWN LANDING DAY</u> - Williamsburg. Jamestown Landing or the Original Site. (757) 253-4838, (888) 593-4682, (757) 253-7236. **www.historyisfun.org**. Sailing demonstrations and interpretive activities explore contact between English colonists and American Indian cultures on this anniversary of the founding of America's first permanent English colony. Free. (May, second Saturday)

SE – <u>CIVIL WAR WEEKEND</u> - Yorktown. National Park Service. (757) 898-2410. **www.nps.gov/colo**. This event features tactical demonstrations, encampments and a Confederate field hospital to interpret the role Yorktown played during the Peninsula Campaign. A special Memorial Day ceremony takes place at the Yorktown National Cemetery and Confederate Cemetery. (May, Memorial Day weekend)

JUNE

NE – <u>ALEXANDRIA RED CROSS WATERFRONT FESTIVAL</u> - Alexandria. Oronco Bay Park. **www.waterfrontfestival.org**. (703) 549-8300. This festival features live music, tall ships, fireworks, children's events, concerts, arts and crafts, and refreshments. This was rated by "Family Magazine" as the best family event in the metropolitan area. Admission fee. (June, second weekend)

NE – <u>JUNETEENTH COMMEMORATION</u> - Alexandria. Black History Resource Center. (800) 388-9119. **www.funside.com**. On June 19, 1865, slaves in Texas first learned of their emancipation more than two years after Lincoln's Emancipation Proclamation. Juneteenth commemorates a joyous day in African-American history. This family-oriented, fun-filled celebration includes music, a reading of the Emancipation Proclamation, entertainment and food. Admission. (June 19th)

NE - MARTHA WASHINGTON'S BIRTHDAY - Alexandria. (703) 780-2000. **www.mountvernon.org.** Anyone named Martha or whose birthday is June 13th will be admitted free upon presenting identification. Mount Vernon's interpreters will share stories and factual information about Martha's role at Mount Vernon. Admission fee. (June 13th)

NE - ASHLAND STRAWBERRY FAIRE - Ashland. Randolph Macon College. (804) 798-8289 or **www.ashlandstrawberryfaire.com.** Guests can enjoy fresh-picked strawberries by the quart or in one of the delicious recipes cooked by the food vendors, who compete for the top honor in the "Best Strawberry Food Contest." Live entertainment. FREE. (June, first Saturday)

NE - CELEBRATE FAIRFAX - Fairfax. Various locations and times. (800) 880-6629 or **www.celebratefairfax.org.** "Virginia's Fair of the Future." Plenty of hi-and lo-tech fun for the whole family, including more than 100 shows on five stages; children's activities and children's stage entertainment; business and nonprofit expo; petting zoo; Frisbee dog competition; senior "net surfing instruction"; County Expo, with dozens of interactive activities; a laser spectacular and light show; and Amusements of America's nationally-renown carnival. Also included are 40 food vendors, a juried arts and crafts show and virtual reality activities. Admission. (June, second long weekend)

NW - ANNIVERSARY OF THE BATTLE OF POINT OF FORK - Columbia. On the south bank of the James River. (434) 842-2277. **www.lynchburg.net./gaskins/PointofFork.** Re-enactment of the Battle of Point of Fork, which occurred on June 5, 1781 between British Colonel Simcoe and American General Steuben. The Revolutionary War era event will feature period music, merchants, military encampment, battle reenactment and batteau rides. FREE. (June, first weekend)

NW - NATURAL CHIMNEYS NAT'L HALL OF FAME JOUSTING TOURNAMENT - Mount Solon. Natural Chimneys Regional Park. (540) 350-2510 or **www.nationaljousting.com.** The exciting sport of Ring Jousting requires horseback riders to spear, on a lance, a series of small metal rings suspended from a wire, as they gallop steadily past the spectators. Admission fee. (June, third Saturday)

NW - BATTEAU NIGHT IN SCOTTSVILLE - Scottsville. James River. (434) 286-4320 or **www.batteaufestival.com.** The annual James River Batteau Festival visits the Historic River Town of Scottsville. Two dozen bateaux will land in late afternoon, and their crews will be dressed in period costume. Other events include music, food, vendors and a period encampment. (June, third Wednesday)

June (*cont.*)

SC – JUNETEENTH - **Hardy**. Booker T. National Monument. (540) 721-2094. This event celebrates emancipation. With the Civil War ending in 1865, approximately four million people of African descent, held in the bonds of slavery, discovered freedom. Admission fee. (June, third Saturday)

SC – LYNCHBURG BATTEAU FESTIVAL - **Lynchburg**. Riverfront Festival Park. (434) 528-3950. Starting in Lynchburg, this eight-day event features authentic replicas of late 18th century merchant boats. Crews pole down the James from Lynchburg to Richmond, camping each night along the way. Music, camps, food vendors and exhibits. Additions to this event are a Civil War re-enactment, American Indian and African-American histories. Admission varies by event. (June, mid-month for 8 days)

SE – AFRICAN AMERICAN FESTIVAL - **Hampton**. Mill Point Park. (757) 838-4721, (800) 800-2202. **www.hamptoncvb.com**. This alcohol-free, family-oriented event is held in conjunction with the Hampton Jazz Festival and celebrates America's diverse African-American heritage. Enjoy ethnic foods, arts and crafts, kids activities and live music. Admission fee. (June, fourth weekend)

SE – BLACKBEARD FESTIVAL - **Hampton**. Downtown. (757) 727-1271. Pirate-themed artists, water-based activities with live actors acting out pirate battles, food and vendors. Arrrr..gg..hh, mateys! (June, first weekend)

SE – NORFOLK HARBORFEST - **Norfolk**. Town Point Park. **www.festeventsva.com**. (757) 441-2345. This festival celebrates the region's rich maritime heritage in grand style. This three-day family event begins with a parade of sail into Norfolk's harbor and continues all weekend with live national entertainment, spectacular fireworks, on-the-water action and an entire area just for children. Free. (June, second weekend)

SE – SEAWALL FESTIVAL - **Portsmouth**. Portsmouth Waterfront. (800) 296-9933, (757) 393-9933. **www.portsevents.org**. This family festival features a children's park, craft show, regional cuisine, golden oldies and beach music. A recreational vehicle park is available for motorcoaches. (June, first weekend)

SE – CHIPPOKES STEAM AND GAS SHOW. **Surry**. Chippokes Plantation State Park. (804) 786-7950. Come celebrate the early days of the modern farm with an exciting and educational weekend. The event includes tractor pulls, vintage trucks, steam engines, kids' activities, demonstrations, farm animals, arts and crafts, a flea market, entertainment, peanut-picking, blacksmithing, food and more. Fee. (mid-June weekend)

SE – UNDER THE REDCOAT, LORD CORNWALLIS OCCUPIES WILLIAMSBURG, Williamsburg. www.colonialwilliamsburg.org. (800) HISTORY. This event re-enacts the British imposition of martial law on the city as a prelude to their eventual move to Yorktown in 1781 and the final battle of the Revolution. More than 250 military re-enactors converge on the town to encamp, drill, and "terrorize" the populace. Admission. (June 29th – July 1st)

JULY

JULY 4TH CELEBRATIONS

- ❑ **NE – Alexandria**. Mt. Vernon. (703) 780-2000. A Red, White and Blue Celebration. Free Birthday cake for all! Fireworks held the following weekend.
- ❑ **NE – Fredericksburg**. Along the Rappahannock River. (800) 678-4748. Heritage Festival. Live music, raft race, food, children's games, fireworks. FREE.
- ❑ **NE – Manassas**. Manassas Park. Independence Day Celebration. (703) 335-8872. Rides, games, entertainment, kids stage, food and fireworks.
- ❑ **NEDC – Washington**, Constitution Avenue. Celebrate the nation's birthday in the nation's capital. Don't miss the parade, with more then 100 marching units stepping out at noon along Constitution Avenue. When that's over, popular music groups entertain from mid-afternoon until the fireworks at Washington Monument. FREE.
- ❑ **NW – Charlottesville**. Monticello Independence Day Celebration & Naturalization Ceremony - The one hour ceremony takes place on the West Lawn. (434) 984- 9822, (434) 984-9800. www.monticello.org. A guest speaker will address people from countries around the world as they take the oath of U.S. citizenship at Monticello's Annual Independence Day Celebration & Naturalization Ceremony. (July 4th)
- ❑ **NW – Lexington**. (540) 463-3777. Balloon Rally & Celebration. VMI parade.
- ❑ **NW – Staunton**. Gypsy Hill Park/Frontier Culture Museum. (540) 332-3972. America's Birthday Celebration. Enjoy games and contests at Frontier Culture. Live music, dance, food, fireworks and parade.
- ❑ **NW – Winchester**. Louden Street Mall. (540) 667-1815. Balloons, walking tours, patriotic ceremonies, parade, free cake and bike decorating contest. FREE.

July 4th Celebrations (*cont.*)

- ❏ **NW – Wintergreen** Resort. (800) 282-8223, (434) 325-8180. Fourth of July Jubilee. Concert and Fireworks.

- ❏ **SC – Bedford.** Libertyfest. Poplar Forest, Centertown, D-Day Memorial. (540) 586-2148. Living history actors, hands-on history, reading of Declaration of Independence, food, clowns, fireworks at Liberty Lake Park.

- ❏ **SC – Brookneal.** Red Hill, Patrick Henry's Home. **www.redhill.org.** Celebrate 4th of July at Red Hill, Patrick Henry's last home and burial place. Patrick Henry was Virginia's first governor and the "Voice of the Revolution." Take a guided tour with costumed docents and participate in Revolutionary drills. Other attractions include Patrick Henry and his stories, live music, arts and crafts, kids' games and a magnificent fireworks display at dusk. Admission per vehicle.

- ❏ **SC – Martinsville** Speedway. (276) 956-1600. Independence Day Celebration. Music, Concerts, food, games and fireworks.

- ❏ **SC – Roanoke.** Mill Mountain Zoo. (540) 343-3241. Celebration. Extended evening hours with regular zoo admission. Overlooks fireworks display at Victory Stadium..

- ❏ **SC – Scottsburg.** (434) 454-7735. Fourth of July Celebration. Parade, music, food and fireworks.

- ❏ **SE – Cape Charles.** Bayfront. (757) 331-2304. Food, contests, entertainment, fireworks on the beach over moonlit bay.

- ❏ **SE – Hampton.** Fort Monroe, Walker Airfield. (757) 727-3151. 4th at the Fort. Fireworks, live music, children's rides and games, food, military exhibits. FREE.

- ❏ **SE – Newport News.** 4th of July. Stars in the Sky. 25,000+ attendance. FREE.

- ❏ **SE – Norfolk.** Town Point Park. (757) 441-2345. Great American Independence Day Celebration.

- ❏ **SE – Portsmouth.** North Landing / Crawford Pkwy. (757) 393-8481. Independence Day. Fireworks between downtown Portsmouth and Norfolk waterfronts over the Elizabeth River. FREE.

- ❏ **SE – Richmond.** Meadow Farm. (804) 501-5520. Old-fashioned 4th of July.

- ❏ **SE – Virginia Beach.** Atlantic Ave. & Beaches between 17th, 24th and 29th street stages. (757) 463-2300. Stars & Stripes Explosion. Fireworks, concerts. FREE.

❑   **SE – Williamsburg.** (800) HIS-TORY. **www.colonialwilliamsburg.org**. A salute to the 13 colonies, a reading of the Declaration of Independence, a garden party at the governor's Palace and a fireworks display as a finale. Admission.

❑   **SE – Yorktown.** (757) 890-3300. The Road to Independence. Rides, parade, food, entertainment, concert and fireworks. FREE.

❑   **SW – Damascus.** Downtown. (276) 475-5261, (540) 475-3831. Country, bluegrass and rock music, games, cakewalk, carnival rides and lots of good food. Fireworks, too.

❑   **SW - Norton.** Main Street. Music in the Park. (276) 679-2655. The city park hosts the region's largest 4th of July celebration with music and fireworks.

❑   **SW – Tazewell.** (276) 988-5091. Join residents for a 4th of July celebration of their coal mining heritage. The event features a fireworks display, food and music.

NE – VIRGINIA SCOTTISH GAMES - Alexandria. Episcopal High School. (703) 912-1943. Celebrate Alexandria's Scottish heritage at one of the nation's largest exhibitions of Scottish culture. The event includes parades, bands, the military, a heptathlon, highland dancing, dog events, clans and an antique car show. Clan tents and the "klikin o'the tartans" church service. (July, third weekend)

NE – ANNIVERSARY OF THE SEVEN DAYS BATTLES AT GAINES' MILL - Mechanicsville. Gaines' Mill Battlefield. (804) 226-1981. **www.nps.gov/rich/home.htm**. The Richmond National Battlefield Park will commemorate the Seven Days Battles with living history programs and ranger-led tours.(Weekend before July 4th)

NE – ORANGE COUNTY FAIR - Montpelier Station. James Madison's Montpelier. (540) 672-2728. This is the only county fair in the nation to be held at a presidential home. Highlights including horse, mule and Jack Russell terrier races; kids' races and challenges; livestock shows, including the popular "Parade of Chickens", cow-milking, blacksmithing, and fiddling contests; live music and stage performances; county fair food; and spirited competitions for the best tomato, homemade pie and cross-stitching. Admission fee. (July, third weekend)

July (*cont.*)

NE-DC – <u>SMITHSONIAN FOLKLIFE FESTIVAL</u> – Washington National Mall. National, even international, celebration of contemporary living traditions. The Festival typically includes daily and evening programs of music, song, dance, celebratory performance, crafts and cooking demonstrations, storytelling, illustrations of workers' culture. The Festival encourages visitors to participate - to learn, sing, dance, eat traditional foods, and converse with people presented in the Festival program. FREE. (first two weekends, Thursday-Sunday, in July)

NW – <u>CELEBRATING AMERICA'S INDEPENDENCE</u>. Charlottesville, Ashlawn-Highland. **www.ashlawnhighland.org**. Meet costumed re-enactors portraying continental soldiers and President Monroe, who was wounded in the Revolutionary War. Open hearth cooking, quilting and spinning demonstrations, hands-on paper quilling workshop, colonial games. Small admission, ages 10 and up. (Sunday before July 4th)

SC – <u>BLUE RIDGE DRAFT HORSE & MULE SHOW</u> - Ferrum. Blue Ridge Institute & Farm Museum. **www.blueridgeinstitute.org**. (540) 365-4416. Draft horses and mules that powered farm work well into the 1900's come together each July for contests of plowing, log skidding and wagon driving. Halter-class competitions highlight the best features of breeds. Other activities: crafts, music & costumed interpreters. (July, last Saturday)

SC – <u>COMMONWEALTH GAMES OF VIRGINIA</u> - Roanoke. Call for locations and times. (540) 343-0987. **www.commonwealthgames.org**. This multi-sport festival is the event's anniversary and is recognized by the United States Olympic Committee and the National Congress of State Games. Olympic style amateur sports festival for male and female athletes of all ages & abilities. 40+ sports offered. Admission. (July, third weekend)

SE - <u>CHINCOTEAGUE PONIES / PONY SWIM, PENNING & AUCTION</u> – Chincoteague. Memorial Park Fireman's Carnival Grounds (tip of Chincoteague Island where it looks onto Assateague Island. **www.chincoteague.com/pony/ponies.html**. (Visit this website on swim day for almost live pictures!). (757) 787-2460 or (757) 336-6161. FREE. Tens of thousands of people from around the world line the banks of Assateague Channel to watch approximately 125 Chincoteague ponies make the swim from Assateague Island to Chincoteague. Part of the immense attraction are the romantic stories of where the wild ponies first came from: Some believe the colonists hid the livestock on the island to avoid taxes. Another theory holds that pirates used the island to hide. And, another (even more) romantic, story tells of them swimming ashore from a Spanish galleon that wrecked nearby. The ponies are auctioned to keep the herd to a workable size so the island ecology system is balanced. The ponies travel in bands, freely, each with a stallion leading the herd. During the month before the swim day, the local fire department holds a carnival with entertainment, rides and food (even clam & oyster sandwiches). Between 7:00am-11:00pm on Wednesday morning, local Saltwater Cowboys round up the ponies, a veterinarian inspects their health, then the cowboys drive the ponies into the water where they take a brief swim to Chincoteague. They reach land, rest a little, and are then driven through the streets to the carnival grounds to be penned and auctioned the next day. By the way, the first foal to reach land is crowned King or Queen Neptune and auctioned for a special charitable cause. Here's the inside scoop for the best day - If you want to see the ponies up close, arriving by 6:00am is a must. Otherwise, you can be a cheerleader from afar (bring some binoculars and arrive by 7:30am, or you'll miss it!) as you watch the 5 minute swim. You do get your chance later to see the ponies up close as they are paraded through Main Street and then penned up at the carnival. The carnival is wonderfully organized and very family friendly. By noon, you may be ready to wander around the islands. Don't forget sunscreen, bug repellant, snacks, raingear if it's damp, and some games or activities to keep the kids occupied while waiting. The free shuttle service is wonderful and highly recommended (although it stops running early afternoon...and it's about a 5 mile walk if you miss it!) (last Wednesday and Thursday of July)

SW – <u>VIRGINIA HIGHLANDS FESTIVAL: ARTS & CRAFTS</u> - Abingdon. www.vahighlandsfestival.org. (276) 676-2282, (800) 435-3440. Attractions include antiques, art and photography exhibits, drama, music, dance, storytelling, a gardening symposium, creative writing workshops, fine foods and wine-tasting, nature walks, historical tours & lectures, hot air ballooning & youth events. (July, last Saturday for 16 days)

SW – <u>CIVIL WAR RE-ENACTMENT</u> - Weber City. The Homeplace Mountain Farm & Museum. (276) 386-2465. This event is a re-enactment of the 1863 Civil War Battle for Moccasin Gap.

AUGUST

NE – FRIENDSHIP FIREHOUSE FESTIVAL – Alexandria. Friendship Firehouse grounds, 107 South Alfred Street. (703) 838-3891. The popular family event features antique fire apparatus, craft booths, displays by Alexandria merchants, and live music. In addition to the day's outdoor events, festival participants will enjoy visiting the Friendship Firehouse Museum, originally built as a firehouse in 1855. Look for the hand-drawn fire engines, leather water buckets, old axes and antique fire truck. Food and beverages are available. Children will receive free fire helmets, meet a real Dalmatian, and are treated to a supervised visit inside the City's fire trucks. FREE. (first Saturday in August)

NE - CHILDREN'S ART EXPO - Fredericksburg. Hurkamp Park. (800) 678-4748. Messy creative fun for children of all ages. Admission fee. (August, second Saturday)

NW – PEACH FESTIVAL - Winchester. Richard's Fruit Market. (540) 869-1455 or **www.valleymarkets.com**. This annual show features a peach harvest with locally made peach ice cream and pie. Free hay wagon rides, kid's games and a bluegrass concert. FREE. (August, third Sunday)

SC – COOL WHEELS FESTIVAL - Roanoke. Virginia Museum of Transportation. (540) 343-5670. **www.vmt.org**. This annual festival features the ever-popular Ugly Pickup Truck Contest, activities for children and families, food, special exhibits and live entertainment. Admission. (August, third Saturday)

SC – VIRGINIA MOUNTAIN PEACH FESTIVAL - Roanoke. Downtown. **www.downtownroanoke.org**. (540) 342-2028. This festival promises to satisfy everybody's sweet tooth and craving for peaches. Other attractions include crafts and entertainment. (August, first weekend)

SC – VIRGINIA PEACH FESTIVAL - Stuart. Rotary Field. (276) 694-6012. **www.co.patrick.va.us**. The festival celebrates Patrick county agriculture and especially, peaches. Local farmers have peaches and produce for sale. There are games and pony rides for the children. (August, second Wednesday)

SE – HAMPTON REGATTA WORLD CHAMPIONSHIPS - Hampton. Mercury Boulevard bridge between Phoebus and Fort Monroe. (800) 800-2202, (757) 727-1102. The Hampton cup is the oldest, continuously run powerboat race in the country and the largest inboard hydroplane race in the U.S. The National Championships, sanctioned by the American Powerboat Association, feature 10 classes of hydroplanes and competition in excess of 140 mph. Live entertainment, concessions and kids' activities are included. FREE. (August, second weekend)

SE – **WATERMELON FESTIVAL** – **Richmond (Carytown)**. (804) 353-1525. Local artists perform, best watermelon costume, watermelon recipes and artwork. (August, second Sunday)

SW – **OLD FIDDLER'S CONVENTION & STREETFEST** - **Galax**. Felt's Park. (276) 238-8130, (276) 238-0668. **www.ingalax.net**. World's best known Old Fiddler's Convention. Competitions for youth & individual instruments. This event features mountain crafts, old time and bluegrass music, dancing and food. Admission. (August, second week)

SW – **BATTLE OF SALTVILLE** - **Saltville**. Main Street. (276) 496-5342. **www.saltvilleva.com**. Four days of music, food and family fun. During the week before Labor Day, residents heat up the town's old salt kettles and boil brine to make salt, just as it was done in the 18th & 19th centuries. (August, third weekend)

SEPTEMBER

NE – **NATIONAL CONSTITUTION COMMEMORATION** – **Colonial Island**. George Washington Birthplace National Monument. (804) 224-1732. **www.nps.gov/gewa/**. The delegates of the Constitutional Convention signed the Constitution on September 17, 1787. As presiding officer of the convention, Washington's influence was critical to the establishment of a people's government, which has lasted more than 200 years. Admission fee. (September, third Sunday)

NE – **FALL FOR FAIRFAX** - **Fairfax**. Government Center. (703) 324-3247. **www.fallforfairfax.com/index.asp**. This is a free fall festival featuring family fun and educational activities on environmental, health & fitness issues. Scarecrows, trains, petting zoo, 3 stages of environment are included. (September, last Saturday)

NE – **GREAT RAPPAHANNOCK RIVER DUCK RACE** - **Fredericksburg**. Old Mill Park. (800) 678-4748, (540) 226-4404. Small, plastic, yellow ducks are released onto the Rappahannock River and race down toward the finish line. All-day festival with crafters, food, kids' games & music. (September, mid-month)

NE – **LITTLE WELSH FESTIVAL** - **Fredericksburg**. 900 block of Charles Street. (800) 678-4748. Enjoy a day filled with Welsh and Celtic poetry, storytellers. Children's activities honor James Monroe's Welsh heritage. Admission. (September, third Saturday)

September (*cont.*)

NE – VIRGINIA INDIAN FESTIVAL – Great Falls. Riverbend Park. (703) 759-9018. Four Virginia tribes - the Mattaponi, Pamunkey, Rappahannock and Chickahominy - demonstrate life skills including tool and canoe making, dancing, cooking and storytelling. Pottery and other native crafts for sale. Archaeology and historical exhibits. hands-on activities for children. Admission. (second Saturday in September)

NE – CONSTITUTION DAY - Montpelier Station. (540) 672-2728. **www.montpelier.org.** This event's activities include ceremonial public signings of the Constitution, reflections on the Constitution by James Madison, colonial games, house and grounds tours. (September 15th)

NW – MONACAN INDIAN FALL FESTIVAL - Natural Bridge. (800) 533-1410. Join dancers, drummers, Native American storytellers and crafts people celebrating their heritage. (third weekend in September)

NW – AFRICAN-AMERICAN HERITAGE FESTIVAL - Staunton. Gypsy Hill Park. (540) 332-3972. This annual African-American Heritage Festival is a celebration of the contributions that African-Americans made to our culture. The event features live music and dance performances, arts and crafts, historic exhibits, ethnic foods and children's activities. (September, third weekend)

NW – APPLE HARVEST - Winchester. Jim Barnett Park. (540) 662-4135, (800) 662-1360. **www.visitwinchesterva.com.** Join the fun in this acclaimed annual festival featuring hundreds of arts and crafts booths, great food, live entertainment and Shenandoah Valley apples. Hayrides, pony rides, petting zoo. Follow the Apple Trail driving tour which takes you through scenic and historic ports of the city using an audiotape as your guide. Stop at the Visitors Center at 1360 South Pleasant Valley Road. Admission fee. (September, third week)

NW – CELEBRATING PATSY CLINE WEEKEND - Winchester. Various times and locations. (800) 662-4135. **www.winchesterva.org.** This weekend of activities is dedicated to the memory of legendary singer and Winchester native, Patsy Cline. (September, Labor Day weekend)

SC – FALL FARM FESTIVAL – Bedford. Rte. 680 North. (540) 586-3707. **www.angelfire.com/va/johnsonsorchards.** Easy to find (look for the 15' Johnny Appleseed watching from the curb!). Festival runs from sun-up to sun-down. Pick your own apples, craft vendors, cider processing, food, apple butter making, antique tractor pull, goat races, and "learning station" tours. (September – mid-month Weekend)

SC – INDIAN HERITAGE FESTIVAL & POW-WOW - Martinsville. King's Mountain Park, Virginia Museum of Natural History. (276) 666-8604. Visitors can enjoy this family fun day with live dancing, exhibits, demonstrations, authentic food, concessions, cultural and educational activities. (September, Saturday after Labor Day)

SC – HARVEST FESTIVAL - South Boston. Downtown. (434) 575-4209. www.soboharvestfest.com. A day of entertainment, food, crafts, people and fun await visitors to this festival. Activities feature four continuous entertainment stages, a scarecrow-making workshop, karate demonstrations, magic shows, pumpkin decorating and tons of fair food. (September, last Saturday)

SE – HAMPTON BAY DAYS - Hampton. Downtown. (800) 800-2202. www.baydays.com. Festivities highlighting the Chesapeake Bay include educational exhibits, a carnival, children's FUNtastic Junction, an Extreme Arena, fireworks and four stages of musical entertainment, including national acts. Also featured are antique cars, the military area and sports events. (September weekend)

SE – UMOJA FESTIVAL - Portsmouth. Old Towne Portsmouth waterfront. (757) 393-8481, (800) POR-TSVA or www.umojafest.org. This event is an African-American cultural celebration, featuring national musical entertainment, an African marketplace, children's activities a community forum, heritage trolley tours, Afrocentric foods, and exhibits. (September, mid-September weekend)

SE – NEPTUNE FESTIVAL / OCEANA AIR SHOW - Virginia Beach. Oceana Naval Station. (757) 427-8000 or www.oceanaairshow.com. Visitors thrill to the sight of aerobic stunts, vintage warbirds and modern military aircraft. Internationally known flying teams. (September, third weekend)

SW - GRAYSON HIGHLANDS FALL FESTIVAL - Mouth of Wilson. Grayson Highlands Park. (276) 579-7092. Visitors can enjoy a colorful autumn weekend in the Heart of the Highlands and go back to a time when horses and mules ground cane into juice to be boiled in sorghum or molasses, when apple cider was the soft drink of the time, when fresh apples were cooked in a copper kettle over an open fire all day long to render apple butter. Saturday night was reserved for fiddlin' and making music with the neighbors. In addition to all this, there is a pony auction and Sunday gospel music. Admission fee. (September, last weekend)

September (*cont.*)

**SW – LABOR DAY FESTIVAL & COAL MINERS REUNION -
Pocahontas.** The parade takes place in town and the reunion is held at the Exhibition Mine & Museum. (276) 945-9522, (276) 988-5091. This annual event is held to celebrate coal mining heritage and includes displays, crafts, food and entertainment. (September, Labor Day)

SW – HOMESTEAD LIVING HISTORY FESTIVAL - Wytheville.
(276) 223-3330. Vendors demonstrate making dulcimers, spinning, weaving, knitting, rug hooking, quilting, soup making, blacksmith, wood and leather works. Food offered over pit fires are beans and cornbread or pressed apple juice. Old time gospel and bluegrass entertainment. Admission. (September, fourth Saturday)

SW – BURKE'S GARDEN FALL FESTIVAL - Tazewell. Tazewell Mall. (276) 988-5091, (800) 588-9401. Visit Virginia's largest historical district and national landmark for a day filled with fun, music, great food and crafts. Also hike part of the Appalachian Trail, bird watch or bike on scenic by-way described as the "Garden of Eden", bowl-shaped paradise. (September, last Saturday)

SEPTEMBER / OCTOBER

NE - GREAT ADVENTURE MAIZE MAZE - Fredericksburg. Belvedere Plantation. (540) 371-8494. **www.belvedereplantation.com.** Cowgirls and cowboys step inside the 14 acre wild-west themed maze, ride 75 foot long zip lines, swing from ropes onto hay piles and take hayrides to the pumpkin patch. Admission (ages 4+). (September/October).

NW - MAIZE QUEST - Mt. Jackson. The Cornfield Maze Adventure. Bridgemont Farms. (Rte. 11 to Rte. 720). **www.cornmaze.com.** (540) 477-4200. Explore Civil War history in a maze of pathways over 2 miles long. Bridges, tunnels, dead ends. Learn history and math / logic. (September/October, Fridays-Sundays)

NW - APPLE HARVEST & APPLE BUTTER FESTIVALS - Nelson County. Each weekend a different orchard (off 56 West or US 29) hosts an event. Call (800) 282-8223 to request a fact sheet on orchards, maps for scenic driving tours and festival dates and times. Hayrides to orchard and pumpkin patches. Cider, ham, music and apple butter making. (September / October)

NW – THE PUMPKIN PATCH – Winchester, Hill High Farm, 933 Barley Lane. (540) 667-7377 or **www.thepumpkin-patch.com.** Pick your own apples, hay rides to pumpkin patch to pick your own, straw maze and farm animals. Fall treats to purchase. Admission. (Labor Day weekend thru October)

SW – GET LOST @ CLINCH HAVEN FARM – Big Stone Gap, 2524 Clinch Haven Road. (540) 523-3276. Tour a traditional working dairy farm, petting area, 7-acre corn maze with observation tower. Pick own pumpkin. Admission. (Labor Day thru October)

SW – WHITT'S CORN MAZE – Jonesville. (276) 346-2652. Corn maze in the path of Daniel Boone. Admission. (September/October)

OCTOBER

NE – FALL HARVEST FAMILY DAYS - Alexandria / Mt. Vernon. Pioneer Farmer Site. (703) 780-2000. **www.mountvernon.org.** Games, wagon rides, music, 18th century craft and harvest demonstrations. Make a cornhusk doll, find way through straw bale maze and meet George. Slave-live interpreters and yummy open-fire cooking. Free pumpkins. Admission fee of $20.00 per family. (October, third weekend)

NE – HERNDON FOLK FESTIVAL - Herndon. Historic Downtown Herndon. (703) 435-6868. **www.town.herndon.va.us.** This annual one-day event includes two stages of folk entertainment, children's hands-on crafts, a children's play land, great food, a petting zoo and the market place. (October, second Sunday)

NE – RAPPAHANNOCK TRIBE AMERICAN INDIAN POW WOW - King & Queen County. Tribal Center. (Route 623 Indian Neck Rd.) (804) 769-0260. Dancing, history orientation, crafts foods. (October, second weekend)

NE - PUMPKINVILLE, Leesburg Animal Park & Pioneer Gardens. **www.leesburganimalpark.com.** Come and enjoy all the activities: Giant slides, moon bounces, hay maze, tree swing, apples, cider and all the critters. Admission. (late September thru early November)

NE – FALL FIBER FESTIVAL & SHEEP DOG TRIALS - Montpelier Station, Montpelier Estate. (434) 973-2222. Sheep shearing, spinning, knitting, a skein & garment contest, Scottish highland dancing, Children's Corner, felt, rug, weaving & a pasture weed class. The Montpelier Sheep Dog Trials run dogs from all over the US & Canada. Many crafters selling their natural fiber clothing and socks. Admission fee. (October, early)

October *(cont.)*

NW – INTERNATIONAL FOOD FESTIVAL - Charlottesville. Downtown Amphitheater. (434) 296-8548. **www.cvilledowntown.org**. This is a celebration of Charlottesville's diversity and neighborhoods with cultural booths, entertainment and foods from around the world. FREE. (October, third Saturday)

NW – CEDAR CREEK LIVING HISTORY & RE-ENACTMENT WEEKEND - **Middletown**. Battlefield & Belle Grove Plantation. (540) 869-2028. **www.bellegrove.org**. Tour the historic Manor House, see re-enactors interpret civilian life and watch battle re-creations. Food and Civil War merchants. (October, third weekend)

NW - WALTON'S MOUNTAIN MUSEUM ANNIVERSARY – **Nelson County**. Walton's Mountain Country Store and Walton's Mountain Museum. **www.waltonmuseum.org**. (434) 831-2000. Stroll amid creative work against the backdrop of the Blue Ridge Mountains and mingle with fans of The Walton's. Other events include hayrides ($1.00 each), face painting, dinners, hamburgers, hotdogs, drinks, apple cider pressing, Bill Bradshaw's antique car & truck display, live music, local crafters and Virginia politicians. FREE. (October, third weekend)

NW – OKTOBERFEST - **Staunton**. Frontier Culture Museum. (540) 332-7850. **www.frontiermuseum.org**. Visitors can enjoy musical programs that share German culture, short plays, and special living history presentations at the German historic farm. Dancing, music and contests. Admission. (October, second weekend)

NW – FALL FOLIAGE FESTIVAL - **Waynesboro**. Main Street. (540) 942-6705. **www.waynesboro.va.us**. This event features arts and crafts by national and regional artists. Apple days-apple butter making, fresh cider, homemade apple dumplings, clowns, entertainment. Open house-tours of the Plumb House, Waynesboro Heritage Museum, & Fishburne Museum. (October, first two weekends)

NW – NORTH-SOUTH SKIRMISH ASSOCIATION – FALL SKIRMISH - **Winchester**. Winchester-Frederick County Visitor Center. (800) 662-1360. The North-South Skirmish Association will be hosting the fall skirmish, featuring competitive target shooting using Civil War firearms. Other activities include period dress competition and large sutler area. (October, first weekend)

NW – <u>SHENANDOAH VALLEY HOT AIR BALLOON FESTIVAL</u> - Winchester. Long Branch Museum in Clarke County. (800) 662-1360. More than 25 hot air balloons launch at dawn and in the afternoon (weather permitting) at this event. Other activities include free mansion tours, powered parachute demos, artisans, and a variety of foods, live music performances, & children's activities. Admission fee. (October, third weekend)

SC – <u>ENCAMPMENT AT LAUREL HILL</u> - Ararat. J.E.B. Birthplace. (276) 251-1833. www.jebstuart.org. See the birthplace of Confederate J.E.B. Stuart. Event features a self-guided walking tour of the property & hosts a Civil War re-enactment. (October, first weekend)

SC – <u>SORGHUM MOLASSES FESTIVAL</u> - Lynchburg. (434) 946-7992. Visitors can watch the making of sorghum molasses while listening to country and bluegrass bands. Other events include crafts, old tractor show and kiddie rides. (October, first weekend)

SC – <u>ZOOBOO</u> - Roanoke. Mill Mountain Zoo. www.mmzoo.org. (540) 343-3241. Visitors can enjoy Halloween at the zoo with a costume parade, scavenger hunts, games, piñata breakings and Papa John's Pizza. The zoo exhibits more than 55 species of mammals, birds and reptiles. Admission fee. (October, last Saturday)

SE – <u>BIRDING FESTIVAL</u> - Cape Charles. Best Western and Sunset Beach. (757) 787-2460. This festival takes place during the Fall migration of neo-tropical songbirds and raptors. It provides an excellent opportunity for birdwatchers to witness incredible numbers of birds congregated in preparation for their flight to the tropics. Festival activities provide a fun-filled weekend for visitors of all ages and interests. (October, first weekend)

SE – <u>FALL FESTIVAL OF FOLKLIFE</u> - Newport News. Regional Park. www.newport-news.va.us/parks. (757) 926-8451. Southeast Virginia's biggest celebration of traditional crafts, trades and entertainment features 200 crafts people, craft demonstrations, free children's activities, food vendors and continuous entertainment. (October, first Sunday)

SE – <u>HARVEST DAYS</u> - Newport News. Lee Hall Museum. (757) 888-3371. www.leehall.org. This event includes hayrides, storytelling, a pumpkin decorating contest, petting zoo and house tours. Admission fee. (October, second Saturday)

October (*cont.*)

SE – <u>VIRGINIA CHILDREN'S FESTIVAL</u> - Norfolk. Town Point Park. (757) 441-2345. Children's events all day. (October, last Saturday)

SE – <u>SUFFOLK PEANUT FEST</u> - Suffolk. (757) 539-6751. Fireworks, commercial, military and county exhibits, arts and crafts, amusement rides and the Nationwide Demolition Derby are featured at this event to celebrate the peanut. Other events include tractor pulls, yo-yo contest and favorite festival foods. "Gooberland" provides an area for family activities. (October, second long weekend)

SE – <u>YORKTOWN VICTORY</u> - Yorktown. (888) 593-4682. Anniversary of Washington's victory over the British at Yorktown. Parade, tactical demos, encampment, hands-on activities, walking tours. Some free, some admission. (October, third weekend)

SW – <u>WHITE WATER RAFTING AT BREAKS INTERSTATE PARK</u> - Breaks. The Breaks Interstate Park. (276) 865-4413, (800) 982-5122. During the first four weekends in October, John Flannagan Reservoir provides white water releases into the Russell Fork River. This creates some of the best white water rafting in the Eastern United States. (October, month-long)

SW – <u>MOUNTAIN FOLIAGE FESTIVAL</u> - Independence. (276) 773-2307. This festival features an art and craft fair on the lawn of the Historic 1908 Courthouse, live mountain music, mountain home cooking, a car show, petting zoo, the toilet paper toss and the Grand Privy Race—outhouses on wheels racing for the Chamberpot Trophy and cash prizes. Admission fee. (October, second Saturday)

SW – <u>RADFORD HIGHLANDERS FESTIVAL</u> - Radford. Radford University's Campus. **www.radford.edu/festival.** (540) 831-5324. An evening ceilidh (celebration) will be held in downtown Radford. Events include a parade, Scottish Highland games, Celtic and Appalachian music, arts and crafts vendors, a gathering of the clans, children's activities, genealogy research and food. (October, second Saturday)

SW - <u>OSTRICH FESTIVAL</u> - Tazewell. Sandy Head Ostrich Farm, Route 3. (276) 988-9090. Music and food accompany the unique farm featuring ostrich birds & llamas. Tours & purchases of ostrich leather, oil soap & meat. (October, third Saturday)

SW - <u>WHITETOP MOUNTAIN MOLASSES FESTIVAL</u> - Whitetop. Mt. Rogers Fire Hall. (276) 388-3480. The highest mountains in Virginia display their fall "coats of many colors". This traditional mountain festival features molasses making, a craft show, live music, dancing and a chicken BBQ dinner. Admission fee. (mid-October, Saturday)

NOVEMBER

NE - <u>FESTIVAL OF TREES</u> - Fredericksburg. Old Town. (800) 678-4748, (540) 371-0831. This event features scores of professionally decorated trees and wreaths, along with luncheons and teas. (November, Thanksgiving week)

NE – <u>TURKEY ROAST</u> - Herndon. Frying Pan Park. (703) 437-9101. Fresh from a last minute pardon, the official "Presidential Turkeys" arrive to enjoy their reprieve from the oven. Turkey "Roast" full of poultry humor, love, and history. Prepaid reservations required one week prior. Limit 100. Some years, the turkeys may go to Disneyland for the Thanksgiving Day parade instead. (November, day before Thanksgiving)

NW – <u>GOVERNOR JEFFERSON'S THANKSGIVING FESTIVAL</u> - Charlottesville. Historic Court Square & Downtown Mall. (434) 978-4466. **www.charlottesvilletourism.org/thanksgiving.html**. More than 50 activities are scheduled at seven different venues to let visitors experience what the community was like during the American Revolution. Events include colonial folk music and dancing, children's games, horse-drawn carriage rides, the "little militia" at the soldier encampment, demonstrations and lectures on history and culture. (November, third weekend)

NW – <u>THANKSGIVING AT WINTERGREEN RESORT</u> - Wintergreen. (434) 325-8780, (800)266-2444. Traditional Thanksgiving feasts, grand illumination of courtyard and trees, kids carnival and olympics, holiday decorating workshops. (November, Thanksgiving weekend)

SW – <u>THANKSGIVING TRADITION</u> - Weber City. The Homeplace Mountain Farm and Museum. (276) 386-6300. Join others for a pioneer Thanksgiving Day tradition, and witness the process of preparing the number one diet staple of the pioneers. (November, Thanksgiving Day)

SE – <u>FIRST THANKSGIVING – PROGRESSIVE PLANTATIONS TOUR & FEST</u> - Williamsburg. (804) 829-6684. After spending the day at Berkeley Plantation, the site of "America's First Official Thanksgiving – 1619," continue the celebration at Edgewood, Piney Grove and North Bend Plantations with a progressive tour and traditional Thanksgiving feast. Admission fee. (November, first Saturday)

NOVEMBER / DECEMBER

CHRISTMAS PARADES

(Thanksgiving weekend or weekend after)

- ❏ **NE – Alexandria**. Alexandria's harbor lights up when brightly lit sailing and power leisure boats cruise along the Potomac River at the City's historic waterfront. Free. 703-838-4200, **www.funside.com**. (first Saturday in December, early evening)
- ❏ **NE - Fredericksburg**. Old Town. (800) 678-4748
- ❏ **NE – Manassas**. Old Town. (703) 361-6599. **www.visitmanassas.org**. (December, second Saturday)
- ❏ **NW - Charlottesville**. Barracks Road. (434) 977-4583
- ❏ **NW – Harrisonburg**. Downtown. (540) 564-3160
- ❏ **NW – Lexington**. Main St. (540) 463-7191
- ❏ **NW - Staunton**. Downtown. (540) 332-3867. (Thanksgiving weekend)
- ❏ **NW - Winchester**. Old Town. (540) 667-1815
- ❏ **SC – Bedford**. Centertown. (540) 586-2148 (first Saturday in December)
- ❏ **SC – Lynchburg**. Downtown. (434) 384-1642
- ❏ **SC – Roanoke**. Downtown. (540) 342-2028 (second Saturday in December)
- ❏ **SE - Chincoteague**. (757) 336-6161. **www.chincoteaguechamber.com**. Enjoy a Christmas parade featuring floats, marching bands, color guards, saltwater cowboys, fire companies from around the Eastern Shore and Santa. (December, first Saturday)
- ❏ **SE – Petersburg**. Downtown. (804) 733-2304. (first Saturday)
- ❏ **SE – Virginia Beach**. Oceanfront beach. (first Saturday, late afternoon)

NE – HOLIDAYS AT MOUNT VERNON - Alexandria. On-site. (703) 780-2000. **www.mountvernon.com** The Washingtons' seasonal entertaining is authentically interpreted daily. Visitors learn about holiday activities at Mount Vernon, as well tour the mansion, including the rarely-seen third floor. Admission fee. (Thanksgiving weekend – weekend after New Years)

SC – HOLIDAY DISPLAY – Bedford. Liberty Lake Park, Rte. 122. (540) 587-6061. 30 acres of drive-thru holiday lights. FREE. (Thanksgiving weekend thru mid-January)

SC – FANTASYLAND - Roanoke. History Museum and Historical Society of Western Virginia. (540) 342-5770. **www.history-museum.org**. This yearly holiday "Fantasyland" exhibit is a collection of holiday scenes and mechanized figures that graced department stores of the area from the 1930's onward. Admission fee. (November, Thanksgiving weekend-Christmas Eve)

100 MILES OF LIGHTS

www.newport-news.org/100milesoflights.htm. (Thanksgiving weekend – January 1st)

- ❏ **SE – Statewide**. (800) 769-5912, (757) 926-7006. Millions of lights and hundreds of holiday events will brighten the holiday season for visitors to the Central and Hampton Roads of Virginia. Drive-through and walk-through light shows in Newport News, Norfolk, Richmond and Virginia Beach are only the start of a season of holiday wonder. Come and experience the world-famous Grand Illumination in Colonial Williamsburg, or a lighted boat parade in Hampton or Portsmouth. There will be events and entertainments for young and old alike in every city along the way.

- ❏ **SE - Hampton**. (800) 800-2202. **www.hamptoncvb.com**. Hampton holiday celebrations include the Coliseum Central Holiday Parade, Holly Days Downtown Illumination and Parade of Sail along the Hampton Waterfront, Hampton University's Holiday Art Marketplace, Venture Inn II Harbor Lights Tours and the Spirit of Hampton Roads Parade. Plus festive Christmas trees in Carousel Park, sparkling lighted boats in the marinas and unique shops with delightful gifts to help celebrate the season. Admission fee.

- ❏ **SE - Newport News**. (888) 493-7386, (757) 886-7777. In Newport News, see leaping reindeer and multi-colored snowflakes and be dazzled by more than 500,000 lights at Celebration in Lights. Shop for unique holiday gifts at Artful Giving and be transported to the skies over Bethlehem 2,000 years ago when you experience Star of Wonder. Learn about Christmas in the nineteenth century at Endview, Lee Hall and The Newsome House or visit a London of years gone by in Dickens' Christmas Village. Holiday Planetarium Show retraces the steps of the Magi in Bethlehem over 2000 years ago. Admission: $3.00 fee per bus or car.

November / December - 100 MILES OF LIGHTS (*cont.*)

- ❑ **SE – Norfolk**. (800) 368-3097, (757) 664-6620. **www.norfolkcvb.com**. In Norfolk, enjoy Garden of Lights and experience the brilliance of the holiday season illuminated by 300,000 twinkling lights along a two-mile drive. The Grand Illumination and Parade includes simultaneous lighting of the Norfolk and Portsmouth skylines, followed by a combined holiday parade. Lighted floats, marching bands, giant balloons, decorated vehicles, dancers and Santa. Close out with a New Year's Eve Celebration in Town Point Park. Admission fee.

- ❑ **SE – Portsmouth**. (800) 767-8782. **www.portsva.com**. In Portsmouth, the spirit of the holidays will come alive with the Olde Towne Holiday Music Festival. From lighted boats, parade along the waterfront to the harpists, jazz trios, brass quartets, choirs, bagpipes and more. Free trolleys will connect visitors to all performance sites. Winter Wonderland at the Courthouse Galleries. The Festival finale is a spectacular fireworks display and a live band performance on the waterfront. Admission fee.

- ❑ **SE – Richmond**. (800) 370-9004, (804) 782-2777. In Richmond, begin the holiday celebration with downtown's annual Grand Illumination where millions of lights and 100 whimsical reindeer will be lighted. Enjoy colorful displays and botanical decorations at GardenFest of Lights at Lewis Ginter Botanical Garden. Other Richmond traditions include viewing the James River Parade of Boats, Richmond Ballet's performance of The Nutcracker and a stop at the Capital City Kwanzaa Festival. Also, Tacky Christmas Lights Tour – townspeople vie for the most outrageous display of Christmas decorations-addresses posted in the local newspaper. Admission fee.

- ❑ **SE – Williamsburg**. **www.visitwilliamsburg.com**. (800) 368-6511, (757) 253-0192. In colonial Williamsburg, celebrate with holiday programs, tours, concerts, feasts, illuminations and incredible decorations along with the annual holiday exhibit of antique toys. The magic of the season comes to life with enchanting holiday décor and an extraordinary cast of musicians, singers and dancers. Admission fee.

- ❑ **SE – Virginia Beach**. (800) 822-3224, (757) 463-1940. **www.vbfun.com**. In Virginia Beach, drive the famous Boardwalk lit from end to end with 500,000 lights for Holiday Lights at the Beach. Admission fee.

SE – JOY FROM THE WORLD - Richmond. Science Museum of Virginia. (800) 659-1727. **www.smv.org**. Visitors can enjoy displays and demonstrations from cultures around the globe and learn how the world celebrates the season of light. Regular admission. (mid-November / December, 9:30 am-5:00 pm)

SW – FESTIVAL OF TREES - Big Stone Gap. Southwest Virginia Museum. (276) 523-1322. **www.state.va.us/ndor**. 80+ beautiful Christmas trees that have been provided and decorated by the community on display. (mid-November / December)

SW - MOUNTAIN TOP LIGHTS - Breaks. Breaks Interstate Park. (276) 865-4413, (800) 982-5122. Self-guided auto tour through lighted mountains, light displays, nature and holiday themes. Evenings. Admission fee. (mid-November/December)

SW – FRONTIER THANKSGIVING AT HISTORIC CRAB ORCHARD - Tazewell. The Park and the Red Barn. (276) 988-6755. Enjoy a Frontier Thanksgiving at the Park with family worship and a potluck dinner held in the Red Barn. Wear pioneer clothing and sing to guitars and fiddles. No Admission fee. (mid-November / December)

DECEMBER

NUTCRACKER PERFORMANCES - No holiday season is complete without Tchaikovsky's The Nutcracker. Enjoy breathtaking scenery, extravagant costumes, and dance that thrills adults and children alike. Admission.

- ❏   **NE – Alexandria** Ballet, (703) 548-0035
- ❏   **NE – Manassas** Dance Company, **manassasdance.org**
- ❏   **NEDC** - American Ballet Theatre: The Nutcracker, Kennedy Center. 202-467-4600, **kennedy-center.org**.
- ❏   **NEDC** - Washington Ballet: The Nutcracker, Warner Theatre, Georgetown. 1299 Pennsylvania Ave. NW. 202-397-7328, **washingtonballet.org**. The Nutcracker bears a striking resemblance to George Washington and the Rat King looks a bit like King George III
- ❏   **SC – Lynchburg** Ballet Theatre (434) 846-8451
- ❏   **SE – Norfolk**. Virginia Ballet Theatre
- ❏   **SE – Richmond** Ballet. **www.richmondballet.com**

December (*cont.*)

NE – <u>CAMPAGNA CENTER'S ANNUAL SCOTTISH CHRISTMAS PARADE WALK WEEKEND</u> - **Alexandria**. The Campagna Center. www.funside.com. (703) 549-0111. This parade honors the city's Scottish heritage. In total, more than 100 Scottish clans dressed in traditional tartans and playing bagpipes march through historic streets of Alexandria, along with living history reenactment unit. Free. (December, first Saturday)

NE – <u>CHRISTMAS IN CAMP OPEN HOUSE</u> - **Alexandria**. Fort Ward Museum. (703) 838-4848). Learn how the holiday was observed during the Civil War with living history interpreters, period music and light refreshments. Admission. (December, second Saturday)

NE – <u>PLANTATION CHRISTMAS & FAMILY HOLIDAY BUFFET</u> - **Alexandria**. Gunston Hall Plantation. (703) 550-9220. Visitors can see how families lived and celebrated the holidays in 19th century homes, aglow in candlelight and decorated with native plant material , fruits and flowers. Cider by the fireplace, open-hearth cooking demonstrations, carriage rides. Buffet of yuletide fare available. Admission. (December, first weekend)

NE – <u>CHRISTMAS IN ASHLAND – TOUR OF HOMES</u> - **Ashland**. Downtown. (804) 798-2728. See the historic homes of downtown Ashland in their holiday splendor. Tour several lovely homes located on or near Center Street, all beautifully decorated. The Hanover Arts & Activities Center serves refreshments and hosts activities for the children in the group. Admission. (December, second Sunday)

NE – <u>A WASHINGTON CHRISTMAS</u> – **Colonial Beach**. George Washington Birthplace National Monument. www.nps.gov/gewa/. (804) 224-1732. The Memorial House at George Washington's Birthplace is decorated for Christmas, candlelit and filled with colonial music. The plantation is busy as costumed interpreters depict holiday preparations in colonial times. Admission fee. (December, Second Day of Christmas – day after Christmas)

NE – <u>BATTLE OF FREDERICKSBURG</u> - **Fredericksburg**. Old Town & Ferry Farm. (800) 678-4748. Battle of Fredericksburg Reenactment, living history, candlelight tours of historic homes. (December, second weekend)

NE - **CELEBRATE THE HOLIDAYS WITH THE MONROES** - **Fredericksburg**. James Monroe Museum & Library. (800) 678-47748, (540) 654-1043. Holiday open house with period music, refreshments & costumed re-enactors. (December, first Saturday)

NE – **GINGERBREAD EXHIBIT** - **Fredericksburg**. Washington's Ferry Farm. **www.kenmore.org**. (540) 370-0732. This annual Gingerbread House Contest and Exhibit features confectionary delights created by area children and adults. (first Saturday thru the end of December)

NE – **YULETIDE 1864** – **Harper's Ferry** Historic Park. Harper's Ferry soldiers attempted to create their own version of Christmas on the battle front. Programs and activities will feature local citizens and soldiers preparing for the Yuletide, a Civil War style Santa Claus dispersing presents to the soldiers, a Victorian Cotillion, Yuletide confections, and special guided walking tours. Admission. **www.nps.gov/hafe/home.htm**. (first weekend in December)

NE – **CARTER'S CREEK PARADE OF BOATS** - **Irvington**. (804) 438-5714. Decorated boats light up the evening scene on Carter's creek in front of the Tide's Resort. Area residents and visitors vie for prizes for the most unusual and most traditional boat decorations. (December, second Saturday)

NEDC – **HOLIDAY HOMECOMING** – **Washington, DC**. Warm up your holiday season with spectacular art exhibitions and lively performances in the nation's capital. Lighting of the National Christmas Tree (White House Ellipse), Discovery Theatre children's performances (Discovery of Light), house tours, Creche Nativity display and Christmas Pageant at National Cathedral. **www.washington.org/holidayhomecoming/**. Some events require fee. (December)

NW – **CHRISTMAS BY CANDLELIGHT** - **Charlottesville**. Ashlawn-Highland. (434) 293-9539. Candle-light tour and re-enactment. Customs, holiday decorations, refreshments, and music. Admission fee. (December, selected days mid-month)

NW – **FORT HARRISON / DANIEL HARRISON HOUSE** - **Dayton**. Cook's Creek. (540) 879-2280. Primitive Valley life at a Christmas Open House. (December)

NW – **CHRISTMAS CANDLELIGHT TOURS AT BELLE GROVE** - **Middletown**. Belle Grove Plantation. **www.bellegrove.org**. (540) 869-2028. Open House. Call for more information. Admission fee. (December, second Thursday-Christmas Eve, 10:00am-4:00pm)

December *(cont.)*

NW – <u>CELEBRATE WOODROW WILSON'S BIRTHDAY</u> - Staunton.
(540) 885-0897, (888) 496-6376. **www.woodrowwilson.org**. Everyone is
invited to celebrate President Wilson's birthday during the annual open
house of the Presbyterian Manse and Museum. Enjoy birthday cake in the
Wilson Museum, listen to live music and find out what's new at the
Birthplace. There will also be special activities for kids. Free. (December,
last Saturday)

NW – <u>HOLIDAY LANTERN TOUR</u> - Staunton. Frontier Culture
Museum. (540) 332-7850. **www.frontiermuseum.org**. Tours leave every
30 minutes to experience holidays in history complete with warm fires,
candlelight and holiday cheer. Travel to four historic farms to see family
vignettes about the holiday heritage of Christmas in 1720 Germany; 1730
Northern Ireland; 1690 England; and the 1850 Shenandoah Valley. A fifth
play in the visitor center ties Christmas past in the present and offers light
refreshments. Admission fee. Advance tickets required. (December, third
weekend)

NW – <u>WINTER WONDERLAND</u> – Winchester, Clearbrook Park. (540)
665-5678. Take a stroll along the park's paved loop to see illuminated
holiday figures and scenes. Enroute, warm up at the bonfire or visit Santa.
Small Admission. (month long beginning early December, Closed the 24th
and 25th)

NW – <u>BLUE RIDGE MOUNTAIN CHRISTMAS</u> - Wintergreen Resort.
(434) 325-8180. Annual Gingerbread House, contests, family concerts,
theatrical presentations, holiday crafts workshops, Santa on the slopes,
Christmas Eve and Day dinners, and New Year's Eve celebrations.
(December, third Friday-New Year's Eve)

SC – <u>SANTA CLAUS TRAIN</u> – Dillwyn. Buckingham Branch Railroad
Station, US 15. (800) 451-6318. Don't miss this opportunity to join Santa
Claus for a special Christmas time train ride! As the train journeys through
the Buckingham County countryside, Santa will pass through the
seasonally decorated train and visit with the children. All tickets $14.00.
(many excursions the first two Saturdays in December)

SC – <u>AN OLD VIRGINIA CHRISTMAS</u> - Hardy. Booker T. Washington
National Monument. (540) 721-2094. Visitors are invited to enjoy a
candlelight tour of the plantation where famous educator Booker T.
Washington celebrated Christmas as a slave child. Learn about his
memories of Christmas while enjoying music, children's activities and
refreshments. Each evening's activities include candlelight tours to the

plantation kitchen cabin, incorporating living history vignettes about how Christmas was celebrated in the 1850's and 1860's, children's games and story time, and a special reading of Booker T. Washington's "Christmas Days in Old Virginia." (December, first weekend)

SC – **CHRISTMAS AT POINT OF HONOR** - **Lynchburg**. Point of Honor. (434) 847-1459. The annual Christmas Open House will re-create a Federal-style Christmas. The house will be arranged for an early 19th century plantation party. Refreshments of mulled-cider and cookies will be served. (December, first Sunday)

SC – **LIVING CHRISTMAS TREES** - **Lynchburg**. Thomas Rd. Baptist Church. (434) 832-2022. Tradition with area music, drama, dance with 33 ft. "swinging choir" tree covered in twinkle lights. Admission fee. (December, 2 weeks before Christmas)

SC – **CHRISTMAS BOAT PARADE** - **Moneta**. Virginia Dare Marina to Bridgewater Plaza. (540) 721-1203, **www.sml-chamber.com**. (800) 676-8203. Spectators may view the parade from the shore. Spectators, please blink your lights to show the boaters your appreciation for their hard work (they will not be able to hear your applause). (December, second Saturday)

SE – **JAMES RIVER PARADE OF LIGHTS** - **Chester**. (804) 706-1340. Celebrate Christmas traditions at the festive 1611 Citie of Henricus. Enjoy the annual James River Parade of Lights as boats compete for the holiday light decorations. (December, second Saturday, 5-9:00 pm)

SE – **CHRISTMAS AT ENDVIEW** - **Newport News**. Endview Plantation. (757) 887-1862. **www.endview.org**. Open House. Visit Endview Plantation and experience a Virginia Christmas in 1861. Greenery and period decorations brighten the house for the holidays. Civil War Re-enactment on second Sunday. Admission fee. (December, second Sunday-end of month)

SE – **LIVING HISTORY PRESENTATION: LEE FAMILY CHRISTMAS OPEN HOUSE** - **Newport News**. Lee Hall Mansion. **www.leehall.org**. (757) 888-3371. Special in-house re-enactments explore the lives of the Richard Decauter Lee family during the holiday season. Visitors can step back to 1860 and watch as members of the Lee family and their friends celebrate Christmas. Caroling, tree trimming and more will delight young & old alike. Reservations required. Admission fee. (December weekends)

December (*cont.*)

SE – <u>CAPITAL CITY KWANZAA FESTIVAL</u>. Richmond Convention Center. (804) 644-3900. Presented by the Elegba Folklore Society in Richmond, Virginia, embodies the principles of the Kwanzaa holiday. This year end celebration features performances, special children's activities, discussion groups and The African Market of eclectic merchandise and African-inspired cuisine. Admission. (December 30th)

SE – <u>LUNCH WITH SANTA</u> – Norfolk, www.spiritcitycruises.com. Lunch with Santa and his elves! Enjoy a holiday buffet and live show, sightseeing on the Elizabeth River, a DJ, and a complimentary photo with Santa (one photo per family). Admission. (mid-December Saturday)

SE – <u>OLD-FASHIONED CHRISTMAS AND LAMP LIGHT TOURS</u> - Richmond. Meadow Farm. (804) 501-5520. The cooks prepare dinner as the Sheppard family greets their guests. Visit with an 1840's style St. Nick along with music, period games and hot cider. Cooking demonstrations, lantern tours of the farm. Free. (December, first Sunday)

SE – <u>VICTORIAN CHRISTMAS</u> - Richmond. Maymont. It's Christmas Day in 1893 with tours of the lavishly decorated House, carriage rides, carolers, bell ringers, Father Christmas, Yule logs, wassail and more. Candlelighting Ceremony & Community Sing. **www.maymont.org/special.** Free. (December, first Sunday)

SE – <u>SNOWLAND</u> – Williamsburg. www.greatwolflodge.com. Great Wolf Lodge. The lodge is decorated in a winter scene. It snows 3x daily, hot cocoa and live music, clock tower sing along, Rowdy the Reindeer Storytime. Attend the North Pole University for Elves. Admission (includes lodging and indoor waterpark passes). (month-long in December)

SE – <u>YORKTOWN CELEBRATES CHRISTMAS HOMES TOURS</u> - Yorktown. (757) 890-4970. Three centuries of private homes and historic buildings are professionally decorated for the holidays. Period entertainment is also featured. Admission. (December, second Saturday)

SW - <u>FESTIVAL OF TREES NIGHT VIEWING</u> - Big Stone Gap. (276) 523-1322. **www.state.va.us/ndor.** Join residents and delight in an evening of walking through a winter wonderland. Admission fee. (December, Saturdays, 7:00-9:00pm)

SW – LIGHTS IN THE PARK - Jonesville. (276) 346-2335, Beautiful light displays, entertainment nightly, crafts, food and photos with Santa can be found at Cumberland Bowl in Jonesville and Leeman Field in Pennington Gap. One admission price to view both locations. (December, first Thursday - end of month)

NEW YEAR'S EVE, (DECEMBER 31ST)

Admission Fee.

❑ **NE – Alexandria.** (800) 388-9119. www.funside.com. A non-alcoholic, family-oriented New Year's Eve with performances along King and Washington streets in historic Olde Town.

❑ **NE – Fredericksburg.** (800) 678-4748. There will be an Open House at the museum with light refreshments served as part of city-wide "First Night" celebration, performing arts, children's activities.

❑ **NE – Leesburg.** (703) 777-6306 or www.bluemont.org. Walk through town to various indoor locations where all types of musical and theatrical performances take place. At midnight, join everyone at the courthouse green for the "Grand Illumination", where participants hold lit candles and sing in the new year. Alcohol-free event.

❑ **NE – Warrenton.** (800) 820-1021. This family-oriented, alcohol-free celebration of the arts welcomes the New Year.

❑ **NW – Charlottesville.** Downtown. (434) 975- 8269. www.firstnightva.org. The mission of First Night Virginia is to bring families together and unite the community in all its diversity through the visual and performing arts in Charlottesville on New Year's Eve.

❑ **SE – Richmond.** New Years Eve Bash. Children's Museum. (804) 474-CMOR or www.c-mor.org. Song and dance, make a hat and fun noise makers and join the CMOR parade. Admission. (early New Years Eve afternoon)

❑ **SE – Williamsburg.** (757) 258-5153. Alcohol-free event, entertainment, fireworks. Enjoy the area's finest professional entertainers including singers, dancers, instrumentalists, magicians, storytellers, puppeteers, jugglers, clowns, ballet, bands, a Big Band orchestra and more! A variety of music is featured, including classical, blues, R&B, Broadway, jazz, country, blue grass, folk and patriotic.

❑ **SW – Galax.** (276) 238-1691. First Night is a major regional performing arts festival created by and for the community to usher in the New Year. The family-oriented, alcohol-free celebration takes place in downtown Galax at multiple venues.

Master
Index

Activity Index

PROUDLY

MADE IN THE USA

Note: Area **NEDC** is Abbreviated **DC**

Note: Area **NEDC** is Abbreviated **DC**

Note: Area **NEDC** is Abbreviated **DC**

Note: Area **NEDC** is Abbreviated **DC**

Note: Area **NEDC** is Abbreviated **DC**

Note: Area **NEDC** is Abbreviated **DC**

Note: Area **NEDC** is Abbreviated **DC**

Travel Journal & Notes:

Travel Journal & Notes:

Travel Journal & Notes:

Travel Journal & Notes:

Travel Journal & Notes:

Travel Journal & Notes:

Travel Journal & Notes:

GROUP DISCOUNTS & FUNDRAISING OPPORTUNITIES!

We're excited to introduce our books to your group! These guides for parents, grandparents, teachers and visitors are great tools to help you discover hundreds of fun places to visit. Our titles are great resources for all the wonderful places to travel either locally or across the region.

We are two parents who have researched, written and published these books. We have spent thousands of hours collecting information and *personally traveled over 250,000 miles* visiting all of the most unique places listed in our guides. The books are kid-tested and the descriptions include great hints on what kids like best!

Please consider the following Group Purchase options: *For the latest information, visit our website:* **www.KidsLoveTravel.com**

❑ **Group Discount/Fundraising** – Purchase books at the discount price of $2.95 off the suggested retail price for members/friends. Minimum order is ten books. You may mix titles to reach the minimum order. Greater discounts (~35%) are available for fundraisers. Minimum order is thirty books. Call for details.

❑ **Available for Interview/Speaking** – The authors have a treasure bag full of souvenirs from favorite places. We'd love to share ideas on planning fun trips to take children while exploring your home state. The authors are available, by appointment, *(based on availability)* at (614) 792-6451 or **michele@kidslovetravel.com**. A modest honorarium or minimum group sale purchase will apply. Call or visit our website for details.

Call us soon at (614) 792-6451 to make arrangements!
Happy Exploring!

- **KIDS LOVE GEORGIA** - Explore hidden islands, humbling habitats, and historic gold mines. See playful puppets, dancing dolphins, and comical kangaroos. "Watch out" for cowboys, Indians, and swamp creatures. Over 500 listings in one book about Georgia travel. 6 geographical zones, 272 pages.

- **KIDS LOVE ILLINOIS** – Explore places from Deere to Dinos, discover Giant Cities and the Mighty Mississippi, or cross the prairie to the Lands of Lincoln and Superman . Over 600 listings in one book about Illinois travel. 7 geographical zones, 288 pages.

- **KIDS LOVE INDIANA** - Discover places where you can "co-star" in a cartoon or climb a giant sand dune. Over 500 listings in one book about Indiana travel. 8 geographical zones, 280 pages.

- **KIDS LOVE KENTUCKY** - Discover places from Boone to Burgoo, from Caves to Corvettes, and from Lincoln to the Lands of Horses. Nearly 500 listings in one book about Kentucky travel. 5 geographic zones. 186 pages.

- **KIDS LOVE MICHIGAN** - Discover places where you can "race" over giant sand dunes, climb aboard a lighthouse "ship", eat at the world's largest breakfast table, or watch yummy foods being made. Almost 600 listings in one book about Michigan travel. 8 geographical zones, 264 pages.

- **KIDS LOVE NORTH CAROLINA** - Explore places where you can "discover" gold and pirate history, explore castles and strange houses, or learn of the "lost colony" and Mayberry. Over 500 listings in one book about travel. 6 geographical zones, 288 pages.

- **KIDS LOVE OHIO** - Discover places like hidden castles and caves, puppet and whistle factories, and workshops of great inventors. Over 700 listings in one book about Ohio travel. 8 geographical zones, 288 pages.

- **KIDS LOVE PENNSYLVANIA** - Explore places where you can "discover" oil and coal, meet Ben Franklin, or watch your favorite toys and delicious, fresh snacks being made. Over 900 listings in one book about Pennsylvania travel. 9 geographical zones, 268 pages.

- **KIDS LOVE TENNESSEE** – Explore places where you can "discover" pearls, ride the rails, "meet" Three Kings (of Rights, Rock & Soul). Be inspired to sing listening to the rich traditions of Country music fame. Over 500 listings in one book about Tennessee travel. 6 geographical zones, 235 pages.

- **KIDS LOVE VIRGINIA** – Discover where ponies swim and dolphins dance, dig into archaeology and living history, or be dazzled by world-class caverns and a natural bridge. Nearly 600 listings in one book about Virginia travel. 6 geographical zones. Includes Washington DC activities. 288 pages.

- **KIDS LOVE FLORIDA** - coming in late 2006. See website for details!

ORDER FORM

KIDS LOVE PUBLICATIONS

1985 Dina Court, Powell, Ohio 43065, (614) 792-6451
For the latest titles, visit our website: **www.KidsLoveTravel.com**

#	Title		Price	Total
	Kids Love Georgia		$14.95	
	Kids Love Illinois		$14.95	
	Kids Love Indiana		$14.95	
	Kids Love Kentucky		$14.95	
	Kids Love Michigan		$14.95	
	Kids Love North Carolina		$14.95	
	Kids Love Ohio		$14.95	
	Kids Love Pennsylvania		$14.95	
	Kids Love Tennessee		$14.95	
	Kids Love Virginia		$14.95	
	Kids Love Travel Memories!		$14.95	
	Combo Discount Pricing			
	Combo #2 - Any 2 Books		$26.95	
	Combo #3 - Any 3 Books		$37.95	
	Combo #4 - Any 4 Books		$47.95	
			Subtotal	
	(Please make check or money order payable to: ***KIDS LOVE PUBLICATIONS)***	*(Ohio Residents Only – Your local rate)*	Local/State Sales Tax	
	☐ Master Card	*$2.00 first book $1.00 each additional*	Shipping	
	☐ Visa		**TOTAL**	

Account Number ☐☐☐☐-☐☐☐☐-☐☐☐☐-☐☐☐☐

Exp Date: ☐☐/☐☐ (Month/Year)

Cardholder's Name _____

Signature *(required)* _____

Name: _____

Address: _____

City: _____ State: _____

Zip: _____ Telephone: _____

All orders are generally shipped within 2 business days of receipt by US Mail. If you wish to have your books autographed, please include a <u>legible</u> note with the message you'd like written in your book. Your satisfaction is 100% guaranteed or simply return your order for a prompt refund. Thanks for your order. Happy Exploring!

"Where to go?, What to do?, and How much will it cost?", are all questions that they have heard throughout the years from friends and family. These questions became the inspiration that motivated them to research, write and publish the "Kids Love" travel series.

This adventure of writing and publishing family travel books has taken them on a journey of experiences that they never could have imagined. They have appeared as guests on hundreds of radio and television shows, had featured articles in statewide newspapers and magazines, spoken to thousands of people at schools and conventions, and write monthly columns in many publications talking about "family friendly" places to travel.

George Zavatsky and Michele (Darrall) Zavatsky were raised in the Midwest and have lived in many different cities. They currently reside in a suburb of Columbus, Ohio. They feel very blessed to be able to create their own career that allows them to research, write and publish a series of best-selling kids' travel books. Besides the wonderful adventure of marriage, they place great importance on being loving parents to Jenny & Daniel.